—— THE ——
BUSH KIDS

KRISTI CLARK

PAGE PUBLISHING, INC.
Conneaut Lake, PA

First originally published by Page Publishing 2019

Illustrated by Dennis Clark

ISBN 978-1-68456-240-4 (pbk)
ISBN 978-1-68456-241-1 (digital)

Printed in the United States of America

This book is dedicated to our beautiful sister Lori, who inspired me to write this true story. She was the eldest.

To my mom, dad, and brothers and sisters, who have always remained close and contributed to all the memories.

Most of all to God, who gives us strength, courage, love, and the gift of salvation.

As for me, this journey back into life in the bush brought both tears and laughter. It enabled me to remember who I really was and where I wanted my journey to end. That place is our homestead in Alaska, where my will to survive first began.

ACKNOWLEDGMENT

A special thank you to my daughter Holli Crouch and childhood friend Beth Valentine for sharing their brilliance in writing and editing this story.

INTRODUCTION

This is a true story of how seven kids and their parents brave the wilds in the bush of Alaska. We were called Bush Kids by a well-known artist and photographer, Doug Lindstrand, who had lived by us for a short period of time. Bush Kids we were—surviving wild animals, fires, and other adventures and trials!

I'm Kristi, the fifth kid, and with lots of help from my siblings and parents, I am here to tell the story that had to be told.

Our homestead next to Goose Creek in Alaska had a magnificent view of Mount McKinley towering among the mountains in the Alaska Range. That is where our family began a new life that would bring both challenges and hardship.

PROLOGUE

EVELYN

D awn's high-pitched attempt to scream rang through the air from the rushing river below us. "Kristi fell in the river!" I think my heart stopped as my younger sister Ginger and I ran down the steep bank where the kids were playing. My adrenaline had reached its peak as I quickly scanned the long bank next to the angry laps of water hitting my tennis shoes! My first thought was, "This can't be happening!" Devan yelled through her tears from down the narrow bank, "I think she went this way!"

We were north of Whitehorse and only a few days away from the border of Alaska when the hitch to the trailer had broken, dragging on the gravel of the Alcan highway. Dennis, his brother Doug, Steve, and Lori (our oldest) were down the road a ways out of earshot repairing the hitch while we made sandwiches.

Ginger and I scrambled through the brush down the bank where my three-year-old twin girls were searching for their little sister. Frantically looking for her blue coat and red curly locks, we screamed, "Kristi! Kristi!" White caps on the waves crashing over the big rocks would surely drown a sixteen-month-old instantly, sweeping her down the river, never to be found. I was crying and screaming for Dennis by now, as I said a desperate prayer, "Please, God, don't let Kristi die!"

1

THE LONG JOURNEY

EVELYN

I t was a beautiful July day in Oregon of 1967 when I gazed into
the small oval-shaped bathroom mirror for the last time. I pulled
my thick red hair back to the nape of my neck with a big silver clip.
Butterflies churned in my stomach, not knowing if I would like living in Alaska, a place that seemed so far away. My husband, Dennis,
and I wanted to get the kids out of the city and into the country
where we could start a ranch and have some solitude.

Turning off the light switches, I took one more look around
our house that had been a comfortable place to live, especially with
five kids. They had a lot of friends in our neat little neighborhood
in Clackamas, which was in between Portland and Oregon City. We
lived at the end of Mable Street with pine-covered hills surrounding us. Big fir and pine trees lined the paved road, giving abundant
shade. We had one of the biggest and prettiest fir trees right in our
front yard. We had been in Clackamas for two years so Dennis could
attend Multnomah Bible College in Portland to eventually become
a pastor.

My sister Ginger spent some time in Alaska, and after hearing
about the long mountain ranges, the fascinating glasslike glaciers, and
the miles of vast land, Dennis's adventurous spirit changed its direction. Dennis also worked in the produce department at the Safeway

grocery store in Oregon City. He transferred to the Anchorage Safeway so he could have a job when we get to Alaska.

Grabbing my purse and the last box, I closed the large brown door and locked it behind me, leaving the key under the mat. Dennis was loading the boxes onto the trailer hitched to our 1957 Bel Air. After securing the tarp that covered the trailer, he checked the brake lights and signals. Then he instructed all of us to load up into the car, including our crazy little Chinese pug, Boots, and our Irish setter, Meardha.

Dennis had bought Meardha at six months old in Lake Oswego after we moved to Oregon and trained her to be a bird dog. Meardha was slender and had long red hair and soft brown eyes. She was a great family dog especially for our five kids. Meardha rode in the camper, where she could lie down and stretch out. Lori, who was six years old now, said goodbye to her neighborhood friends. Our only boy, Steve, who was five, was climbing into the car with the twins and Kristi, who sat in the back seat, already dozing off.

Dennis at twenty-six and his nineteen-year-old brother Doug secured Dungo, our four-year-old stallion, and our white mare into the small barn next to the house. Dennis's brother Dewey was planning to stay at our house with the horses until we were settled in Alaska and until the house sold. Doug and Ginger would drive our 1954 Ford pickup up to Alaska with us.

The trip would take at least a week with frequent stops for the kids and the dogs. Dennis had made a camper for the pickup a month before our journey to Alaska. The big camper was made of pine wood nailed securely together, with a window in the front that lay over the cab. After cutting a door into the back, the camper was sanded and painted baby blue. Inside the camper there was a big bed over the cab where all five kids would sleep. The small wood table Dennis had installed folded out to be a small bed where Dennis and I would sleep on the trip.

Looking out at the house on Mabel Street before we drove off, I prepared myself for the inconveniences of being cramped up in a wooden camper with no stove or refrigerator. We had a small camp stove and ice chest with sandwich items and water.

My husband, Dennis, is a direct descendant of the explorer William Clark, with an adventurous spirit yearning to be challenged by nature. He's a handsome man at six feet and a few inches tall with navy-blue eyes that twinkle when he smiles. Dennis is a proud man, never to go out without his cowboy boots and his black velvet Stetson positioned on top his thick brown hair. He is a Christian by faith, not to be reckoned with by anyone but liked by everyone. I am proud to spend the rest of my life with him.

Raised on a ranch in north Idaho, Dennis worked the fields, rode many horses, and built a fence by the time he was five. He and his four brothers made an ideal team of ranch hands for his dad, Austin. Dennis's dad was a stern man who didn't hesitate to whip the horses or the boys when they got out of line. The many chores the boys had to do came before play or schoolwork.

*   *   *

Austin watched Dennis from afar and saw that he had a special touch with horses that was as natural as he had ever seen. The sleek large animals seemed to draw to his voice as if they could understand what he was saying. Dennis seemed to have a natural love for horses, not afraid of them at all as he talked to them softly and walked with ease around them.

Without halters or lead ropes, they followed him around the corral with their noses nudging his small shoulders. Austin put Dennis to work every day after school tending to the horses and training the colts that soon would be at the race track. There was no time for his love of art either, and he was not encouraged to pursue it even though he had a natural talent. Dennis's four brothers—Dave and Dewey, who were twins, Norman, and Doug—were good riders too but were always in awe of their brother's ability to "whisper" to the horses.

*   *   *

Dennis and I met in high school in Newport, Washington. I remember him sitting on the steps leading to the principal's office with a friend. He saw me walk by and said, "How about stopping by and having a chat?"

I stopped and looked at the cocky, handsome redneck, smiled, and walked on to class. I was not interested in chatting with one of the Clark boys as they had a reputation for being rowdy. Dewey, Dennis's older brother, punched the principal in the face one day, and he and his twin brother, Dave, quit school to join the Navy. Dennis had a love for art and told me later that he would lie under a big fir tree in the woods with no one else around to create his drawings and paintings. The agriculture teacher in the one class we had together took an interest in Dennis's art and asked him to display them in the classroom. I thought the paintings and drawings of horses and cowboys were beautiful and he was very talented. I started to see another side of him.

What really made me fall for him was when he came to Bible study at the First Baptist Church. It was across from the high school and was led by our teacher who taught Latin. My heart skipped a beat when he stood up and gave his personal testimonial. Dennis shared that he went to church with his mother, Viola, almost every Sunday and was recently saved at the Blanchard Community Church. That was something I was hoping to hear, being a Christian myself since the seventh grade.

I was the oldest of four sisters and lived on a one-hundred-and-sixty-acre farm near Newport, Washington. Dennis would seek refuge at my house when his father was angry with him, oftentimes helping my dad, Vern, with his unruly colts. Dad had his doubts about Dennis, especially when he heard him curse, but he saw the good in him also. I had an enormous crush on the hardworking, artistic boy and soon fell in love with him.

We were inseparable and married the summer of 1960 in Spokane at the Crestline Nazarene Church with my uncle Leland officiating. Both of our parents gave us their blessing.

The very next year, on May 2, we had our first baby at the Newport hospital, a pretty baby girl named Lori Virginia. Everyone said that she looked just like Dennis's Irish mother, Viola, with her ivory skin, green eyes, and dark-red hair. Dennis thought Lori was beautiful and would gaze down at her lovingly as he held her often.

One year after, I gave birth to our second baby on July 19, 1962, in Newport. I remember Dennis bursting into the hospital room after work, shouting, "Do you know what you gave me? A nine-pound baby boy!"

Stephen Douglas was brought into the world with curly red hair, an abundance of freckles, and golden eyes like me. Baby Steve's nose was smashed to one side when he was born, and he cried loud and frequent.

Almost two years later in 1964, after a hard labor and a risky delivery, I gave birth to our twin girls at the Deaconess Hospital in Spokane. Dennis had a job at the hospital as the janitorial manager. We didn't know we were having twins until two weeks before they were born. The way I found out was overhearing the doctor tell the nurse "It's twins!" while looking at an x-ray that was taken. The doctor ordered my x-ray because the baby I was carrying was just not coming, and I was huge and way overdue.

My mom sat by my side all night until our first twin girl was born. Seven minutes later, her tiny twin sister finally came. Dennis named our first twin Devan Vi after his mother, and our tiny twin he named Dawn Bright because he said she had bright eyes. Dawn had a shorter umbilical cord, getting less nutrients, and was underweight with her skin hanging off her bones. We were worried she wasn't going to survive while Devan was a healthy, happy baby. The hospital room was full of interns and nursing students wanting to see a set of twins be born. After they were both naturally delivered, I started to hemorrhage badly and nearly went into shock. I was thinking, "I can't leave Dennis with these two babies." I remember a Christian nurse at the head of the bed rubbing my head, comforting me. My mom poured out her prayers and tears all night for me and baby Dawn. She said, "Is Dawn going to make it?" Everything turned out fine, and they were both cute and curious with their blue eyes and strawberry-blond hair.

A year after the twins were born, Dennis moved us to Oregon. We had spent a year there earlier at the college, living in separate dorms right out of high school. I had been accepted into the nursing program but eventually gave that up to become a wife and mother.

This time we were moving back to Oregon with four little kids. Dennis would be the only one going to college and work.

Our fifth child was born in Oregon City in the spring of 1966. I named her Kristine Joyce after my little sister Joyce, who was also pregnant at seven months. She sat by my side until I gave birth to a blue-eyed baby girl with big feet and curly red hair. "Yes! Another girl!" my doctor said. "These are the longest feet I've ever seen on a baby!" Kristi was born sunny side up, so the delivery was very excruciating. It was the first delivery I had ever had anything given to me for pain. When Dennis got to the hospital after working at Safeway, he came into the delivery room where I was holding baby Kristi. I must have had a disappointed look on my face, because he said, "What's wrong, Evelyn?"

"It's a girl, and she has red hair and big feet!" I said sobbingly, feeling like I was disappointing him knowing he really wanted another boy. Dennis laughed as he sat on the bed beside me, taking Kristi into his arms. Looking down at her, he said softly, "I think she's perfect." When we took her home, Lori, Steve, Devan, and Dawn gathered around as I held her in the easy chair as each one of our small kids had their hands on her.

THE ALCAN HIGHWAY

The minutes seemed like hours as Kristi was nowhere in sight! I noticed farther down the bank, it sloped up to a tablelike surface with a large drop-off. Ginger had run up the bank the other way, searching the rushing river for any sign of her. I knew if we didn't find her soon, it would be too late! The twins were right behind me as I scampered up to the drop-off, flopping down onto my stomach to look over it. The deep white-capped waves lashed out angrily at the bank, splashing the freezing water into my face. Even if she fell off this steep bank into the water, she could not have survived. Hanging out over the dirt ledge and straining to see through the sunrays, I saw no sign of her blue coat and red hair. Just as I was about to lose all hope and face the terrible truth, I thought I heard a little voice from below! Devan and Dawn held onto my legs as I hung farther out over the flat ledge to be able to see below it. As I was leaning over the tip of the ledge, I couldn't believe it when I heard, "Mommy!"

Under the ledge was hollow and had a big flat rock that was embedded into the side of the dirt bank. There was little Kristi, sitting Indian-style on the flat rock with her hood on, looking up at me, smiling as if nothing was wrong. The big crashing waves were only a few feet from her as she just sat there below me within arm's reach. Instantly I reached down and grabbed her hood, pulling her up into my arms.

"She's okay! She's okay!" I yelled so Ginger could hear as I scooted back off the bank, holding little Kristi close to me. "Praise the Lord!" Ginger yelled as she ran over to us.

It was as if she had fallen off the ledge of the bank and her guardian angel had sat her on that flat rock until I could find her. I thanked the Lord and then gave the twins a spanking for not watching their little sister.

The 1957 Bel Air was purring like a kitten through the Yukon on the Alcan highway. The road was all gravel, winding back and forth like a snake on flat ground. Dennis was driving our Bel Air, with me in the front seat and all five of our kids in the back seat, sitting quietly as instructed with our pug snuggled down in between the twins. Even though the kids knew the outcome, a jab or two between siblings made its way into the unsupervised moments. Lori was in charge of keeping the other kids quiet. Dennis was a strong disciplinarian and believed children should be seen and not heard.

The trip took eight days from Oregon to Alaska with frequent rest breaks for us and the dogs. Staying overnight was a challenge with only one camper for all seven of us to sleep in. My sister Ginger had her own tent, and my brother-in-law Doug slept in the back seat of the Bel Air. So far on the trip, we had found nice places to park along the way where we could stop for the night.

This one particular evening in British Columbia, we were having a hard time finding a place to pull over, when we came upon a state park with lush green grass and beautiful maple trees. "That looks nice, Dennis. Maybe we could stay there for the night." I was hoping he would pull over and check it out. There were lots of room for the kids to run and play and get rid of some of their energy. Dennis pulled into the beautiful park, and Doug and Ginger pulled the three-quarter-ton pickup in behind us. There were a lot of fancy people standing on the newly mowed green grass, playing a sport that looked like lawn bowling. We must have looked a sight, with the kids pressing their noses on the inside of the car windows to see out and our big blue homemade wooden camper mounted on the pickup behind us. With very few baths, we were looking pretty haggard also. The fancy people all looked up at the same time from their game, and then their mouths dropped at once. "I don't think we can stay here, Dennis," I said, feeling embarrassed by the people staring at us. Dennis adjusted his cowboy hat and put the Bel Air into drive. He waved to his brother out the window to follow us as he left the beautiful park and continued to drive up the highway a few miles.

It was getting late, so Dennis decided to pull over into a turnout off onto the right of the highway. "We are stopping here for the night, so you kids go to the bathroom and climb in the camper." Dennis got out of the car, and walking back to the pickup, he told Doug and Ginger to settle in for the night. Doug helped Ginger set up her tent. Lori was a big help getting the twins and Kristi in their pajamas and tucked into the big bed at the top of the cab. Steve was outside helping Dennis lock everything up. Soon they were in the camper also. We didn't know there was a train track next to the turnout, and all night the loud and vibrating trains kept coming with bright lights shining through the windows to the camper. Ginger's tent became transparent from the light stealing any chance of privacy. At some point we were all so tired we tuned it out and fell asleep for a few hours.

We finally crossed the border of Canada and into the land of the midnight sun! It was so exciting for all of us to know we were only hours away from our new home that we had never seen. Alaska was so beautiful with such magnificent mountain ranges everywhere and more wild animals than people.

The kids stared out the windows, barely able to sit still and keep quiet. Dennis said, "We need to gas up one more time before we get to Palmer. There is a gas station ten miles up the highway. We'll stop there." We stopped at a Chevron station, where we got gas in both rigs and the kids and I used the bathrooms. The kids said they wanted to ride in the camper, so Dennis said it was okay until we got to Palmer, which was two more hours still, then another hour to Anchorage.

When we got to the small city of Palmer, Dennis said we were going to stop again to let us stretch our legs. We pulled off the highway into a Dairy Queen parking lot that had a large dirt area, and everyone got out of the rigs and began walking around. Dennis exclaimed, "Where's Steve?" As we looked around, I turned to the kids and said, "Wasn't he in the camper with you girls?" Lori's face turned pale, and her big green eyes got wide as she said, "I thought he was in the car with you!" I felt like I was going to lose it again as I said loudly, "If one more thing happens on this trip, I'm going back to Oregon!" Dennis looked upset as he said, "Load up, we are going back! We had to have left him at that Chevron station." Doug and Ginger stayed with the pickup in Palmer.

I couldn't help but cry all the way back worrying about little Steve, who had just turned five years old and had to be scared to death all by himself. Hopefully, he would remember what we had taught him about not going with strangers no matter what. Once again I remembered to pray and hoped his guardian angel was with him also.

It seemed like forever before we got back to the Chevron station, and I was out of the car before it had even stopped. Steve was nowhere in sight outside the station. Dennis and I ran into the building, and there was our son sitting at the only table in the corner of the room, coloring. The attendant knew he had been left behind. He asked a kind lady to watch over him until hopefully his parents came back for him. Steve jumped up from the table, grinning big, glad to see us, and said, "I was scared, but I knew you would come back for

19

me." We were so grateful Steve was safe and thanked the kind people over and over. This time we made sure all five kids were in the car with us before leaving. Steve didn't even mind sitting next to his four sisters.

After going through Palmer again, we finally made it to Anchorage, where we stayed for a few days. The first day the kids stayed with Doug in the camper. Dennis and I drove north of Anchorage to the Talkeetna area, one hundred miles, to choose between two properties we were interested in. One of the properties was on a hill next to the highway with a sturdy house. I thought it was nice and would have been my first choice.

The other house was in need of repair but on more property and next to the Susitna River. When we got to this old shack, which was a two-mile drive in on an old dirt road, we took a hike down to the slough on a narrow trail. After cutting down a long trail south, we saw the most beautiful creek that was wide and crystal clear called Goose Creek.

On the way back, the vista of Mount McKinley and the sixty acres of emerald-green field stopped us in our tracks as we knew we were finally home.

Dennis and I bought the 155 acres in the bush next to the river with the old house for twenty thousand dollars with two thousand dollars down. My sister Ginger stayed in Anchorage to attend Victory Bible Camp, run by Arctic Missions, and Doug also stayed there to work but would come out to the homestead when he could.

2

THE SHACK

DENNIS

S pring was behind us, and so was life in the city that would soon be forgotten.

Our dirt road was barely visible off to the left of Parks Highway at mile marker 95. Turning off the gravel highway, Evelyn, who was now driving the Bel Air with our girls, followed me. Steve was riding with me in the blue Ford pickup with the camper.

We had stopped five miles back at Lloyd Lankford's house to let them know we had made it. He and his wife, Betty, were the original owners of the homestead and were our closest neighbor. They were kind enough to invite us all to have dinner with them later this evening at six o'clock, which I was happy to accept.

As the pickup bounced through the deep, wide ruts on the narrow dirt road, Steve was hanging out the window. We talked about the different kinds of trees that grew with thick underbrush along both sides of the road. The spruce trees grow in a variety of sizes, but the closer to the Alaska Range, the bigger they get, which was to the north of our property.

The cottonwoods are gigantic, with branches high and low, and thick, rough bark that turns a grayish color as it ages. The tall birch tree has white and sometimes pink bark also that peels off easily and has many branches, the oldest of all the trees in the area. The birch is a large river tree with carvable bark used for the salve of Gilead.

A half mile in on the rugged road, we came upon the Alaska Railroad tracks that ran north and south as far as the eye could see. I knew it was important to teach Steve about all possible dangers out here so he could protect himself and his sisters. I really wanted to make all of them tough!

Looking both ways and then driving over the narrow crossing, I said to Steve, "The Alaska train runs often and fast, and there are no crossing arms so make sure you always look!" Steve looked at me when I was talking to him. His golden eyes were shining with excitement, and his short red hair was moving in the breeze, and he said, "Yes, Dad, I'll remember!" He was my only boy and was already my right-hand man. Meardha sat between us, panting and drooling on the seat. Looking out my window, I noticed low bush cranberries barely ripening in the moss along the banks of the train tracks. In my rearview mirror, I could see our girls with their heads out the open windows as Evelyn drove the Bel Air down the dusty road.

Steve noticed the blueberries that grew thick in bushes on the floor of the forest next to the narrow road. The bears especially were known for enjoying the blueberries and all other berries. I knew this was grizzly country and would need to prepare the family for surviving situations that might involve bears, wolves, and other dangerous animals. There were even wolverines in this part of the country. In Alaska, the moose were the largest in the world, and if charged by one, it could be more dangerous than a grizzly bear.

Suddenly we rounded a corner, and just on the right side of the road, the forest ended and turned into a large overgrown field. Towering behind the field was a spectacular view of the gigantic McKinley Mountains with snow-capped peaks in July. It is also known as Denali, with an elevation of 20,320 feet, making it the highest peak in North America.

"We've got work to do on this field, because it will produce a lot of hay for the horses," I said to Steve, who was pointing at one of the windrows out in the middle of the field. Steve leaned out the window a little farther and said, "What are those?"

As the truck hit a couple of ruts in the road, I answered him, "Those are called windrows. When the field was cleared, the brush and trees were pushed into rows."

"Sure would make good forts!" Steve yelled at me above the noise of the truck.

I yelled back, "The wild animals like them too!"

"Dad, will you teach me how to shoot your guns?" Steve looked serious, like he was already becoming a man.

"You bet, son. Some winter I'm going to take you out ptarmigan hunting and show you how to handle a gun. Then you can eventually go with me moose and caribou hunting."

I was about Steve's age when my dad taught me how to hunt, I thought to myself as I answered him loudly.

The narrow unruly road came to a sharp right corner where a large cottonwood tree with big knots marked the bend in the road. We continued driving with the field to the right of us and the thick forest on the left side. It was two miles in from the highway, but the idea of having plenty of land right by the river was exciting to me.

Minutes later the dirt road veered to the left in somewhat of a circular driveway in front of an old dark-brown shack nestled in a forest of trees. There was a large white birch tree right in the middle of the defined driveway directly in front of the house. Growing birch trees sprouted up all around the cleared area. Massive amounts of willow brush and weeds blanketed the shack and covered the windows in an eerie way.

Steve spoke up with excitement, "Is this our new house?"

"Yep, let's unload. We have lots of work to do!" I told Steve as I climbed out of the pickup. It felt really good to finally be out here on our own land.

Evelyn and the girls were getting out of the car as Steve and I walked over to the shack to get a closer look.

The dark-brown cabin facing north was built sometime in the nineteen twenties by homesteaders that had a sawmill and used birch from the property to build it. The wood had been weather damaged, bowing over time, leaving cracks in the walls. I could see the sawdust that had settled to the bottom that was used for insulation.

I thought to myself, I would have to get some Visqueen to put on the outside of the shack to keep the cold air out for the long winters.

An old gray garage made of birch overwhelmed the shack, as if protecting and hiding part of it. The homesteader used it for an airplane hangar by taking the wings off the airplane and storing it in the garage. It had two big wooden doors on one end that had a long wooden handle that fell into open metal brackets. Lloyd said there used to be an airstrip in the field before there was a road.

There was a door going into the shack next to the attached garage near the field facing the long mountain range. It was brown and had a framed-in window and was elevated off the ground and at one time probably had steps.

We walked to the left where the garage doors were, and behind the garage, which was up against the thick forest of trees, called the woods in these parts. There was another brown wooden door that was tucked in behind the garage with a well-worn path covered in grass and brush. The worn-out door had a glass square window that was framed in and a tarnished round silver door handle.

The roof of the shack was pitched in the middle and covered with tar paper and had two chimneys, one on each side of the roof. Behind the shack about a hundred yards in the woods was what looked like an outhouse made out of birch wood, tattered and beaten up by the weather. By now Evelyn and all five of our kids were standing behind me, not knowing where to start. Looking at them, I saw my beautiful wife looking a little overwhelmed but ready to go to work. Steve was smiling and eager to help, with his freckles poking through his rosy cheeks. Lori with her long straight red hair was growing tall and thin. Our twin girls looked alike at a glance but definitely had their differences and stayed together most of the time. Lori was holding curly haired little Kristi on her hip, careful not to let her down. Looking at them under my cowboy hat, I said, "We're all going to pitch in and make this a ranch home for our big family! Nothing wrong with a little hard work, is there? Dawn, you watch Kristi and start unloading the car, while Steve and I unload the camper. Lori and Devan, help your mom start clearing the willow brush and weeds away from the doorways so we can get into the house after we get unloaded."

The girls got right to work with Evelyn pulling up the weeds and willows around the shack by hand, throwing them into a pile.

After that we unloaded the pale-blue wood camper onto wood flat pallets in a clear dirt spot up against the woods near the house. We would have to sleep in the camper for now until the shack was made into a home. The camper was large enough to stand up in and had several windows.

Being summer, it was light out most of the night hours, providing enough time to prepare for winter by haying the fields, cutting firewood, gardening, and making the house weatherproof. I would have to commute to Anchorage to work at Safeway, Monday through Thursday, in the produce department. I could pick up some supplies to start repairing the shack. The badly damaged kitchen floor would have to be replaced and also the broken windows all around the shack. I would have to wait on some of the projects until I received a paycheck from work. Priority for me was having a safe, warm place for us to stay, water for drinking and baths, and plenty of food for the winter.

I grabbed my thirty-thirty, one-shot rifle out of the truck, which was smaller than my other rifle and could be taken apart and packed. After motioning for Steve, we walked behind the shack about thirty yards through the underbrush and grass to the outhouse. The birch walls were weather worn but still standing with a flat roof and an old rusty piece of tin on top of the six-foot-high structure. The thick door, made out of plywood and two-by-fours, had broken hinges and was hanging open. Inside the outhouse were piles of wet leaves that had collected over the years around the wood bench with a round hole in the middle. "Steve, go get our gloves out of the pickup and come right back!" I said. While he was running to the pickup, I looked down into the hole that was meant to be sat on with no seat. There was still a bag of lime in the corner and a roll of toilet paper, brown and shriveled up, next to the hole. Steve came back with our gloves, and we both cleaned all the leaves out by hand. The old outhouse would need new plywood on the walls, hinges for the door, and a regular toilet seat to sit on. Being at the edge of the woods and a ways from the house, the kids would need to have Evelyn or me go with them, but at least we would have a place to go to the bathroom.

Having to be a hundred miles away to work, I was worried about Evelyn and the kids being in the bush by themselves. There would have to be strict rules about not going too far from the house, especially in the trees and brush.

Lloyd had told me of a natural spring that was about a quarter mile from the shack back in the woods. In a few days, our water supply would run out for us and the animals.

After raking the brush from the entry to the house, I opened the already ajar door, holding my rifle, not knowing if it was inhabited by a wild animal. Handing Evelyn my pistol and instructing her to stay outside with the kids, I went into the shack alone. The scratched, worn-out brown door creaked open to a big dark room with a linoleum floor that was at least twenty years old. The floor was thick with hay strewn about and bear scat. There was an open attic above the big room that had some dusty boxes that were barely visible. It was dark in the house and hard to see, so I yelled to Steve to grab a flashlight and come in the house.

After Steve came in and looked around the floor with the flashlight, he yelled out to the girls, "I see bear poop!" Giggling, they could hardly wait to come in.

The large room was probably the living room. It was connected by a partial wall with a large square opening to another room, maybe the kitchen, that had a counter and a black woodstove. There were two small built-in bunks on the partial wall to the left side of the narrow entry to the kitchen.

It was hard to walk through the rubble, but we made our way through the two large rooms, checking for wild animals that might still be inside. There was a lot of dust and dirt on the smooth tan counter in the kitchen that was next to the door going out to the driveway.

A small wood-framed window was above the kitchen counter with a view of the driveway and part of the field. A well-used black iron woodstove in the middle of the room but against the back wall had a stove pipe going up through the hole in the low ceiling.

Back in the living room, I noticed another hole in the ceiling that was closed off, by the front door for a woodstove. The walls were all made out of birch wood and were dark brown.

Evelyn and the girls came in squealing as a long ermine ran through the rubble and out of the house next to them.

I knew this was a lot for my wife and kids to take in after having all the conveniences at our Mabel Street house and now being in a shack with no power or running water. It was my job to toughen them up and teach them to appreciate the real blessings in life, like faith, family, and food on the table. I spoke to my family, all looking at me for guidance. "We'll take it easy today and only work a couple hours more, then clean up and go to the Lankfords' for supper."

Evelyn and Lori swept and dusted the house, raking the hay and remnants out the doors. Devan kept pulling weeds, while Dawn and Kristi raked them into a pile in the front yard.

Later we all piled into the Bel Air and drove down our dirt road to the Lankfords' for moose roast with low bush cranberry ketchup and fresh vegetables from their greenhouse. It was almost midnight before we got back to our homestead and still light out. We all buckled down into the camper to get some rest before the long day of work ahead of us. I felt a sense of accomplishment already.

With a deep sigh, I fell asleep listening to the quiet sound of the leaves on the trees around us blowing in the breeze and the howling of wolves in the distance.

3

THE FAMILY BATHTUB

LORI

With no well for water or plumbing in the old hunter's shack, now our home, Dad said there was a natural spring about a quarter mile from the shack on a narrow trail through the woods. The spring water would have to be packed up by buckets and stored in a larger drum for drinking, baths, and cooking. The plastic gallon jugs of water we had stored in the camper under the table were getting low. We kids only drank water and occasional powdered milk Mom mixed up for us. She made coffee on the camp stove with the silver percolator for her and Dad.

With my light-blue pedal pushers, a yellow blouse, and slip-on tennis shoes on, I pulled my long straight red hair back in a cloth headband. Dad handed Steve and me each an empty five-gallon bucket that were white with black handles that were almost as tall as us.

The spring was south of the cabin, through the thick forest with somewhat of an overgrown narrow trail.

I was enjoying smelling and admiring all the wildflowers along the way—miniature red roses, dandelions, bluebells, and many other pretty flowers I didn't recognize. My eyes gazed at the tall purple flowers that had buds growing slowly up the plant and blooming into pretty purple flowers. The leaves bowed low under the pretty buds and were long, skinny, and dark green. Dad told us that they were called fireweed. When the purple buds blossom all the way to the top of the plant, Alaskans believe there are only six weeks to snowfall. The smell of the grass covered with dew mixed with tree bark aroma filled my senses. My somewhat large ears could hear Goose Creek introducing itself with the consistent but unpredictable waves dancing across its rock bed moving west.

We barely spotted the trail off the steep bank to the right of us where the natural spring bubbled up. Looking down, we could see the reflection of the sun off the top of the water buried in tall thick grass and large ferns. Dad, Steve, and I hiked down, breaking willow branches along the way to make a wider trail. The stickery raspberry bushes poked at my pant legs and scratched my arms as we made our way down the steep bank. Dad stopped at the clear water coming up out of the almost perfectly round small hole on the ground. He told Steve and me, "You two kids are responsible for making sure we have enough water at all times. Stay alert and make noise! There's a lot of grizzly bears in these parts, especially in the brush and near water."

Steve and I looked at each other, hoping Dad wasn't serious, but we both knew he was.

The high dirt bank to the left of us had large cave-like holes under the tree roots that looked like animal dens. The massive thick willows created a jungle-like feeling, hiding its inhabitants.

The clear and pure liquid tasted so good on my parched tongue and lips as I scooped some into my cupped hand and drank from it several times. Only ever having water from a faucet, it was as if God was giving me a drink straight from his creation. Steve and Dad did the same, and then we filled the two five-gallon buckets with the clear glacier water. It was record-breaking heat this summer, and today it felt like it was ninety degrees. After splashing our faces with the ice-cold spring water, we hiked back up the long quarter-mile trail to the shack with Dad behind us, feeling refreshed. He was carrying one of the five-gallon buckets of water and his large rifle.

Steve and I carried the other bucket between us, sharing the large handle, careful not to spill a drop of the precious liquid. The buckets were getting heavy, so we stopped along the trail for a minute to rest. I picked some of the pretty bluebells and dandelions to take for Mom.

As soon as we got back to the shack, Dad showed us how to empty the buckets of water into a thirty-gallon white plastic drum he had bought in Anchorage. The drum was kept by the shack outside the kitchen door.

After having a quick peanut butter and jam sandwich, we hiked back down the hidden trail again, finding it a bit easier, this time with Mom and the girls to show them where the spring was and to refill the buckets. Dad showed us some thick, high, beaten-down grass that trailed off into the woods and said, "That's a recent bear trail! Keep your eyes out!" Our clan made plenty of noise as we made it there and back with no problems.

When we got back to the shack with more water, Meardha started to bark at a pickup with two people inside that had pulled up into our circular driveway. "Meardha, stop barking and come here!" I yelled, slapping at another huge mosquito that was biting my arm. Boots was left in the house and was barking also. He had a strange bark, very high pitch. When we walked a little closer, Dad recognized the pickup owned by the Lankfords. Lloyd Lankford was a stern, short, and stout man who wore a bill cap over his short brown hair. Betty was shorter than Lloyd and a little on the hefty side with shoulder-length curly brown hair. They were from Oklahoma, and being in Alaska only five years, they still had a drawl. The Lankfords had three kids: two boys and a girl. One of the boys was only a few months old. Lloyd walked over and met us in front of the shack, carrying a fifty-pound sack of potatoes. Setting the bag of potatoes down, he shook Dad's hand and said, "These potatoes need to be eaten, and go great with salmon."

Betty was carrying a big round galvanized tin tub in her arms, and you could barely see her face over it. With all of us kids standing behind Mom, she handed it to her, saying, "I thought you might need this, not having plumbing and all. Ya'll will need something to bathe in."

The shiny gray tub was perfectly round with an oblong metal handle on each side that could move freely in their hinges. It had ridges on the outside all the way around, forming a standard pattern. The tub was a foot deep with a flat bottom that had nine rings forming ridges. I noticed a number 3 in the very center of the nine rings. Mom graciously accepted the tin tub that looked brand-new, telling Lloyd and Betty thank you.

Betty also brought us some jars of raspberry jam she had canned last summer, which she had fetched out of their pickup. She told Mom that canning was a necessity out here and she would teach her how to do it this summer.

*   *   *

We had been here at the property three weeks now and still sleeping in the camper. I had been wondering how we were going to bathe, even though we dipped into Goose Creek, which ran off into the slough. "Dad said the mighty Susitna River supplied all the creeks nearby such as Sheep Creek and Montana Creek."

Not having much money, Dad had even prayed about having enough food last night over supper. Our dinner tonight consisted of some humpy fish he had caught at the creek. Mom cut them into steaks and cooked them on our camp stove outside the camper. Humpies were small dark salmon with pink meat and a hump on its back. Mom made cornbread in the iron stove and pinto beans to go with it. Dad liked dessert every night, having a sweet tooth, so Mom made skillet cobbler with the blueberries we had picked one day in the woods.

After working on the homestead for a week or so, we hiked down to Goose Creek after Dad had got home from work one late afternoon, to try to catch some salmon as our food supply was getting low.

Our main road coming into the homestead curved to the right past the house and followed the field on up to the slough. The whole family hiked up the dirt road with deep ruts in it that was overgrown with willow brush and ferns. The big grassy field was on the right side of the road, and the woods were on the left side as we hiked to the slough. Mr. Lankford had told Dad it was about a half-mile hike.

Looking down on the side of the road under the many tall trees, I saw large blueberries ripening and said, "Mom, can we pick some berries and eat them?"

"Go ahead, but put some in the cans I brought, for dessert tonight," Mom said to us kids walking in between her and Dad. Mom had Dad's .41 magnum pistol on her waist in a gun belt, and Dad had his old rifle with a strap over his shoulder. Steve was right behind Dad, and the twins were holding hands behind Steve. Being the oldest kid, I had to take care of Kristi most of the time and help watch the twins as well. Kristi was too little to keep up with Dad's fast pace, so I carried her on my hip, trading sides as she was getting heavier.

Our mouths blue from eating all the blueberries we could about halfway to the slough, Dad said, "All right, break's over, let's go!" When Dad told us to do something, we knew we had better jump! Towering over us at six feet with his black Stetson on and his tan Western leather coat with fringes, his navy-blue eyes pierced ours with both sternness and concern.

We had just started walking again when Dad stopped in the middle of the road, put his hand up, and hushed us. My breath left me for a second as he looked around us in the brush and up in the tall trees. He quietly pulled his large rifle off his right shoulder, loading a bullet into the chamber. Dad pointed his finger up at the top of a tall spruce tree where a black bear cub had climbed and was on a branch hanging on to the tree trunk. The cub's mother was nowhere in sight. Protective mother bears were called sows, and knowing she was close by, Mom pulled Dad's already loaded pistol out of its holster and held it pointed at the ground. I put my hand over Kristi's mouth to quiet her and motioned to Devan and Dawn to keep still. Steve held each of the twins' hands as they looked very frightened.

Without any present danger and not to show a threat to the cub, Dad waved at us to keep going behind him. As Dad led us the rest of the way up the road, he yelled back to us, "Make some noise!" It was one of the only times we were allowed to be noisy, and that was when we were walking on trails or through the woods, to give the wild animals a chance to scatter and not feel threatened. Mom led us in a chorus of "Onward Christian Soldiers" as we made our way down the brushy road that ended above the bank of the big slough. We stood on the bank to look down at the silty river water that ran off from the glaciers. The dark and murky water ran wide and long and had a greenish color. Dad told us fishing would be good in the slough where the water was clearer.

There was a barely visible trail that hooked to the left of the slough that took us to the mouth of Goose Creek toward the Susitna River. Along the way to the creek, looking over the bank off to the right of the trail, I could see logs piled up in a tangled sort of way on the bank of the slough down by the water. I asked Mom, "Who would stack wood like that?"

Mom laughed and said, "The beavers! That's their home! They are called beaver dams." I thought the logs might be fun to climb on. Steve elbowed me, smiling, knowing that's exactly what we would do later.

Goose Creek was awesome! The crystal clear water flowed over a wide rocky bed with a thick bank of cottonwood and poplar trees on each side. Poplars have olive-green bark and are skinny with large paper-thin leaves. We kids would discover later on they made excellent toilet paper!

The tall fireweed on the bank created a magenta blanket as far as I could see. I had never seen anything so beautiful as I took a deep breath of the fresh natural breeze that touched my face.

Devan and Dawn already had their tennis shoes off, wading in the water. They were so cute with their short strawberry-blond hair and chubby cheeks. Both were pointing and giggling at the hundreds of silver salmon and dark humpies that swam by them in schools. You could almost walk on the top of the fish; they were so thick.

Dad said, "You girls stay with your mom and wash off in the creek, while Steve and I will hike up the bank a ways and do some fishing. We'll rinse ourselves off over there after we fish. Evelyn, keep my pistol close, make lots of racket, and holler if you see anything.

We won't be far." Dad and Steve took the rifle and the fishing poles and disappeared down the bank through the willow brush.

After laying a stack of towels in the grass, Mom undressed Kristi and handed her to me, while she took her own clothes off behind a large cottonwood. Tiptoeing naked across the brush on the bank, she took Kristi from me and waded into the middle of the creek, which was up to her waist. Mom told me to help the twins get undressed, and then she let us go into the water up to our waist. We had a blast splashing each other with the cold clear water and collecting different types of rocks from the bottom of the creek bed. With not another soul around, you could hear the echo of our laughter ringing through the thick green trees.

Mom held Kristi tightly as she dunked her and herself all the way down into the cold water, coming back up quickly. Kristi gasped for air as she came up, wrapping her little arms around Mom's neck.

Devan, Dawn, and I sat down into the water, holding hands, letting our heads go under. When we hit the rock bottom, we opened our eyes and could see each other. It was neat to watch the bubbles seeping from our mouths under the clear water.

Getting later and cooler, we were all shaking and our lips were turning blue from the cold water. Mom got out of the creek, wrapping herself and Kristi in a towel, and told us to do the same.

A few minutes after we all got our clothes back on, there was a rustling sound in the bushes down the bank. Mom reached for the big pistol and cocked the hammer back. Just then we heard a voice and saw Dad and Steve come out of the brush down the bank. "It's us, Evelyn, don't shoot!" Dad yelled. Steve was carrying the poles, and Dad had the rifle and a string of eight large humpies he had caught. Dad looked worried and said, "Let's get going with these fish before the bears come down for dinner." That's all he had to say, and we girls had our shoes on, walking quickly down the trail behind them. On the way back to the shack, Mom had us all singing "I'll Fly Away."

That evening Steve and I helped Dad clean the guts out of the humpies and cut their heads off. Mom and Dad had started a small garden when we first got here on the edge of the field that had a few vegetables barely growing. Mostly squash, cucumbers, and lettuce. Steve and I carried the fish guts in a big bucket, out the kitchen door, to the small garden area by the field and buried them with a shovel in the dirt to serve as fertilizer.

Several days later, Dad said we would heat water from the spring on the woodstove in the kitchen for bathing in our new family tub. After Steve, Devan, and I gathered some loose dry birch behind the camper, Dad showed Steve and me how to start a fire in the woodstove in the kitchen. We crumpled newspaper to put in the stove first, then small pieces of birch called kindling crisscrossed over the newspaper. Dad let Steve light the stick matches and start the newspaper on fire. As the fire started burning, we added larger pieces of birch Dad had cut from a dead tree. Then we filled a large pot with water and heated it on the stove, dumping the water into the galvanized tub that we put on the floor in the kitchen, until it was almost full.

Mom got to use the clean water first, then Dad, then me, and on down to the youngest. I had to give Kristi a bath, so after Dad came out of the house, I grabbed two clean towels, our jammies, and Kristi and headed into the dark house. Kristi was playing with jacks and marbles in the driveway under the big cottonwood with Dawn, covered in dirt.

Dad had lit a kerosene lantern, and it was on the counter in the kitchen. Even though it was still light out at 9:00 p.m., the house was dark and empty. I couldn't help but feel like I was being watched. "Oh well," I told myself, "it must be that this is a strange house to me." After taking Kristi's dirty pants off and her shirt and socks, I undressed also and looked into the small tub, wondering if we could both fit. Stepping in one foot at a time, I crossed my thin legs in Indian style and told Kristi to come over to me, and when she did, I picked her up and put her in the middle of my legs. Kristi was a somewhat mischievous, good baby, and she usually listened well. Her curly red hair was bouncing as she splashed the water with her chubby hands and laughed. "Don't get water on the floor. You'll waste it!" I said to her. After washing her hair and body, I set her outside the tub with a towel wrapped around her. Washing my own hair was a challenge in the perfectly round tub, so I got on my knees and leaned forward, dipping my head into the water, washing it with the shampoo Mom had left by the tub. "Lori, Lori," Kristi was pointing at the stove as she called for me. She couldn't say her *r*'s yet but was talking quite a bit. "That's hot! Stay away from it." I told her sternly, climbing out of the tub, so Steve would have warm water. Besides, Dad would give me a lickin' if I let Kristi burn herself, so I quickly dried her off and put her jammies on.

After I got my ankle-length white cotton nightgown on, we made our way through the dark, empty living room to the front door. Steve came into the shack as we were going out and took his bath by himself. Then Devan and Dawn went in together and came out in their nightgowns not long after they went in.

Dad and Steve went in the shack and took hold of the tub handles and dumped the dirty bathwater outside the kitchen door. It was almost midnight and dusky outside. Alaska is called the land of the midnight sun. I think God made it that way so we could have a lot of time to get ready for winter. I snuggled in the soft bed at the top of the camper with my three little sisters in between Steve and me; it felt good to be squeaky clean again.

4

THE LONE WOLF

EVELYN

It was a beautiful Sunday morning when Dennis and I woke up to the bright sunlight seeping around the dark curtains through the windows in the camper. We both climbed out of the bed I had made on the fold-down table. Stretching and yawning, we pulled our everyday clothes on for cooking and doing chores.

Dennis tugged on Steve's small bare foot sticking out of the covers from the bed in the cabover and said, "Time to roll out and do the chores! We're all going to church in Talkeetna after breakfast!"

Betty had told me the Talkeetna Bible Church service started at 11:00 a.m., and I was thrilled we already had a church to attend. I also thought it would be great to meet some new folks and see Talkeetna for the first time. That, and it was the nearest town within fifty miles.

Steve poked his head out of the covers and sprang up out of the crowded bed, jumping down to the camper floor. The girls heard their dad and sat up in bed, knowing they had to get up also and do their chores. Lori was to help Kristi get dressed, use the outhouse, and brush her baby teeth. Devan and Dawn could get themselves dressed and brush their own teeth and hair. They weren't allowed to go the outhouse by themselves, so Dennis or I took them.

After all the kids were dressed and washed up, Lori and the twins helped me make breakfast. To eat, we all sat at the wood picnic table outside the camper that Dennis had made the first week. He had just enough of the lumber he bought for the badly damaged kitchen floor for a large table.

We were all excited about going to church and seeing Talkeetna for the first time. It was the second week of August, and we had been living here on the property, in the camper, for a month now.

The second week Dennis took me out behind the house with his thirty-thirty rifle that was a single shot he could take apart and pack. It could kill a large grizzly at close range. He taught me how to shoot it, aiming at some old cans he had found in the shack. The rifle had a kick to it, so I had to learn to brace my feet and keep my elbows up, and was hitting most of the cans by the time I finished.

After eating salmon with syrup, eggs, and blueberry pancakes I had cooked on the camp stove, we took turns going in the camper to dress in the cleanest clothes we could find. Thank goodness we had plenty of clothes, because most of them were dirty! I knew I was going to have to do laundry at some point soon. I wore my light-green pedal pushers and a long-sleeve white cotton blouse. I had nylons on under my pedal pushers with white slip-on tennis shoes on my feet.

We had our weekly bath last night, on Saturday, so my short, thick, wavy red hair was easy to comb out. Dennis looked handsome in his blue wrangler jeans, his thin brown long-sleeve Western shirt with pearl snaps, his black cowboy boots, and his black Stetson.

Grabbing our Bibles and my white shiny purse, I gathered the kids and loaded them into the car. Dennis closed Meardha and Boots into the shack, and then he drove us in our Bel Air down the dirt road, this time heading for town.

Turning left on Parks Highway, which was gravel, he drove five miles north to the Talkeetna turnoff. Another fourteen miles and we drove into the historical town of Talkeetna.

The first thing we saw on the right side of the gravel road at the beginning of town was an old miniature log cabin. Beside one of the windows was a wolf hide stretched out and nailed to the logs on the outside and caribou antlers over the front door.

In front of the small cabin on the very corner of the main street going into the small town was a big wooden sign that said "Welcome to Beautiful Downtown Talkeetna." The unique sign had the letters in yellow paint on four separate pieces of long, flat brown wood nailed on top of each other on a tall post. There were pretty yellow daisies growing all around the bottom of the post.

Dennis kept driving down the main street through the small town as we took in the sights. Right after the Talkeetna sign, on the right side of the street, was a large white building with green trim and several windows. It had a large sign on the front that read "Fairview Inn."

Across from the hotel on the other side of the main street was a small old general store made out of red painted logs. The big square white sign on the front of the building said "B&K Trading Post, since 1921." Next to the store was a big two-story white building with a bar and restaurant called the McKinley Hotel.

On the right side of the street across from the Fairview was a log building with big windows with a sign that read "Talkeetna Laundromat." It had a little service station attached to it with one gas pump.

As we were coming to the end of the street, I noticed a sign on the left side that said, "Sheldon Air." I asked Dennis, "Is there an airport here?"

He replied, pointing off to the left of the main street, "Don Sheldon is a well-known pioneer pilot in these parts and has a small airstrip right over there behind that little red building, which is the grade school."

Lori's head poked out the back window, straining to see where she would start school. The pretty red one-room schoolhouse stood back a ways from the main drag close to the airport. Dennis turned right at the end of the main street and drove over the railroad tracks.

Being at the base of Mount McKinley, Talkeetna consisted mostly of mountain climbers, trappers, miners, sourdoughs, and fishermen. Sourdoughs were old native Alaskan miners that lived mostly off the land. Don Sheldon flew locals and tourists in and out of the Alaska Range and the Talkeetna mountain range. Going only a short distance, Dennis took a right down a long dirt road on the outskirts of town. "Where is Talkeetna Bible Church?" I asked Dennis. Just then we came to a small road off to the left of the street with a sign at the entrance that read "Talkeetna Bible Church, service at 11:00 a.m., Pastor Lloyd Dean."

The parking lot was small and full. The church was a small red Quonset hut. It was dark red and had a white roof, white framed windows, and a big white door with an eve.

People were arriving and looking at the "new people" as they got out of their cars and pickups. Dennis got out first and then opened all the doors to the Bel Air, and out we climbed, all seven of us. I told Dennis, "Well, I guess we're here to praise the Lord and fill the pews!"

He laughed and told our five kids standing quietly by the car, "You kids better mind your manners, and be on your best behavior!" I took Kristi from Dawn's arms and carried her across the parking lot with Dennis in the lead and the rest of the kids behind me. When we got to the door, one of the deacons was there to greet us and gave us a program. The deacon's name was Dick Smith, and he was about our age, in his late twenties, shorter than Dennis with dark hair and glasses. Dennis introduced all of us as we walked by him through the big white door into the warm and inviting church.

The sanctuary had maroon carpet and white metal folding chairs in several rows facing a wooden podium with a cross engraved on the front. After meeting several members of the church, we met pastor Lloyd, who was an older gentleman about seventy, and his wife, Ruth, who was older also. We filled a row of six seats toward the middle of the sanctuary. Dennis and I were on the end of the row with Kristi, and the rest of the kids next to us with their hands in their laps as instructed. Dick Smith led the congregation in a series of gospel songs out of their red hymnal book that they had under each chair.

After the praise, Dick announced children's church to be held at this time out of the sanctuary into a hallway in which the pastor's wife, Ruth, was teaching. Dennis motioned for Lori, Steve, Devan, and Dawn to go with her and several other children.

Pastor Lloyd gave a solid sermon on paying your debts and being honest, out of the King James Version of the Holy Bible. Then to our surprise, he started preaching about how it is a sin to have too many children. He was looking right at Dennis and seemed to be singling us out since we had five kids already and we're still young enough to have more. I was proud of Dennis as he just sat in the folding chair, holding little Kristi, smiling, knowing the sermon was meant for him and possibly other families in the congregation.

After church and telling the pastor we enjoyed his sermon, Dennis and I went down the hall to get our kids. In one room there was a Ping-Pong table, a small kitchen, and several small rooms for children's church. Devan and Dawn came running up to us, showing the pictures they had colored of Jesus with all the children around him. Lori and Steve had learned the verse "Let the children come unto me, saith the Lord."

We all loaded back into the Bel Air and drove back home, having enjoyed the day in town at our new church. When we arrived back at the shack, there was a white official-looking jeep in our driveway. Dennis recognized the vehicle as the game warden. The man with a brown uniform and hat stepped out of the vehicle as we all climbed out of the car. He introduced himself and shook Dennis's hand and said, "There are a lot of people that will try to come in through here to the slough and fish illegally. If you don't want me snooping around on your property, then I'd appreciate it if you would help keep them out."

Dennis said, "I sure will. I don't want people trespassing on my property anyhow!" The nice game warden and Dennis talked for a while, and then he sped off down our road.

Lori and I made tuna fish sandwiches, while Dennis and Steve worked on putting a new floor into the kitchen using plywood and nails.

The girls and I hiked down the trail through the woods to the spring to get more water and pick raspberries that were big and ripe. Kristi was in a baby pack strapped onto my back, and I was carrying the single-shot rifle also across my chest with a leather sling Dennis made for me, keeping my hands free and making it easy to grab and aim if necessary. Lori, Devan, and Dawn were in front of me, picking raspberries along the trail off the stickery branches, putting most of them into the cans I gave them. "Don't go into the brush, stay on the trail. There's more berries by the spring." I warned my little girls, who were getting so big.

Keeping my eyes on the brush along the trail and looking into the trees, I saw several large and smaller dark figures in the woods to the left of the trail almost to the spring. Hushing the girls and waving them closer, I pulled the double-barrel shotgun down, and put shells in the chamber. Devan's mouth hung open, seeing the large moose in the woods about a hundred yards from where we were standing. The big animals were interesting, breaking branches from the birch trees and didn't seem to mind we were there. Some of the moose had the biggest antlers I had ever seen. They all had dark hair, long skinny legs, a big drooping nose with little ears, and a flap of skin under their chins.

I told the girls quietly to move on down the trail to the spring. With their help, we filled the two five-gallon buckets up with fresh water and started back up the hill from the spring, hiking back quickly to the shack. Thankfully, the large moose were still in the same spot and were busy eating. Dennis had told us that if there were calves around, the cow moose were viciously protective like any other animal. A bull or cow moose can kill a human by stomping them to death with their hooves. When coming upon moose, he said to be quiet and get away. If necessary, we would have to climb a tree.

Keeping the rifle handy while carrying a five-gallon bucket of water, and Kristi on my back, I kept walking swiftly up the trail to the house. Lori and Devan carried the other bucket in front of me, and Dawn was holding the two cans of raspberries they had picked.

Finally, the blue camper and the shack came into our sight where we saw Dennis standing at the end of the trail with his rifle. Meardha and Boots came running up to us, jumping on the girls. "What took you girls so long?" We were about ready to go looking for you," Dennis said.

Taking my floppy brown hat off and shaking my head, I said, "Well, we saw some large moose in the woods by the spring!"

Dennis was excited about the moose and said, "I'll hike out tomorrow, and maybe I'll shoot us a moose for the winter." As we walked back to the camper, he continued, "It's getting late. We should have supper and buckle down for the night after I show you what I made for washing clothes."

After Steve and Lori heaved up the buckets of fresh water into the large drum, we all walked over to the garage, and Dennis opened the big doors and pulled out a handmade washboard. To my dismay, he was so proud of the washboard he made for me and proceeded to tell me how he made it and how I would use it. The kids giggled, knowing how I was used to using an electric washer and dryer and actually had a set we brought from Oregon in the backyard we couldn't even use. Dennis told me, "I took this piece of three-foot plywood here and sanded the corners so you don't get splinters. Then Steve and I cut some willow branches, and I split them. See?" As he showed me the split willows nailed to the plywood, he continued, "I took each willow branch and split it straight down lengthwise, creating a flat surface to nail to the plywood, so the smooth round part of the ten branches face up. You should be able to get the clothes nice and clean on this, and I made it fit so you can put it right down into the bathtub!" I didn't want to seem ungrateful, so I thanked Dennis and decided I would have to give it a try.

Dennis dipped a big beautiful Dolly Varden in flour and cooked it on the camp stove outside the camper on the table. He had caught it a few days ago in Goose Creek when he took Steve fishing. He promised to take me and the other kids fishing soon.

I made rice and beans and cornbread to go with the trout, and raspberry cobbler for dessert in the iron stove. Dennis led us in a prayer of thanks for the food and shelter provided to us, as we held hands under the blue sky as the night started to cool down.

I told the girls to get their PJs on after Lori and Devan did all the dishes in the two plastic basins we bought in Anchorage. Dennis and Steve put Meardha and Boots in the unfinished house and then fed them some dog food.

After the girls were tucked into the large bed in the camper, I walked outside to get a breath of the clean fresh air. Dennis was on his way back from building a horse corral with railroad ties when he stopped and turned to look out at the field with little Steve right next to him. Dennis planned to bring our two horses from Oregon next spring and was trying to prepare a place to keep them. I walked over to my husband and son to the edge of the field under the huge McKinley Mountains, and my breath was taken away! My eyes froze upon the beautiful gray-and-black sleek wolf that stood alone, tall and proud in the middle of the green grass. The big long-legged animal was close enough to see its dark eyes looking at us above its long black striped nose. Steve got closer to Dennis as his big gold eyes lit up wide. He kept quiet as not to scare the big wolf away or make it feel threatened.

Dennis pulled me into his side as the wolf ran off farther into the field. He said quietly, "I understand and respect him, the lone wolf, that's how I feel sometimes."

5

BOOTS!

DENNIS

R ed, orange, yellow, and gold were the pretty colors of the large
fall leaves. They were floating in the breeze softly to the ground.
The colorful leaves were shedding from the branches of the birch and
cottonwood trees everywhere on our homestead.

It was already the end of September, our first year here and
almost in our new house.

The plywood floor in the kitchen was finally finished and covered in light-blue linoleum I had bought in Palmer, which was sixty
miles away. Before putting the new linoleum down, with Steve's
help, I used my handsaw to cut an eighteen-inch square hole in the
wood floor. Then I dug into the ground below the floor about two
feet down and around to use for a root cellar, providing a cool place
where we could store some perishable food items. Using the piece of
the floor I had cut, I made a lid with two hinges and a small handle.
The cellar was to the left of the woodstove several feet, in the middle
of the someday dining area.

We were still in need of furniture but had the wood table I had
made out of plywood with benches that would work nicely in our
kitchen right over the cellar door, since it had enough room for all
seven of us to eat. Evelyn had wiped out the two small white cupboards that were above the kitchen counter and cleaned the smooth

tan-colored surface that was four feet long. It had a large porcelain sink and a small window above it with a thick wood frame and a wide, deep windowsill. It was old and rustic but made well to last for years.

The squeaky brown wood door in the kitchen that went out to the driveway had a worn-out round copper doorknob. The old door had a small framed window that I had repaired in August, along with the other two windows that were broken out in the shack.

With the scrap lumber, Steve and I had made a wood porch outside the kitchen door with wood railing on each side with two steps. Then we built a small roof over the whole thing. It felt like going through a tunnel to go in or out of the kitchen to the front yard.

Repairing the old outhouse was a priority and was another one of the many projects that needed to be finished before winter. It was already in use but needed to be weather tight.

Evelyn and the girls dusted, swept, and mopped the living room nesting in their new house. They were busy hanging dark curtains and talking among themselves, planning our sleeping arrangements. They were all tired of being cooped up in the camper and were looking forward to making the old shack their home as long as we all stayed together.

In August I had repaired the large garage that was attached to the house by closing in the holes the weather had caused in the siding and the roof. There was an opening in the ceiling of the garage that was an attic going all the way across to the rafters above the living room.

We had noticed a couple of old cardboard boxes up in the loft above the living room when we first came. Giving Steve and Lori a boost, they climbed into the rafters. After they dusted the cobwebs off the boxes, Steve dropped them down to me, and then they climbed back down, jumping onto the couch. The two boxes were filled with old yellow newspapers from the nineteen thirties. Without a television, the whole family enjoyed looking through the delicate papers for several weeks, then I stored them in the garage.

Just in time with the colorful fall leaves, after a warm summer, the weather was starting to turn also. Droplets of water on the saturated grass and the large puddles in the driveway were evidence of the sufficient amount of rain this season. The large leaves that lay on the wet ground were covered in frost and crackled under my boots.

Repairing the shack enough to live in, with the whole family's help, took most of the summer, and we still had work to do on the outside of the house to keep the cold out. We would have to wait to build a barn for the horses until next summer, with time and money running out.

I overheard the other day in town at B&K Trading Post the owner saying, "The farmer's almanac says it's going to be a tough winter, record-breaking cold and a ton of snow!" Hearing that worried me, knowing we weren't ready for a hard winter, much less any winter.

Steve stacked the pieces of wood we had unloaded off the bed of the pickup against the house to the left of the front door, while Boots, our little Chinese pug, ran in between his legs. It was Saturday morning, and Steve and I had taken the pickup into the woods, off the dirt road, and cut several dry birch trees down for firewood.

Sipping a glass of instant ice tea Evelyn had made, feeling worn out from cutting each log and piece of kindling by hand with my large ax, I watched my small boy stack the wood eagerly. "You're doing a great job, Steve, keep it up. It'll make you strong!" I told him, proud of how he knew how to work hard already.

Our next project today was to take the rusty fifty-five-gallon metal barrel that we had found behind the house in the brush and make a barrel stove with my welder and torch.

I would cut a round hole to insert a stove pipe that would go up through the ceiling connecting to the chimney. I would need to weld metal legs onto the bottom of the stove to hold it up off the floor. The barrel stove would burn hot, keeping the house warm on the cold winter nights, and with the ceiling being higher in the living room, there was less chance of a fire.

The new kitchen floor was higher than the living room floor, causing the kitchen ceiling to be lower, with a step up into kitchen from the living room, making the ceiling in the kitchen about seven feet from the floor and almost eight feet high in the living room.

Evelyn and the girls drove the Bel Air to Anchorage this morning to find some winter clothing, including boots and gloves. Using the rest of my last paycheck from Safeway, I told her to pick up a six-foot stove pipe for the barrel stove, and several rolls of plastic Visqueen to nail to the outside of the house to keep the cold air from seeping through the many cracks in the old birch siding. The rumors of Alaska blizzards and severe cold temperatures permeated my thoughts.

The barrel stove took an hour or so to finish but was sturdy enough to burn several pieces of birch for many hours. The girls weren't back from Anchorage yet, and it was already early afternoon and cold and windy.

A couple of months ago, Evelyn and I hiked up to the slough, and we caught a couple of large silver salmon using salmon roe I had dried out on a board by the house. When we got home, Steve helped clean them and then bury the guts in the garden like I told him to do.

When we all lay in bed in the camper that night, we could hear the grizzly's shrill sound as they fought over the salmon in Goose Creek and the slough at dusk. The bone-chilling sound broke the silence of the night for hours on end.

That night after eating more salmon for supper, and the last of the carrots and beets picked from our small garden by the field, the wind picked up, with a chill in the air, as it was almost October. I said to Steve, "It's getting dark. Lock the dogs up in the shack." Steve put Boots and Meardha in the house after playing with them in the yard for a few minutes.

Evelyn was tucking the girls into the bed when Steve and I walked into the camper, shutting the door quickly to keep the cold air out. After a few giggles from the bed above us and the music of the wolves, we all started to fall asleep as the camper swayed in the strong wind.

As I was just dozing off, I heard in the distance a shrill yelping sound. Evelyn sat straight up in bed and said, sounding frightened,

"What was that sound?" Lori and Steve were still awake and heard the yelping also and sat up in bed.

"Stay here, I'm going to check the animals," I told them as I grabbed my rifle and flashlight. Throwing my coat over my long johns, I slipped my boots on and headed outside the camper. I walked into the circular driveway where I didn't notice anything.

Heading back to the camper, I decided to check on the dogs in the house even though they couldn't have gotten out. Opening the living room door, I shined my flashlight at Meardha, who was lying on the floor right inside the door. I didn't see Boots, which was strange because he usually ran up to me. I looked around the living room and then went into the kitchen and saw the door was halfway open. The kitchen door must have been left open and Boots must have run outside. I stepped into the circular driveway calling for him and could not see him anywhere. I realized the shrill yelp must have been Boots fighting for his life against some big grizzly or maybe a wolf. The hard part was to go inside the camper and tell my kids their little pug was gone. Maybe it could wait until morning.

When I stepped inside the camper, Evelyn, Lori, Steve, and the twins were sitting on our makeshift bed, hoping for good news.

Tears filled Steve's eyes, and Lori and the twins started to cry when I told them Boots got out of the house and could not be found. Maybe he would come back. The kids knew he had been killed, by the shrill sound he made, probably by a grizzly. They all went to bed sobbing quietly.

We never did see our little pug Boots again and never even found his remains. The next day I noticed the part of the garden by the field where we had been burying the fish guts had been dug up by an animal. Even though the kids missed Boots, the thought of their brave little warrior pug challenging a big grizzly bear over fish guts somehow made him a hero in their memories forever.

6

MOOSE AT THE DOOR

LORI

Snowflakes bigger than I've ever seen were rushing sideways outside the kitchen window in a whirl of cold wind. Soon I was lost in my thoughts in a trancelike state, trying to make sense out of my new life as I washed the dishes. I was tall for six but still had to stand on a chair.

I thought about how Dad had made the house weatherproof just in time for a mid-October blizzard with a foot of snow sticking to the ground already. The barrel stove he had made that was in the living room was putting off a lot of heat with the help of the iron stove in the kitchen.

A few weeks ago, Dad and Steve put Visqueen on the outside of the house to keep the cold out of the cracks in the birch siding right before the bad weather set in. Knowing I was tired of being in the house and taking care of my sisters, Dad let me hold the Visqueen up in place on the old boards that sided the house while he hammered the nails. Steve unrolled the Visqueen against the house as it was needed and retrieved things for Dad, like nails.

Going to Talkeetna Bible Church almost every Sunday, we met some nice local families. Glenn and Janet Valentine had kids our age who went to children's church with us. The Valentines had heard from someone at church that we didn't have any furniture yet, and a few weeks ago, they brought us a queen-size bed, a couch, and an easy chair for Dad.

I was happy that they had brought their kids, Chad, Amy, and Beth, along, not having company for months. They had never seen our homestead before.

It was so great to finally be out of the camper and living in our house, even though, with only two large rooms, it was crowded with all seven of us. Dad and Mom put the queen-size bed in the dining room area in the kitchen for them to sleep in at night.

Dad had met a man named George McCullough and his wife, Delores, who lived in Talkeetna. Delores had kind eyes and a big smile. They seemed to care a lot about us, hugging us often.

We kids all slept in the living room next to the rusty big barrel stove Dad had welded together that put off lots of heat, keeping the house warm. The twins and I got the two small beds by the built-in bunk that Kristi slept in. Steve had to sleep on the couch across the room.

"Lori, are you done with the dishes yet?" Mom's voice startled me back from gazing at the large snowflakes twirling by the window. I handed Devan, who was standing on a wood stool next to me, another plate to dry to put on the toweled counter. With only one sink, I used our small plastic basin on top of the counter for wash water with dish soap, and the large porcelain sink had hot clear water for rinsing. I used spring water out of the big drum to heat in a big metal pot on the barrel stove for the supper dishes.

It was Saturday evening, and we had to have our baths even if the cold weather and snowstorm kept us from going to church tomorrow. When Devan and I finally put the last dish away in the two cupboards, I took the basin of dirty dishwater, and with Devan holding the kitchen door open, I threw the dishwater off the side of the small porch. As I turned to go back through the door in the kitchen, Devan said, looking outside through the door, "Look, Lori, there's a moose!"

Whipping around to see if she was teasing me, there in front of the porch not far from the steps was a large black moose looking straight at me with its big dark-brown eyes, as if it wanted to come in. Running back in the house and shutting the door, I yelled for Dad, who was sitting on the couch in the other room, cleaning his guns, with Steve watching. "There's a big moose outside the kitchen door!" Dad jumped up off the couch, making his way through the kitchen, while Devan, Steve, and I got out of the way.

Dawn was helping Mom fold the clean clothes they had washed in Talkeetna yesterday while I was in school. Kristi played with her spinning top toy next to them in the living room.

Dad looked out the small kitchen door window at the large animal blocking our porch and said, "Strange, it's by itself and it looks hungry. Let's leave it alone. Maybe it'll take off, looks pretty thin." We were all trying to look out the door window at the same time, so Steve and I got up on the small step stool to look out the window over the sink. The black hairy moose just stood there watching us, sniffing and scuffing in the snow, while the big flap under its long nose was wiggling back and forth. Meardha was barking at the door, wanting to get out to chase the large animal.

With the thick scruffy hair on the back of the moose's neck standing up, it scuffed its feet and took off running by the garage toward the woods. "All right, the excitement's over. Everybody had better use the outhouse before we take our baths," Dad said as he told Meardha to lie down by the stove and then continued, "Steve, heat up some water in the metal pot on the stove for our baths. We'll have to get more water from the spring as soon as this storm blows over."

Mom put her new snow boots on and her heavy coat with the Savage rifle over her body in the leather sling to take us to the outhouse. Dawn asked me quietly as she put on her little boots, "Lori, don't you miss Boots?" I almost wanted to cry again, remembering our cute little pug we brought from Oregon, who only lasted a couple of months out here. "I miss him really bad, Dawn. We all miss him," I answered her, holding my tears back. I was learning a hard reality of life.

"Let's go, girls," Mom said as she headed for the front door with us girls behind her, me carrying Kristi. Mom opened the front door going out of the living room, and there right in front of the door was the big moose again! His big nose was inside the door frame and was so close Mom could have reached out and put her hand on it! The wind and snow blew in around him as Mom yelled and jumped back, almost landing on us! She was so startled, and so were all of us kids. Dad and Steve jumped up off the couch again, and we all stood there staring at this huge but frail moose at our front door as if he wanted to come in. Mom bravely said to him, "Well, come in if you want to!" The moose, to our surprise, actually put his right front large hoof over the crevice onto the linoleum. Meardha jumped off the big easy chair that was red cloth with wooden arms and started to bark at the big hairy animal coming into her house and near her family.

We all quickly took several steps back as Dad put a shell into the rifle. With Meardha barking and now in front of the moose, it backed up quickly out of the door frame but stood its ground outside. I felt kind of sorry for the frail moose shaking the snow off his coat, trying to survive.

After shutting the living room door, Dad said, "Evelyn, take the girls out the kitchen door and go around the back of the house to the outhouse. I'll keep an eye out on the moose this way." Mom and we girls headed through the partition for the kitchen door, and when Mom opened the door, there was the moose again! This time it was charging at us, almost coming up the steps! "It's over here again, Dennis!" Mom yelled into the living room. Dad came running with Steve and Meardha behind him into the kitchen. We all knew Dad was going to shoot him as there was no other way to get rid of him. Besides, we needed more meat. I still felt bad for the hungry moose.

Dad told us to go into the living room and then fired one shot, dropping the moose right in front of our porch outside the kitchen.

After Dad shot the moose, Mom took us girls out the living room door to the outhouse in the whiteout of snow and wind. We could barely see ahead of us as we made lots of noise talking about the moose at our door.

Dad and Steve dragged the dead moose's carcass into the three-foot snowbank, and Dad skinned its hide back with his large butcher knife. Then he cut the four large quarters of meat off the carcass without even gutting it, while he had Steve hold on to it to keep it from moving. After putting the quarters of meat into a package of butcher paper and masking tape, Steve carried each of the four large packages into the kitchen and put them in the hole in the ground to keep them cool. I watched as Dad quickly carried the dead moose carcass over to the field. He hooked it out into the snow, as far as he could for the large wolves to eat. Dad told us the reason he butchered the moose that way, and threw it into the field, wasn't just to feed the wolves, but to keep the grizzlies that had not hibernated yet away from the house.

The new snow was coming down in buckets covering the bloodstained snowbank, as layer by layer of the cold flakes fell to the ground.

When Mom and we girls got back to the house, we shook the snow off our coats and stomped our feet to get it off our boots before we went into the living room. Mom and Steve filled the round bathtub, this time putting it behind the partition where there was some privacy. Dad was still in the garage, so Mom took the first bath, then us girls. The two kerosene lanterns hummed loudly as they glowed with a soft yellow light from their wicks. It was a comforting sound and made me feel safe and warm with the snow outside blowing around the windows.

The twins and Kristi and I were all ready for bed and in our nightgowns when Dad and Steve finally came in, stomping and shaking the snow off, and then took their baths also.

The next morning the wind had stopped, but the snow was still coming down hard, so Dad said we would stay home and stay warm today. Sitting around the iron stove in the kitchen after Dad blessed the food to our bodies, we all had one of Mom's big Sunday breakfast of homemade blueberry pancakes, salmon, and scrambled eggs. Since Dad was working in Anchorage, he brought home fresh bread, eggs, and milk every week when it was cool enough to store in the ground. Sometimes after church he would stop at the B&K store for small items and let us kids all pick out a piece of candy.

The snow continued to fall off and on the rest of October, leaving four feet of snow on the ground at all times. Dad had to climb up on our roof and shovel the heavy snow off several times. Wearing his leather fringe coat, a black stocking cap with ear muffs, and his knee-high black snow boots, Dad made paths through the deep snow from both doors with the wide snow shovel he had bought in Anchorage. Safeway had gone on strike a week ago, so he stayed home and hunted for meat for the family.

Uncle Doug hiked in from the highway one weekend, and he and Dad hiked across the field to Montana Creek, where they could hike out to the little islands on the big Susitna River. Dad shot a big moose on one of those islands. He and Uncle Doug packed it out through the thicket, taking all night to get it home. Mr. Lankford let Dad store the meat in his freezer, and Dad was glad to give him a share.

Halloween wasn't the same this year, stuck out at the homestead in the snow. The last few years we got to trick or treat in our quiet neighborhood with our friends on Mabel Street, and I missed that. The never-ending mysterious beauty of our new homestead healed my longing.

On Halloween night, Mom let us all dip our own apples into melted caramel she had put on the iron stove in a small cast iron pot. We kids sat around the stove eating the caramel apples and telling ghost stories with the wolves and the wind howling outside.

Dad came in from the garage and handed each of us a small bag of candy corn he had bought at B&K Trading Post. While I lay in bed that night, I thought this was a pretty good Halloween after all.

7

WINTER IN ANCHORAGE

EVELYN

D ennis and I both knew we weren't ready for the record-breaking winter that was promised Alaska this year, our first year at the new homestead. It was mid-November, not even winter yet, and there was still snow coming down almost every day with temperatures at night below zero. Dennis parked the blue Ford pickup at the end of the two-mile road by the highway so he could hike out if necessary. Without a plow or snow machine, we were stuck at the homestead now for a month, not even able to do laundry.

Last week Lori and I washed some of our clothes in the kitchen sink with the homemade washboard Dennis made for me, and we hung them by the woodstoves to dry. We needed to go to Anchorage for more food and supplies, as our food supply was starting to get low besides meat. Thank God Dennis and Doug had shot another moose, and we still had salmon and the fifty-pound bag of potatoes that were almost gone.

Waking up next to Dennis in the dining room next to the woodstove with the snow reaching our windowsills on the outside of the house, I said, "How are we going to get the kids to school this year?" Dennis looked like he was lost in thought when he said, "We're going to have to move into Anchorage this winter until I make enough money to buy a snow machine and build a barn." He continued after propping himself up on his side, "I have a friend in Anchorage I worked with at Safeway that manages a trailer park. You can hike out with me to the Lankfords' today, and I'll try and get a hold of him."

I gave him a kiss on the cheek and jumped out of the bed, happy to hear he had a plan to get us out of here for the winter. I was worried Lori and Steve wouldn't be able to go to school at all this year.

Waking all the kids up, I told them the good news about moving to Anchorage for the winter. I think we all had cabin fever and were excited about getting to go to the big city and live for a few months.

After breakfast of salmon, fried potatoes, coffee, and powdered milk, Dennis told Lori and Steve to keep everyone in the house, while he and I hiked the long ways to the Lankfords'.

The Lankfords were glad to see us and invited us into their warm cabin right away. Dennis made phone calls while I warmed up by their woodstove and chatted with Betty and Lloyd. After Dennis finished his phone calls, he came in the room and said, "It's all set. My friend Tom that manages the Penguin trailer park in Anchorage is going to rent us a trailer for the winter for cheap."

"Praise the Lord!" I exclaimed, feeling relief from possibly being snowed in all winter.

Lloyd and Betty understood our dilemma, and Lloyd offered to help Dennis get us out to the highway as the weather was supposed to lighten up for a few days.

On the way back, the winds had calmed, quieting the forest, leaving only the sound of a large snowshoe rabbit darting in between the spruce on the snow surface. I have to admit, I was falling in love with the natural beauty of this rugged country that brings out a certain survivalist instinct in your spirit. The enormous and strong mountain ranges, the wide and rushing rivers, and the dangerous wild animals made a human feel small and unprepared.

We passed a few moose by the barely visible train tracks only a short distance from us. The large moose ignored us as they continued to dig in the snow for vegetation.

Steve asked Dennis as we were eating supper that evening, "Dad, can we take Meardha?" The rest of the kids stopped eating and looked at Dennis, waiting for an answer. "Yes, we are taking Meardha." Dennis told all of us, knowing he would miss her too.

The next morning Lloyd showed up with his snow machine, pulling a large sled. He and Dennis made a trip out to the highway with all of our belongings where our Ford pickup was parked, then came back for all of us.

After shutting down the woodstoves, Dennis helped the kids and me into the large sled. The kids were bundled up in their winter clothes down in the sled with Meardha and me in front of them. The sun had come out today and was glistening off the snowbanks as we made our way down the trail Lloyd had already created with his snow machine.

With only the pickup for all of us to ride in to Anchorage, some of us would have to ride in the back. I sat in the bed of the truck with Meardha and Steve and Lori, huddled together up against the cab, in the freezing cold weather, the whole hundred miles.

The big blue sign at the entry of the trailer park said in large white letters "Penguin Court," with a character of a penguin with a blue suit on and a top hat and a cane. Our trailer was white with tan trim around the windows and door. It had two bedrooms, one bathroom, a living room, a kitchen, and a little mudroom going out the front door. There was a big cottonwood tree by the door with large branches that covered the trailer.

What a blessing to be out of the snowdrifts to being in town again with running water, electricity, and a washer and dryer at the park. Dennis's brother Doug also stayed with us often.

The next day I took Lori and Steve to the Anchorage Elementary School and enrolled Lori into the second grade and Steve into the first grade. The school district was hiring a maintenance manager, so with Safeway on strike, Dennis took the job and went right to work five days a week for the school district.

Still interested in nursing, I took a position at the Anchorage general hospital as an aide in the OB-GYN department four days a week.

There were a lot of nice people that lived in our trailer park, including a lady my age that had three kids of her own, whom I hired to watch the twins and Kristi while Dennis and I went to work. We wanted to save enough money to buy the equipment for the homestead we needed. To be able to go back out there next spring and stay for good.

One day while we were all gone, Meardha got out of the house and onto the main highway through Anchorage and got hit by a car. Thankfully, Dennis had got tags for her to wear with the number to his work, and someone called to let him know she had been hit but was still alive. Dennis rushed to Meardha and put her in the car, taking her to the animal hospital. She had a broken pelvis and could barely get around. The kids and Dennis all babied her back to health like one of the family.

While working at the hospital, I met a nurse who worked in the same department named Jean Lok. We instantly became friends and got together frequently with Dennis and me, and her husband, Barry, who was Chinese and owned a Chinese restaurant in Anchorage. They introduced us to Joe and Jeanette Seale, who also became good friends to us. The Loks came to our trailer for a delicious feast I had prepared with the girls' help on Thanksgiving.

Before we knew it, Christmas was only two weeks away, and the kids were excited about Santa coming to put gifts around the six-foot pine tree that we had decorated together. The store-bought ornaments, lights and candy canes, and the strings of popcorn the kids set up and worked on for evenings on end filled the tree, putting us in the holiday spirit.

A few days later, after a long day assisting with newborn babies at the hospital, I walked in the front door of the trailer. I found Dennis sitting down on the couch with a concerned look on his face. I rarely saw him sit down in the afternoon, and the kids were all in their bedroom.

After hanging my coat up, I set my purse on the coffee table and asked him, "What's wrong, Dennis?" He looked up from a letter he was reading and said, "You had better sit down, Evelyn. You have received a telegram by delivery from your folks in Washington."

Dennis continued as I sat on the couch next to him. "It's about Joyce. Maybe I had better read it to you," he said.

I nodded and my heart started to race as he read the words on the telegram exactly as written from Mom and Dad. "Joyce has been in a train accident-stop-she is in Holy Cross hospital Spokane-stop-critical condition-stop." The tears were welling up in my eyes as I thought of my little sister, only twenty-four years old, being in critical condition. "What could have happened?" I asked Dennis through my tears. He looked upset also as Joyce was his sister-in-law and said, as he gave me a hug, "I'll get you a plane ticket."

The very next morning I flew out of the Anchorage airport to Spokane, Washington, with Kristi, waving goodbye to Dennis, Steve, Lori, Devan, and Dawn, just ten days before Christmas.

My dad, Verne, my mom, Gloria, and my other younger sisters, Ginger, who was twenty-two, and Wendy, who was only twelve, picked us up at the airport in Spokane. Dad told me that my sister Joyce had left her children, Joy, who was the same age as Kristi, and Dougie, who was only eight months old, with their father Norman to go into town and pick up a suit that was being dry cleaned. My grandma, Anne Salisbury, who was mom's mother, had just had a stroke and died two weeks ago at the age of eighty-five. The suit was for the service that was to be held the day after Joyce's accident. Joyce and Norman lived in Newport, right next to Dennis's parents, Austin and Viola. We thought it was strange she left her two kids with Norman, as they meant the world to her, and she rarely left them behind even for short errands. The shaken engineer told Dad that when Joyce drove her Buick across the train tracks with a big feed store blocking the view and no crossing arms, she froze on the tracks. The engineer said, "I saw her look directly at me, but she wouldn't move off the tracks."

Dad went on to tell me that Joyce was in a coma and her kidneys were failing fast.

When we walked into the critical care unit where Joyce was lying in a small private room, I rushed into her room to her side, hoping to see her better. My beautiful sister with her curly blond hair poking out of a gauze wrap around her head with her face badly bruised lay there unresponsive and unaware of what was going on around her.

After several dialysis treatments, my sister's kidneys completely failed, and she remained in a coma. The whole family held hands and prayed for Joyce, hoping she would recover. We talked about the things we would do after she got well.

Then the doctor came into the room and told Mom and Dad the worst news a parent could ever hear. Joyce had brain damage and kidney failure, and if she survived, she would be like a vegetable.

Several days passed as our mom lay on her bed and cried for her daughter. One by one we spent time with our beautiful, gentle Joyce, praying and crying at her bedside. I whispered to my little sister, "I love you, sis." I kissed her tenderly on her bruised cheek, bursting into tears as I left the dark room.

Dad and Mom had to make the decision to take her off the ventilator and let her go.

My sister Joyce went to her savior Jesus Christ. Her funeral service was held the next day in Elk, Washington, at the country church where Mom and Dad attended. A lot of relatives attended, including cousins on Mom's side. Pastor Green officiated the beautiful service for my little sister. It seemed unreal that she was actually gone so young.

Mom said Joyce had told her for some strange reason several months ago that if anything ever happened to her, to take care of her kids. Dennis's distraught brother Norman reluctantly signed over custody of his and Joyce's kids, Joy and Dougie, to Dad and Mom, knowing he couldn't take care of them. My sister Joyce met Norman in high school and started dating him their junior year. Joyce thought he was handsome and smart. They were married in Blanchard Idaho a few years after Dennis and me.

When Dennis picked Kristi and me up at the airport in Anchorage the night of Christmas Eve, he told me a funny story. He had given Meardha too much milk of magnesia for constipation because of her broken pelvis. I laughed for the first time in a week when he said a few hours later she sprayed the house with dog diarrhea! I was grateful Dennis cleaned up the mess before I got home.

The kids all got out of bed when we walked in the door of the trailer, happy to see us after a week and a half. They were all talking at once, and I heard Lori say, "Mom, look at the stockings Dad hung for us!" There hanging by the woodstove in the living room were five of Dennis's big dirty gray wool socks with the red rim at the top, one for each of our kids, who all went to bed hoping Santa would know where they were this Christmas.

Before we knew it, the new year was upon us, and the twins were going to be four years old in a few days on the nineteenth of January. Dennis was planning to go to Oregon in April with Steve to get our four-year-old stallion, Dungo, and the white mare, Blue. We would hopefully be able to get back to our homestead by the end of May.

Staying in Anchorage was convenient and nice for the time, but we still wanted to raise our kids in the country. Dennis and I will have saved enough money to buy a snow machine and start other projects around the property by May. He would have to continue to commute to Anchorage, as work was hard to find in Talkeetna.

Dennis came home late from work with an early birthday present for the twins. All the kids, except Kristi, were still up and excited to see him walk in with a medium-size black-brown-and-white dog. "He's a sheltie, and his name is Pete," he told the kids as they immediately surrounded the shy dog. "Do we get to keep him?" Devan and Dawn asked at the same time while petting the friendly dog, who was licking their faces. Dennis looked at our kids playing with the new dog while Meardha joined in, trying to get some attention too, and said, "Yep, we are keeping him. Got him from a shelter here in Anchorage. He was rescued from a house where he was chained up and teased." The little dog seemed happy, wagging his tail and running in circles with Steve and Lori and the twins chasing him around the living room and Meardha barking at them. In all the commotion, Kristi woke up crying, and Dennis carried her into the living room where she squealed with delight at our new dog Pete.

The twins had a nice birthday at home with cake and ice cream and gifts. Their babysitter came over with her kids also for the party, and they all played pin the tail on the donkey.

The rest of the cold winter went by quickly, as Dennis and I continued to work, take care of our kids, and visit with our new friends in Anchorage. Before we knew it, spring had come, along with Kristi's second birthday in March.

I gave notice at the hospital in April as I would not be able to leave the kids alone at the homestead or commute to work. During that time, Dennis and Steve had just gotten back from Oregon with Dungo and Blue. He left them at the homestead with Doug until we could return.

We had a wonderful Easter at the Loks' house after church and we said our goodbyes, as we were leaving the day after. The kids carried in their baskets the two dozen Easter eggs they had proudly colored for the occasion.

We were all excited to get back out to the homestead and out of the city once again, even though the conveniences such as power and water were something I enjoyed and definitely appreciated!

8

CANTANKEROUS STALLION

STEVE

Lori and I got to ride in the bed of the blue pickup by ourselves all the way from Anchorage back to the homestead. We huddled down with our backs against the cab, behind the boxes of clothes and groceries, and Meardha and Pete wagging their tails with excitement.

It was almost May, and we had the whole spring and summer to get ready for winter this year, hoping we could finally stay at our new homestead. We kids hadn't been back all winter. Early April Dad and I drove to Oregon with the pickup and went to our old house on Mabel Street. It had sold already and seemed so different from the trailer in Anchorage. In a way I missed our old neighborhood. Dad and I spent two weeks there before having to leave. Dungo and Blue rode in the blue-and-white horse trailer Dad had rebuilt by welding it strongly together all the way back to the homestead. Dungo's registered quarter horse name was Dungaree, and he was a four-year stallion. Dungo's dad was a well-known race winner in Portland named Whistle Britches.

While Dad and I were out at the homestead with the horses for a few days, we built a large corral for the horses made out of railroad ties and bailing wire. I got blisters on my hands from digging the holes and tamping the posts in the frozen ground. Dad said it was part of learning to work hard. Uncle Doug would be taking care of the horses until we returned to the homestead.

After a long drive from Anchorage, Dad turned our Ford pickup onto our road off the Parks Highway. Lori and I jumped up and looked over the cab. Even though it was spring, it still looked like winter with snow still covering the ground. Dad stopped the pickup and told me to get out so he could show me how to turn the hubs on the wheels of the pickup, to put it into four-wheel drive. I noticed the trees that lined our road still had long thick icicles hanging from the branches where the snow had tried to melt in the still-freezing temperatures. Some of them were bigger than my little sister Kristi.

When we got to the train tracks, Dad stopped suddenly as a big blue-and-gold Alaska train was coming from the south with the engineer blasting its loud horn. The big train came rushing through the crossing right in front of us faster than I've ever seen anything go. Lori and I stood up to see the train over the cab of the pickup, and Devan and Dawn got to look out the open windows. The long train finally went by, then Dad made sure no other trains were coming before crossing the tracks, and kept on driving down the rough road. We came to the right hook in the road where the big cottonwood marked the start of our field. There were still patches of snow on the field, and the huge Mount McKinley was in full sight with snow still covering it like a blanket. Mom told me that the mountains here in Alaska always have snow on them year-round. I felt a certain fear in my young mind about being back in the bush with the wild animals and the hard work ahead of us.

Finally we were back at the homestead and making the circular driveway when Dad put the pickup into park right in front of our house. Lori and I jumped out of the back of the pickup onto the driveway. Meardha and our new dog Pete had already jumped out over the tailgate and were chasing each other around the yard. Dad, Mom, and the twins got out of the cab, while Mom picked Kristi up, who had fallen asleep.

Bending down to retie my black-and-white sneakers, I heard Dad call my name through the sound of my noisy sisters talking and giggling. I answered quickly, "Yes, Dad?" Dad was unloading the big boxes from the bed of the pickup as he told me, "Go and open the garage doors and let Dungo and Blue out so they can go out on the field."

Uncle Doug had left a couple of days ago after staying with the horses. He had left them in the garage for shelter and protection with plenty of feed until we were to get back today.

Reluctantly, I walked over to our big gray wood garage that was attached to the house. I couldn't deny Dungo made me nervous, being a big strong stallion, but I knew I had better do what I was told. Mom and the girls had all gone in the house, putting our stuff away after staying in Anchorage all winter.

I wished Lori would have stayed outside and helped me let Dungo out of the garage. She was like my best friend because she liked to do things I did, like ride horses and go fishing. We always watched out for each other at school and in our neighborhoods.

Reaching up for the big wood handle that kept the garage doors closed, I could hear Dungo scraping his hooves on the concrete floor and snorting loudly. Slowly pulling up the long wood handle out of the iron brackets, the big wood doors creaked open. There was our big stallion Dungo standing at the back of the dark garage with his ears back and his head down. Blue, our white quarter horse mare, instantly ran out of the garage and barely missed me as she whisked by. Dungo was looking straight at me with his big dark eyes! Scraping his front hooves on the concrete, he seemed like he was mad and hungry. Not seeing any feed around, I knew I needed to get him out of the garage so he could graze on the field.

Even though Dad taught us not to show fear around a horse, I was shaking in my shoes and beads of sweat began to appear on my forehead. I heard Dad yell from the truck out front as he was still unloading, "Everything all right, Steve?" My small hands trembled opening the big wood doors all the way, hoping the dark red horse would come out on his own. He didn't seem to care about coming out of the garage and just stood his ground. I clicked my tongue, trying to get him to come out with no success. I walked slowly into the garage, talking to Dungo, "Come on out, Dungo, come on out!" I slowly reached my left hand out to him, and suddenly the big angry stallion was lunging at me! His head came at me as I ducked down and tried to get away from him. Then Dungo's big mouth opened up and clamped down on the top of my head!

My head felt numb, and my body went limp as he picked me up off the concrete floor by my head with his large teeth! Then he threw me against the wall and then ran at full speed out of the garage!

The almost six years of my life were swirling in my mind as I thought I was dead lying on the hard floor. I heard Dad yell loudly for Mom as I could see him running into the dark garage, "Evelyn, come quick! Steve's been hurt!" The next thing I remember, Dad was carrying me in his arms out of the garage and Mom was crying, saying, "His head is bleeding bad, Dennis!" Dad told Mom to get some wet towels and bag balm, and then he put me down in the metal folding chair outside the front door of the house. I felt like I was going to faint as I tried to sit up in the chair. The blood from my head was spurting up like a fountain and was dripping down my face. Lori came running out of the house with a cold wet towel, handing it to Dad as he put it right on top of my head with great pressure.

Because of the blood drenched into my red hair that was dripping into my face, I could barely see my sisters all standing around me, wondering what had happened.

Mom ran out of the house with the bag balm and packed it onto my head after Dad got the bleeding to stop. Lori was giving me sips of water from a plastic glass and helping to hold me up. Dad and Mom wiped my face and then put a gauze wrap around my head. Dad said, "He'll be fine, just a few lacerations. If Dungo wanted to really hurt him, he would have bit down hard and broke his skull."

Mom looked really upset still and said, "What in the world made him bite Steve?"

Dad said, "The gal that I bought Dungo from, when he was two, in Oswego, Oregon, kept him in a dark stall most of the time. Being contained in this dark garage for days at a time probably made him get cantankerous." Dad looked like he felt bad and continued, "I should have let him out myself!"

Devan and Dawn were still crying, as Lori and Mom helped me get off the metal chair. They walked me into the house, where I lay on the couch the rest of the day.

Lori told me that Dad went out to the field where Dungo was and caught him up with a halter and rope. After saddling him and putting his bridle on, Dad ran Dungo hard through the field, making him obey different commands, showing him he could not dominate us.

This was one time my little sisters were really nice to me, bringing me things to do and chatting with me all day. Kristi even handed me her stuffed rabbit to hold, "Make you better," she said. Mom told them to keep me awake while she and Lori worked around the house.

No matter how bad I wanted to go outside and run around, my throbbing head made me lie still.

A couple of days later, Dad took the bandage off my head and washed my scalp with peroxide. He said the lacerations were healing nicely and we could leave the bandage off and I could even run around outside.

While I was laid up, Dad and Mom had gone into the woods and cut down a bunch of spruce and poplar trees for Dad to build a barn for the animals and to store hay. Lori and I had to straddle the logs and scrape the bark off so Dad could use them for the walls of the barn. I used a long blade Dad had with wooden handles called a draw knife to pull back on the bark to peel it from the spruce logs. The strong smell of fresh peeled bark filled the air as my hands slid across the slickness of the sap.

Mom held the boards up for Dad, after he built a strong frame for the walls, while he nailed each one close together to keep the cold air out. After a couple of days and several blisters later, Mr. Lankford came over one day and helped Dad put the roof on the barn. They used the smooth poplar logs and large sheets of tin. The front of the barn was taller than the back, making the roof slant so the snow would slide off to the ground. It had two big wood doors on the front but was barely tall enough for Dungo to find shelter.

Dad nailed whole poplar logs across the inside of the barn from one wall to the other to make two stalls and a small tack room on the right as you walk into the barn. The tack room was closed off from the stalls with sheets of plywood and would be fun to hide inside.

The small barn, which Dad called the cowshed, was a short distance from the house next to the main dirt road.

My head was finally almost healed after a week, and I was able to take my bath on Saturday night and wash my crusted thick hair.

Sunday morning Dad woke us all up early to do our chores and have breakfast before church. It was May 2, Lori's seventh birthday, and we were all excited to go to Talkeetna Bible Church to see our new friends again.

Dad and I headed out to the corral to let Dungo and the mare out onto the field that was starting to grow again after a long winter. He told me to go open the gate and let them out while he stood outside the large round corral and watched. He talked to the big horses in a strong low voice as I opened the wooden gate with wire strung across it, "Easy, easy now."

My heart was racing and my hands were shaking, but I knew Dad wanted me to get over my fear of Dungo, and I had to obey him. After I swung the gate open, I clicked my tongue at the big stallion, hoping he would come out. He pranced over to Dad for a pat and then threw his head up in the air and ran out of the corral and onto the field at a full run, paying no attention to me standing outside the gate. The big mare followed behind.

Dungo could go wherever he wanted on the property during the day because Dad had put up an electric wire behind the house, up against the woods that went all the way behind the camper to the trail going to the spring. He didn't want Dungo or the mare to get into the woods or the creek, where any wild animals could hurt or kill them. Dad used a twelve-volt fence charger to hook to the single thin electric wire that he strung from each tree, tied securely to yellow plastic hooks he nailed onto the birch trees. He had me tie small white pieces of sheet every few feet on the wire Mom had cut up to keep us and the horses from getting shocked.

After Dad and I fed the dogs, we went back into the house for breakfast that Mom and Lori had made. We had hotcakes and scrambled eggs with the last dozen we had brought from Anchorage.

The powdered milk we drank tasted funny and weak after having cow's milk all winter. We didn't have electricity for a refrigerator to store milk or eggs in the summer, so it was a treat to have them in the winter when we could keep them cold.

Dad said we might get chickens this summer after he could build a coop to keep them in and have fresh eggs most of the year and chicken meat also.

When we got to Talkeetna Bible Church early, I saw my friend Chad Valentine with one of the Smith boys playing outside on the swings. He seemed glad to see me and waved to me as I walked up the white steps into the red Quonset hut church. Dad shook hands with Mr. Smith as we walked through the door into the sanctuary, where he and Mom talked to the other adults we had met last year. I tugged on Mom's long coat while looking up and asked her, "Mom, can Lori and I go outside and say hi to our friends?" She looked down at me from her conversation with Mrs. Smith and said, "Go ahead, but only for a few minutes. Church is getting ready to start soon."

Lori and I walked out to the playground that was on the right side of the small church and walked right up to Chad to say hi. Tyler Smith was mine and Chad's age also and had an older sister named Farrah, who was seven like Lori. They played on the big metal swing with us, along with Chad's sister Amy, who was four, and Tyler and Farrah's little brother Landon, who was the twins' age. Mr. Valentine's first name was Glenn. He came out of the church and called to us all to come inside.

After the singing and announcements, the whole church sang "Happy Birthday" to Lori and to other people in the congregation that had a birthday this week. Children's church was a lot of fun learning verses out of the Holy Bible. We colored pictures of people and animals that pertained to the stories Mrs. Smith read us out of the big children's Bible.

I got to sit in between Chad and Tyler during children's church and felt grown-up and proud to have two good friends of my own already. When the adults got out of church, Dad let us all play on the swings for a short time while they visited. Soon we were pulling out of the church parking lot in our Bel Air and heading home for afternoon chores.

Before we left Talkeetna, Dad stopped at the trading post, B&K, and let all of us kids pick out an ice cream out of the freezer case and sit outside on the wooden deck and eat it before we left. Mom picked out some groceries, including a cake mix, butter, and powdered sugar, to make Lori a birthday cake.

Back at the homestead after we all changed into our everyday clothes, Dad took me out to the cowshed and handed me Dungo's blue halter and his lead rope. He looked down at me under his black Stetson with his stern eyes and said, "Go and catch Dungo up, and put him up in the corral."

My face flushed and my heart started to beat fast, and it felt like I was going to throw up. The vision of the big stallion coming at me with his big teeth and throwing me kept me from doing what I was told.

I knew I had better move but felt frozen and couldn't get my feet to take a step. Dad's words snapped me out of my inability to move, and quickly I ran out of the shed and headed out to the field. "You want a lickin'?" Dad had asked me sternly.

Dungo and the mare were grazing about a hundred yards out on the thick green grass that was up to my hips. Our stallion's large muscles rippled and shone in the sun. He picked his head up and looked at me with his big dark eyes. I looked back at Dad watching me from the edge of the field. I bravely walked slowly up to Dungo with the halter and lead rope behind my back. He started to walk away from me like he knew I was going to catch him up. Remembering what Dad had taught me, I told Dungo sternly, "Whoa, Dungo, Whoa!" The well-broke horse knew that meant to stop, and he did. I walked up to his big neck, and with my small trembling hands, I wrapped the lead rope around it so he would stand still. While he was chewing on a bite of grass, I slipped the halter over his nose and fuzzy ears and fastened the buckle under his chin as quickly as I could.

Dungo sniffed my red hair, as I took hold of the lead rope and nudged the big animal forward toward the shed. Powerfully, the red stallion took big steps through the field with me hanging from the lead rope, unable to keep up with his fast pace. Blue followed close behind, trotting gracefully.

When we got to the corral, Dungo took off ahead of me with the lead rope burning my hands as the rough rope slipped through them. Dad came running past me and yelled at Dungo in a commanding voice, "Whoa! Knock it off!" The big stallion stopped in his tracks at the sound of the voice he knew and respected. Dad grabbed his lead rope and jerked on it once, and Dungo immediately brought his large head down. Dad looked over at me and said, "Come over here and hold on to him while I put the saddle on." Feeling safe with Dad right there, I held on to Dungo's rope and started to pet him, even his head.

Mom and the girls came out of the house to the outside of the corral and watched as Dad made me get on Dungo into the saddle and take hold of the long leather reins. He kept hold of the lead rope as I trotted the big stallion around the corral, making him stop when Dad told me to.

After several times around the corral and making him turn and back up, Dad unlatched the lead rope from the halter and let me take control.

I knew that Dad wanted me to get over my fear of Dungo by riding him, or I would always be afraid. Blue watched tied up on the outside of the corral.

That night before we all went to bed, we sat on tree stumps by the field out under the big dark sky, gazing up at the millions of stars.

I got up and walked over to the corral and put my hand through the fence out to Dungo, who was eating his grain. He picked his head up and walked over to the side of the corral where I had my hand out, smelling me. I reached up and pet his big soft nose and noticed my small hands weren't trembling this time.

I said quietly to Dungo, "I know you don't want to hurt me." As I walked back to my family, I looked up and saw my dad watching me with a proud smile on his face.

9

LITTLE RED MERRIE'S PUPPIES

DEVAN

Something hurt real bad! I was dreaming, and something was stabbing me in my side. Dad's voice woke me up, "Rise and shine!"

Waking up in our bed right against my twin sister, Dawn, I realized her elbow was jabbed into my ribs and she was still asleep unaware of my pain.

Steve and Lori were dressed already and heading outside to let the horses out of the corral with Meardha and Pete at their heels.

Our pretty mom came into the living room in her green robe and stoked the barrel stove. Her long thick red hair was tied back, and she had her horn-rimmed glasses on. Even though it was almost summer, it was still cold at night. She said to me, "Wake your sister up and get dressed so I can take you all out to the outhouse."

I nudged Dawn, and she opened her greenish-blue eyes that looked just like mine and swept her short straight strawberry-blond hair out of her face. Even though Dawn and I look mostly alike, we are mirror twins and have several differences. For instance, I am left handed and Dawn is right handed. I am taller and bigger boned than she is. She is shy and quiet, and I am not. Not that I don't like having a twin, it has its benefits, like always having a friend to play with who thinks just like me and will do anything I want her to do.

Kristi was big enough to get out of her built-in bunk by herself and had climbed on top of the couch in her PJs. She was always climbing on something, especially furniture. I was worried she was going to get hurt someday. After getting my cotton pants on and the blue cotton T-shirt I wore yesterday, I helped Kristi get dressed.

Mom and Dad bought each of us kids one new outfit a year, and we were also starting to get Lori's hand-me-downs. Since Kristi had three older sisters, she got all our hand-me-downs.

Mom had brought her Singer sewing machine from Oregon and said she was going to start making all our clothes. She liked Dawn and me to dress in same outfits, which confused people.

While we followed Mom down the grassy trail to the outhouse by the woods, Mom said, "I'm going into Talkeetna today to the Laundromat to wash our dirty clothes. Do you girls want to go?"

Dawn and I squealed with excitement and said at the same time, "Yes please!"

Kristi wasn't sure what we were jumping up and down for, but she joined us anyways.

Dad had told Steve and Lori to stay home and start raking an area for a garden next to the field. Mom loved to garden and was really good at it; she could make anything grow.

Even though Dawn and I were getting bigger, it was still hard to get up on the outhouse seat to go to the bathroom. We had to jump up on the hard white toilet seat that was over the hole on the high wood base. The toilet seat was not nailed down and had a handle so that in the winter we could take it in the house and put it by the woodstove to warm it up.

After Mom and Kristi went, we walked back to the house to get ready to go to town.

Meardha and Pete came running, wagging their tails and barking, almost knocking Kristi over. Her long red curls bounced around as she struggled to keep her balance and squealed, "No, Merrie!" We all loved our tall Irish setter Meardha, or "Rhubri," which is Meardha in Gaelic, which meant "Little red Merrie." This spring she started to look like she was getting fat. Dad told us he had her bred in Anchorage to a registered male Irish setter, and she was going to have puppies soon. My siblings and I couldn't wait to play with little puppies, which we had never seen before.

Mom had made some oatmeal in a cast iron pot on the black woodstove in the kitchen with raisins and cinnamon. Steve, Lori, Dawn, Kristi, and I sat around the small card table in the kitchen and ate our oatmeal with powdered milk. We knew it was good for us, but all of us made faces at the mushy cereal as we ate every bite.

Mom gathered up all the dirty clothes and put them in cardboard boxes. She told Steve and Lori as they loaded the boxes of dirty clothes into the bed of the blue pickup, "You two be careful and stay close to the house. Don't go any farther than the garden area. We'll be a while since there are a lot of clothes to wash."

I pushed Dawn up into the cab of the pickup, then picked Kristi up and handed her to Dawn so she could sit it in her lap. Mom drove the pickup down our muddy road to the highway, sliding around and driving through big puddles as all three of us girls bounced and laughed with joy.

I was so excited I could hardly stand it when we finally made it to the sign that said "Welcome to Beautiful Downtown Talkeetna." Mom pulled into the front of the log building on the right side of the narrow gravel road that ran down the middle of town. The sign on the front of the building said "Talkeetna Laundromat," which was also a gas station with one pump. I jumped out of the pickup and helped Dawn and Kristi out, then we helped Mom carry the big boxes into the Laundromat. Being taught at a young age that work comes before play, Dawn and I knew we had to help Mom sort the dirty clothes and load them into the seven washers we needed, before we could ask to go to B&K store across the street and get some candy.

Mom told us to look both ways crossing the street to go to the store with red painted logs, a white door, and white framed windows. The three of us held hands skipping across the street and up onto the old wooden deck in front of the store. As we opened the creaky door, I looked up and noticed a big moose rack over the top of the door nailed to the logs. Inside, the floor was made out of wood, too, with several shelves of candy right in front of the counter. A nice older man with a gray beard behind the counter was looking at us with curiosity and said, "Are you Dennis Clark's kids that live by Goose Creek?"

Dawn hung on to Kristi's hand and kept quiet while I smiled and eagerly talked to the man. "Yes, sir, we have a brother and sister at home also. Mom is at the Laundromat washing our dirty clothes because we don't have electricity to run a washer or dryer," I answered, divulging more information than I should. I loved to talk to people and continued rambling on, "Dad made Mom a washboard out of plywood and willow branches so she could wash our clothes by hand, but it didn't work for very long and fell apart."

The nice man was looking at me as if he wanted to hear more, so I kept talking, "My name is Devan, and this is my sister Dawn, and our little sister Kristi, who's only two."

The tall man grinned big through his mustache and gray beard at me and said, "Well, very nice to meet such nice polite kids." He pointed at Dawn and me and continued our conversation, "You two must be twins!"

I felt like I had a new friend and answered him, "Yes, we are twins, but she's the shy one."

He laughed thunderously and said, "Pick out some candy from those shelves and get some for your brother and sister at home. It's on me this time!" After thanking the nice man, who said his name was Joe, Dawn and I looked over the rows of candy carefully. We picked out some bazooka gum and cherry Jolly Rancher sticks for us and Lori and Steve, and a grape tootsie roll pop for Kristi. When we got back to the Laundromat, I gave Mom back the change she gave me and told her about how nice Joe was. She just shook her head, knowing sometimes I was too social with strangers. Taking most of the day to finish the ten loads of laundry, we didn't get back to our road until late afternoon, and it was starting to rain. The clothes were beginning to get wet in the back of the pickup, so Mom drove as quick as she could down the muddy two-mile road. She had to put the truck into four-wheel drive by getting out in the pouring rain and turning the hubs on the wheels. Dad was home when we got to the house, and he and Steve were in the house, stoking the barrel stove.

I noticed right away that Meardha was lying on her red blanket by the barrel stove and didn't get up to greet us like she always did. Our sheltie dog Pete was barking at us while we all helped carry in the clean clothes in the wet boxes, putting them by the woodstove to dry. Lori was kneeling down by Meardha, petting her head and talking softly to her. Dad saw us girls standing around her, looking worried, and said, "She's about ready to have her puppies! Give her some room to breathe and help your mom make supper. Steve, go out and bring Dungo in from the field, put him in the corral, and throw him a flake of hay."

Lori looked up from Meardha and asked Dad, "Can the twins help Mom with supper tonight so I can go outside with Steve?" Our brother Steve looked relieved when Dad said she could, since it was the first time he had to catch Dungo up without Dad there. They headed out the kitchen door with Pete into the rain after putting their coats and boots on. Mom told Dawn and me to start peeling potatoes as she fried moose steaks in a large cast iron skillet. Kristi wasn't old enough to do chores and got to sit on the floor by Meardha. Dad felt her belly to see how close she was to having her puppies and yelled into the kitchen, "Evelyn, you better warm up some water and get a few clean towels. She's getting ready to give birth."

Dawn and I said to Mom at the same time, "Can we watch Meardha have her puppies?" Mom was cutting the potatoes into small cubes to boil in a pot on the camp stove that was on the counter and warming water on the iron stove for Meardha. "Yes, but first grab your dad some clean towels from the boxes of laundry." We both scrambled off the step stool that was up against the sink where we were peeling potatoes for supper. We ran into the living room quickly, grabbing towels on the way to where poor, frail Meardha was whining in pain and was trying to get up. Dad affectionately petted her all over and spoke to her softly to calm her down, as she lay back down on the flannel blanket.

Lori and Steve came in the living room door and threw off their coats, excited to nudge their way into the circle of all five of us and Dad around Meardha.

Then something amazing happened as she pushed out with all her might a beautiful golden wet little puppy that Lori said was a boy, as she got to wrap it in the clean towel.

Meardha pushed out another miracle as we all squealed with delight to see another healthy puppy that had dark-red hair like her mommy. I couldn't contain myself any longer as I asked Dad, "Is there any more? Can I wrap the next one up in the towel, Dad?" He winked at me as another wet puppy came sliding out of Meardha into Dad's hands. It was light red and was a little girl with the smell of a newborn puppy. As he handed me the tiny miracle into my small chubby hands, I could feel her heart beating and the warmth of her soft breath on my skin. I wrapped her in the clean towel to dry her and then laid her next to her mommy by the warm stove. Our whole family watched our frail Irish setter give birth to her babies right there in the living room of our shack.

We all held our breath, with our eyes wide to see if Meardha was done having puppies. We kids were talking all at once about the three beautiful Irish setter puppies that were squirming around next to Meardha with their small eyes still sealed shut. Meardha just lay there still, not interested in licking her puppies like maybe something was wrong.

Then she took a deep breath and pushed one more time. We all stopped talking as one more puppy came out. It was smaller than the other ones and was dark red also like Meardha. It was a cute little boy, and Dad said as Steve got to wrap this one that it was the runt of the litter.

As Meardha licked her puppies one at a time, their red hair started to dry as they tried to get up on their short wobbly legs.

We kids were sitting closely around our new family members, fascinated as Meardha lay on her back, letting her puppies drink milk from her nipples. Dad noticed we were practically on top of the them and said, "Let's leave Meardha alone with her puppies so they can eat and maybe we can too."

Mom was already in the kitchen mashing the boiled potatoes and heating up the canned peas. "Supper's ready!" she said loudly, hoping to pull us away to eat as it was already eight o'clock and getting dark.

Soon it would be summer solstice in June and would stay light out most of the night, giving us extra time to get ready for winter, and we kids got to stay up until midnight.

Mom put a big moose steak on Dad's plate and a pile of mashed potatoes and peas as he sat at the card table, waiting for her to cut up some meat for Dawn and Kristi and me. Lori and Steve could cut up their own steaks and get their own vegetables.

There wasn't much room at the small table, and I was left handed, so I rubbed elbows with Dawn, who was squeezed in on my left side. Dad loved dessert, and so did we kids.

Mom whisked a bowl of chocolate pudding with powdered milk until it thickened, and then gave us each a small bowl of it to eat. We savored every bite and licked the bowls until they were clean. Dad said that we got more on our faces than in our stomachs.

After Dawn and I cleaned up the table and finished the dishes, we had to use the outhouse and get ready for bed. Lori already had Kristi in her PJs and tucked into her built-in bunk as she rubbed her eyes and went to sleep. Lori, Steve, Dawn, and I went over to the puppies every chance we could as we got ready to go to bed. Looking at them sleeping next to their mommy by the warm stove, cuddled together next to her warm belly, looking so cute, we all wondered if we were going to keep them.

Dad turned down the damper on the barrel stove that was crackling as the birch wood burned hot, and said, "You kids go to bed now and stay in bed. Don't be picking the puppies up! They can't be held for a few days, or they will get sick."

After we all climbed into bed, Dawn and I took turns lightly tickling each other's backs so we could fall asleep. Our sheltie Pete lay by our bed, feeling left out as we gazed over at Meardha and her puppies.

The next morning Dad woke us up early like usual before the sun came up. It was Saturday, and he wanted us all outside to help with the garden and the greenhouse. My eyes opened to the sound of the puppies making squeaking noises on the blanket by the stove.

Dawn and I jumped out of bed and scrambled over to see the new puppies again. Lori and Steve were already next to them, trying to figure out names for each of them, while Meardha was outside taking a break.

Dad told us as he stoked the fire, "You kids can name the puppies if you want, but we are only keeping one. I'll even let you kids pick which one we keep."

Lori and Steve looked at each other, and then at me and Dawn, not knowing which puppy to choose. Lori said, "I think we should name the male golden one that came out first Shane, and keep him!" Steve was fond of the last one, the runt, and said, "I want to name the little red one Mickie."

"Dawn and I get to name the last two," I said, not wanting to miss out.

"I want to name that one Devan!" My twin sister pointed at the dark-red female that looked a lot like Meardha.

"I'm going to name the light-red girl Lucy!" I said loudly.

Mom came into the living room with Kristi after using the outhouse and told us, "Okay, kids, let's leave the puppies alone. Meardha is going to feed them."

After chores and breakfast, Dawn and I took Kristi out to the garden area. We helped Mom and Lori rake the patch of dirt by the field next to the greenhouse Dad had started to build.

With Steve's help, he was framing the walls and the roof with two-by-fours. He and Steve built wooden boxes up on shelves inside the greenhouse to plant vegetables in.

Dawn and I created rows in the dirt using long-handled hoes to plant vegetable seeds for Mom's outside garden. The tall green grass in the field that was next to the garden was higher than me and looked like it would be fun to play hide-and-seek in. I nudged my twin when no one was looking and whispered, "Look how high the grass is. Let's play hide-and-seek sometime when we aren't doing chores."

Dawn shook her head at me and said quietly, "We better not, Devan. I don't think we're allowed." Going back to hoeing the rows,

I thought about what a weakling Dawn was. If I didn't toughen her up soon, she would always get picked on.

For the past hour I had been fighting the urge to go to the bathroom and asked Mom, "Mom, I have to pee. Can I go to the outhouse?"

Dad was nailing the wood boxes to the shelves inside the greenhouse and heard what I had asked Mom and said, "The twins are old enough to use the outhouse by themselves now, as long as they go together and take the dogs."

By now I was trying to hold it and was dancing around, as I told Dawn, "Come on, slowpoke. I have to go bad!"

Dawn dropped her hoe and finally followed me.

We ran across the circular driveway around the garage to the back of the house and down the grassy trail to the big wood outhouse. When we got to the big wood door that was shut, I had to jump up to release the wooden latch that worked on both sides of the door. We were supposed to keep the outhouse door shut so no animals could get inside.

I told Dawn to wait outside with Pete as I stepped up into the dark outhouse and pulled my pants down to get onto the toilet seat.

I jumped up on it and went as quick as I could when suddenly I heard a buzzing sound around my head.

Pulling up my pants in a hurry, I saw a huge bumblebee flying around inside of the outhouse!

I fumbled with the wood handle to get out and away from the bee that was still buzzing by my head, but it wouldn't open.

By now I was screaming, when the door flew open with Dawn on the outside staring in at me.

Then suddenly I felt a bad stinging pain on my stomach under my T-shirt!

"I've been bit! I've been bit!" I screamed as I ran down the trail back to where Mom and Dad were working.

Pete was barking, and Dawn was running close behind me. I couldn't help but cry from the stabbing pain on my stomach.

The whole family heard me and stopped what they were doing until they found out it was only a bee sting. Mom got some mud from the road and pasted it on the bite, taking the sting and redness out right away.

Dawn rubbed my back, trying to make me feel better, and Kristi brought me a dandelion. Lori and Steve called me a cry baby and made fun of me the rest of the day.

After the frame and the door of the greenhouse were finished, Dad nailed white plastic Visqueen over the whole thing to keep the heat and moisture in to help the lettuce, cabbage, and radishes grow. After that, he and Mom put the big thirty-gallon metal barrels on each of the four corners to help keep the Visqueen on and to collect rainwater.

It felt good to be outside with my family on the last day of spring even if we did have to work. Mom and Dad had taught us that you have to work for what you eat, and that's what we did.

I knew, despite getting stung by a huge bumblebee, I was grateful for them. Without bees there wouldn't be all the beautiful different-colored wildflowers blooming everywhere that I loved so much.

10

PULLING THE TRIP ROPE

STEVE

Summer at our homestead on Goose Creek meant a lot of work to do from morning to midnight. That's when we went to bed along with the rest of Alaska.

Even when Dad went to work, he left us chores to do while he was gone and expected the job done when he got home. I felt like the muscles on my arms and legs were getting bigger every day.

Lori, Mom, the twins, and I had been working in the greenhouse, and it was now planted and already growing vegetables. We planted tons of swiss chard in the outside garden, and it was sprouting already. Mom said it tastes like spinach and makes kids stronger.

Using small metal buckets, we dipped out of the barrels that were on the corners of the greenhouse to catch the rainwater for multiple purposes. This time of year in June, we had plenty of rain and lots of puddles.

One of our chores was to weed the garden every day, which none of us liked to do.

One day at the end of May, Dad and I rode the horses to a man's house that Dad said wanted to buy Blue from us. Dad and I made our way through our sixty acres of wet grass, him riding in the big leather saddle Grandpa Austin had given him and me in Dad's old leather saddle. My feet did not reach the stirrups, so I gripped my knees and kept one hand on the saddle horn. We rode north of Willow Creek to the house of a man named Ron and then right up into his yard. Dad and I stayed mounted as he came out of his house to greet us with two large huskies beside him. Ron was a tall local man with long brown hair tied back in a ponytail and a baseball cap on. The two large huskies started barking at our horses while he and Dad were talking. Blue started dancing around, and Dungo began snorting. Before I knew it, the huskies were behind me and Blue, barking and jumping up on her. Then she got her head down and went to bucking around the yard. I pulled back on the reins and hung on for dear life. I could see Dad trying to get close to me with Dungo, who was fighting against the bit, wanting to run with his big neck bowed against Dad's steel grip. Ron called off his dogs, and Dad pulled us in close with my lead rope. We both noticed the wounds on Blue's hind quarters and understood why she was bucking. After Ron came back out of his house, he looked up at Dad still on Dungo and said, "There is no way I am buying a bucking horse!" Dad was proud I didn't let Blue take off running, and we talked about it all the way home. A few weeks later, a man in Palmer bought Blue from Dad.

The native grass in the field was dry and growing tall, and Dad said we needed to hay the field in July during a dry week. Mr. McCullough sold Dad a big dump rake this spring for cheap that was made in the eighteen hundreds when they were pulled by horses. It was eight feet wide with several big round tines. The dump rake had big wheels and a round metal seat on top. Dad was going to use the Ford pickup to pull it around the field to pick up the cut grass.

It was the Fourth of July, and Dad had a three-day weekend off work at the Anchorage schools. Mom had made breakfast, and we all sat down at the picnic table outside to eat biscuits with moose gravy and fried potatoes, when Dad said, "Looks like it's time to put my John Deere tractor to work and get this field cut before it rains! I'm going to teach Steve how to drive it so he can pull the rotary scythe behind it and cut the grass. Then I'll hook the dump rake to the pickup and pull the hay into shocks in the field. After the grass is cut, we are going to need everyone's help making the shocks of hay."

Eagerly I sat up in the metal folding chair and said to Dad, "I get to drive the tractor?"

He winked at me and said, "Well your sixth birthday is coming up, and I was driving a tractor when I was your age."

Mom didn't seem to look worried, and Lori wanted to know if she could ride on it with me.

Mom said, "Lori, you and the twins need to help me clean house before you go outside, because the Valentines are coming over later for an early Fourth of July supper." We were all excited about having our new friends from church come visit.

Dad took me to Palmer last week to find a tractor, and I helped him pick it out. It was in a tractor sales lot with shiny new ones and old used ones. He couldn't afford a new tractor and found an older used one that was faded green and yellow with the front wheels close together. It was a John Deere Model A. It was missing the seat and the steering wheel.

Dad and I stood there and looked at the big white for-sale sign on the tractor that read, "For Sale—Runs good—Perfect for someone who's lost their ass and doesn't know which way they're going."

I've never seen Dad laugh so hard at the message on the sign, and he knew this was his tractor. So Dad bought a steering wheel and a seat and bought the used tractor for five hundred dollars. He also bought a new Holland rotary scythe that was six feet around and low to the ground with sharp blades for cutting grass. Mr. Lankford loaned Dad his big hauling trailer to get the tractor and the rotary scythe home from Palmer.

On the way home, we stopped at the Sheep Creek Lodge, which was about five miles from our road off Parks Highway. Dad and I sat up at the bar and had a Coca-Cola together while he talked to the other people inside. He was a social person, making friends fast, as they seemed to admire and respect him.

Dad got up on the John Deere tractor and turned the key and started the loud motor that began to spurt black smoke out of the stack on the front. He backed it up to the new rotary scythe and then hooked it up to the tractor with the hitch.

Jumping back on the big metal seat of the green-and-yellow tractor, Dad yelled to me, "Climb up here, and we'll take it out on the field and see how it runs." Bracing my black sneakers on the runner, I grabbed Dad's hand and jumped up on the tractor and stood right next to the big metal seat.

Dad tilted his black Stetson back on his thick brown hair and pushed the black knob on the gear stick on the floor straight up and then pulled the long handle on the steering wheel down, making the tractor go forward as I hung on to the back of his seat. The old tractor had huge back tires with yellow wheels and tiny front tires that were really close together. It had a big smokestack on the front of the long body of the tractor.

Mom had closed the dogs and the puppies in the house, while she and the girls came outside to watch us drive our new tractor.

I felt proud to be on the loud machine with my dad heading into the sixty acres of field that was ours. Looking back as we bounced around over the bumps in the field, I watched the many sharp blades on the scythe spin fast in a circle around the long metal tube they were attached to, making a loud whirring sound. The low-to-the-ground scythe cut the grass right above the roots so more grass could grow and we could hay the field year after year. Dungo had been grazing, but now he was running around the field, startled by the noise of the tractor and the scythe.

Starting at the left corner of the field by our heavily treed road going up to the slough, Dad headed north in a straight line, cutting grass all the way across the field toward Mount McKinley.

Turning the tractor at the end and starting another row heading toward the house, Dad looked like he was enjoying himself on this beautiful day, feeling a sense of accomplishment. He showed me the gears, which there was only forward and reverse, while he cut the high grass with the scythe on his new tractor. I bounced up and down on the tractor while it made its way through the deep grass and uneven ground.

Dad had me stand by him next to the seat and shift the gears when he told me to. Then he told me to get up on the big metal seat while he stood next to me. Dad had me steer the tractor with the big steering wheel and keep it straight as it ran slowly, pulling the loud scythe down each row, cutting the high native grass and forming raised rows of hay.

Dad went into the house to get us some lemonade while I sat on the big seat and steered the big loud tractor by myself.

The sun was getting warmer, and the mosquitos were starting to bite me. It seemed like Dad had been gone in the house for a long time, when Lori came running out of the house onto the field toward me. I turned the tractor around to start my sixth row. Lori made it out to me, panting, handing me a plastic glass of lemonade, and said, "Dad said for me to come check on you and ride with you if it's okay?" Chugging down the cold lemonade, I thought about how lonely it was riding up and down the huge field on the tractor all by myself, even though I enjoyed it for a while. I yelled above the noise of the tractor, "I'll let you ride if you go get me some mosquito dope!"

"Okay, Steve, I'll be right back!" Lori yelled to me as she turned and ran back to the house.

I felt bad for Lori because I knew she wanted to be outside all the time with me. She was stuck in the house helping Mom cook and take care of our younger sisters.

Dad had come out of the house and was over at the dump rake by the small barn, getting it ready to hook up to the pickup.

As I was almost to the end of the sixth row and turning the tractor to start the seventh row, which was right next to the large windrow, my big sister came running back out into the field past Dungo grazing and waved for me to stop. I pulled up on the long handle on the steering wheel to make the tractor idle, and Lori jumped up on the runner and then up by the seat, standing next to me. While I was spraying mosquito dope on my thick red hair, face, neck, and arms, Lori said, pointing at the windrow next to us, "Let's make a fort in there sometime!" I knew we would have to ask Dad, but I was thinking the same thing as Lori and was hoping he would let us.

Heading back down the row toward the house, I saw Dad at the edge of the field with the dump rake hooked to the pickup. He was waving at me to come his way, and Mom and the twins were with him.

I kept the tractor steering straight toward the edge of the field. Dad motioned me to turn the tractor around to start a new row, which was heading straight toward the windrow, and then stop the tractor.

I did what he wanted me to do, then pulled up on the long handle to put the tractor in idle. As Lori and I jumped off, Dad said, "You're doing a great job, Steve. Shut the tractor down for a bit. We are going to pull some of this loose grass up into shocks of hay."

Dad had Mom drive the blue Ford pickup slowly down the row of loose grass, pulling the dump rake behind. I was on the big round metal seat that was on top of the dump rake. I had to hold on to the thick rope that was attached to the handle that tripped the rake when the tines were full of grass, releasing it into a shock.

Dad walked alongside of the dump rake, and when it had enough loose hay in the tines for a shock, he would yell for me to pull up on the trip rope to release the hay into a pile and then lower it back down to start a new pile. Lori and the twins stayed behind the dump rake using pitchforks and their hands to pull the loose hay into a tight shock.

Dad yelled up to me, "You guys keep doing this while I run the tractor for a while to cut more grass. Be careful, Steve, and let your mom know if you need to stop and I'll switch off with you to give you a break."

Wiping the sweat off my freckled face, I yelled back to Dad, not wanting to seem tired, "Okay, Dad!" Lori watched the dump rake from the ground and let me know when to pull the trip rope, while Devan and Dawn had fun scooping up the loose hay and throwing it into the shocks. Kristi had her face pressed up against the back window of the cab of the pickup, watching and waving at us while we worked. It was too dangerous for her to be around the heavy equipment since she was only two years old and liked to be into everything.

Mom kept driving the pickup in front of the dump rake, while I bounced in the big metal seat, pulling the trip rope over and over.

My arms were getting tired as Lori yelled, "It's full, Steve!" I pulled hard on the trip rope again, but this time the short rope gave way! The dump rake sprang back, catapulting me off the metal seat into the air!

Next thing you know, I was flipping head over heels doing backward somersaults in the field! Lying in the grass, trying to catch my breath, I could hear Lori yelling, "Dad! Dad!" I could see Mom and the twins running toward me. Mom knelt down beside me in the grass and asked me, "Steve, are you all right?"

Shaking, I sat up and looked at everyone standing around me and said, "I guess I'm all right." Dad crouched down beside me and felt my head and told me to move my limbs, making sure I wasn't hurt bad. Then he laughed and said, "Must have been pretty scary flying off the dump rake! Well, it'll toughen you up!"

Devan said, "He flew really high!"

Lori and Dawn helped me up off the ground and brushed the grass and dirt off my clothes while Devan gave me a drink of water. Dad and Mom walked back over to the dump rake to see what had gone wrong. Turns out the pin in the handle that tripped the rake after pulling the trip rope, popped out, causing the tines to lift and spring back, sending me on a one-way flight. One thing I knew about my dad was, he would make me get back on the dump rake so that I wouldn't be scared of it just like with the horses.

After he put the pin back in securely, Dad told me to do a few more rows then we would quit for the day. Wanting to show Dad how tough I was, I climbed back on the big metal seat again. Dad walked beside the dump rake, letting me know when to pull until we finished the last few rows of loose hay.

The Valentines came driving up in their white minivan into our driveway just as we were covering the large shocks of hay with tarps. Chad jumped out of the van after they parked and ran out into the field where we were working and yelled, "Hey, Steve, can I help?" Dad had heard him and nodded yes that he could. As Chad ran up to me with his sisters, Amy and Beth, I said, "Hi, Chad, I'm glad you came over. We might be able to play for a while." I continued catching my breath. "I'll ask Dad when we get through working."

My sisters were excited to have company too and already asked Dad if they could show Amy and Beth around. Dad told them to go have fun, and off they all ran and played "Simon Says" in our yard.

Sometimes I wished I wasn't the only boy in the family, having to do most of the work outside with Dad.

Mr. and Mrs. Valentine met Mom and Dad at the edge of the field while Chad and I finished tarping the shocks. Then Dad told us we could go play for a while, but stay close to the house.

For the next couple of hours, I showed Chad the small barn and the greenhouse we had built. We pet Dungo from outside the corral. Then Meardha, Pete, and the puppies chased us around the yard, fetching sticks we threw as far as we could.

Mom and Dad hiked with Chad's parents up to Goose Creek and back, and then we all ate together outside at the picnic table with the small card table next to it where the adults sat.

Supper was my favorite meal, and Mom was the best cook in the world. Everything tasted so good! I put bite after bite in my mouth of moose burgers, potato salad, green beans from our garden, and juicy watermelon the Valentines brought.

I could hear Mom telling Chad's parents about me being catapulted off the dump rake. Lori heard them and started telling the story at our table about me flying through the air and doing somersaults in the field. The adults and all the kids except Kristi, who was sad I got hurt, laughed hysterically.

Swallowing my food hard and laughing along to not seem like a baby, I really didn't think it was funny, and my sore body didn't either.

After a berry cobbler with whip cream, all of us kids got to wave sparklers around even though it wasn't dark. The Valentines said goodbye and went home after a long, fun Fourth of July.

Dad's twenty-eighth birthday was on Sunday, July 11. After church he took us all to lunch at the Fairview restaurant in Talkeetna. We all gave him a shiny new big silver belt buckle with a bronc rider on it, and Mom got him new wool socks.

When we got home, he took me out behind the house and showed me how to shoot his .22 rifle. Dad stood close behind me, helping me get the rifle in my arms with my elbows up and my feet apart. He showed me how to look through the sight to aim at the cans he set up on a fallen tree up against the woods. Then I squeezed the trigger slowly and fired my first shot, hitting the old soup can I was aiming for. Dad yelled, "Good shot, son! Try another!" The next one missed, but then I hit the last three cans in a row!

Dad and I walked back to the house as Mom came out the front door and said, "Well, how did he do?"

Dad patted me on the back proudly and said, "He's a steady sure aim!"

Mom smiled and said, "Let's have some birthday pie."

Exactly eight days after Dad's birthday was my sixth birthday, so Dad took the day off and took me fishing up at Goose Creek for silver salmon. We hiked up the half-mile trail through the woods to the slough and then down the short heavily bushed trail to the creek. Dad and I caught several large salmon, enjoying the day together. He was packing his .41 magnum in the holster on his hip, and his twelve-gauge rifle was propped up on the tackle box along with his .22 rifle he let me pack.

When we got back to the house, Mom and the girls had a birthday supper ready for us. Deep-fried humpy with homemade tartar sauce, corn bread, and fresh green beans. Mom made a chocolate cake with chocolate icing and six candles to blow out as my family sang "Happy Birthday" to me.

My sisters had wrapped the two gifts I opened, and to my delight, one of them was a jar of Skippy peanut butter. They all knew I loved peanut butter. I could eat it by the tablespoon!

Lori had decided she was going to give all of us kids a nickname. I was the first to get a nickname that everyone agreed on, Skippy!

The other gifts were a Monopoly game that all of us kids couldn't wait to play tonight and some neat plastic army soldiers that were small and stood up by themselves.

After I opened my gifts and thanked everyone, Dad and I went out to put Dungo in the corral for the night. When we got back into the house, he said, "Steve, I have one more gift for you." I felt my eyes getting as big as saucers as he pulled his .22 rifle up that was leaning against the living room wall. He walked over and held it out to me.

Gulping and reaching out for the rifle, I said, "My own gun?"

Dad said, "It's yours if you respect it and take care of it."

I couldn't believe it was mine and suddenly felt grown-up holding the long heavy rifle in my small hands.

11

OFF TO THE RACES

DAWN

The Alaska State Fair was finally here! That meant we were going to the fair for the first time ever!

It was mid-August 1968, and Dad had been running Dungo, our five-year-old stallion, through the fields every day since we got back out here to the homestead in April.

Using a bridle with a bit, Dad rode him bareback, working his large sleek muscles into a lather, getting him ready for the horse races.

Mr. Lankford was the one that told Dad about the horse races in Palmer. They came out to our place and saw what a powerful horse Dad had in the corral.

When we lived in Oregon, Dad tried to enter the horse races there. One of the racehorse owners got word of how fast Dungo could run. He found a way to keep Dad out of the races in Portland on the rule that he wasn't a professional racer.

Dad was excited to race and finally be able to let Dungo show everyone what he was made of. Besides that, first place was a three-hundred-dollar purse.

Steve wasn't allowed to ride him the last month before the races because Dad said that he didn't want anyone to mess him up.

Dad did let Lori and Steve brush Dungo down every night until the dark-red hair on his rippling muscles shone in the sun.

The big registered quarter horse snorted anxiously as Dad and Steve loaded him into our horse trailer, shutting the metal gate behind him. It was hitched to our blue Ford pickup with the light-blue wooden camper on top just like when we traveled here from Oregon.

Devan really liked it here, but I missed our nice house on Mabel Street with faucet water and electric lights. Devan and I had a bedroom with Lori and baseboard heaters for the mild winters. There were paved streets in the cute neighborhood with no grizzly bears. I was scared of this eerie place and thought maybe there were monsters or snakes under the bed at night.

I had frequent nightmares about snakes. When we lived in Oregon, two of the mean neighbor boys put a bunch of snakes down my pants when I was only three! Dad drove up from work as it was happening and got out of his truck and spanked the naughty boys. Then he sent them home where they got in more trouble with their parents.

Devan told me there weren't any snakes here, but we should pray about it anyhow when we were snuggled close together at night. Mom put dark curtains on the windows of the house to keep the midnight sun out, and it made it really dark while we lay there in our bed we shared with Lori. Praying to God to keep the monsters and snakes away seemed to help, and soon we would fall asleep.

Butterflies tickled my stomach with excitement to go to the Palmer state fair for a week, and we got to sleep in our camper again! Off we went to the races as Dad drove out to the Parks Highway and then sixty miles south to Palmer. All five of us kids lay on the bed in the cabover of the camper, looking out the small window at the other cars and scenery. We played a game called "I spy" something blue, for example, and then the others try to figure out what it is. We could see the horse trailer hitched to the pickup behind us out the back-door window. Being up in the camper, we could talk as loud as we wanted, and lying on our stomachs enjoying the bumpy ride, we did just that.

Lori talked about dad racing Dungo and hoped he would win, while Steve said he might want to be a jockey someday. Devan and I were mostly chattering about the carnival rides.

We finally arrived in Palmer, making our way through the small city out to the fairgrounds. We could feel the jolt of the horse trailer every time Dad was stopped at a stop sign from Dungo stomping around. He could probably smell the many other horses at the fairgrounds close by.

Dad pulled into a camping area close to the horse stalls where there were several other campers, horse trailers, and a large grassy area with picnic tables.

Dad and Steve unloaded Dungo from the horse trailer and took him to the stables where all the racehorses were kept.

Devan asked Mom if we could go on some rides by ourselves, and Mom said we could. Our family got free carnival ride tickets because of Dungo being in the race.

As we were getting ready to run toward the Ferris wheel, Mom told us, "Be back by noon, stay together, and don't talk to strangers."

Devan and I held hands as we ran across the grass to the carnival rides next to the race track. The line to the Ferris wheel was long already so early in the day, and there were a lot of people everywhere around us.

Feeling dizzy looking up at the gigantic Ferris wheel, I said to Devan, "Are you sure you want to go up in that? It looks so high up."

My twin sister looked at me, disgruntled, and told me, "I want to ride the Ferris wheel, Dawn, and you are going with me!"

Devan wasn't afraid of heights like I was, so she didn't understand why I was so scared. My legs were shaking as I stood up to the wood squirrel with the measuring tape drawn on it.

To my disappointment, we barely made the required height for the ride.

Devan and I sat close together in the big seat with the red umbrella as the carnie snapped the safety bar across our stomachs. My knuckles turned white gripping the bar as the Ferris wheel began to move upward. It stopped just a little ways up to pick up more riders. The wind was making the seat move, and the minutes seemed to go by as we would stop a little farther up, each time going a little higher, suspended in the air to load more people.

Devan was having a great time already, bouncing up and down, causing the chair we were in to swing back and forth. The Ferris wheel jerked forward again, this time taking us all the way up to the top, and then around and around we went. Devan was screaming with delight as terror gripped my whole body. I just knew the pins holding the chair onto the ride were going to break any minute, and so I said loudly, "Devan, please don't rock the chair. It might break!" Reluctantly, she stopped rocking the chair, but the last time we went around, the ride stopped with us right at the top of the Ferris wheel! Gripping tightly to Devan's arm and praying to Jesus, I started crying in a panic. I felt like something bad was going to happen, and I could barely say to Devan, "Make them put us down please. I don't want to ride anymore!"

Other kids on the ride were straining their heads to look at us, and it was embarrassing Devan, so she pried my hands off her arm and told me sharply, "Quit being a baby, Dawn!"

The Ferris wheel jerked one more time as it took us around and then stopped and finally let us off. Still sobbing, I climbed out of the chair after my sister, looking down, not making eye contact with anyone.

After we got away from the Ferris wheel, Devan wiped my tears away and said sweetly, "I know you're scared, Dawn, but I'll always protect you." She continued, "We have time to ride more rides before noon. Let's try the Octopus!" Not wanting to be the big baby she thought I was, even though the Octopus sounded awful, I said quietly, "Okay, Devan, let's ride a few more rides."

Turns out, to my relief, they wouldn't let us on the Octopus ride, which was big and scary, because we weren't tall enough. We decided to ride the carrousel on the horses, which was a great ride.

After lunch at the camper, we took Kristi on the carrousel several times, while Lori and Steve rode the Octopus.

As we rode the rides every day, Dad ran Dungo around the track, getting ready for the Saturday and Sunday race, and then Steve walked him around and brushed his shiny coat.

I was really worried for my dad and was praying he wouldn't get hurt racing our powerful stallion.

Mom took lots of pictures of Dad in his English saddle on Dungo with her polaroid camera the first day of the race. We siblings just stood there in awe of our dad looking so young and handsome in his black Stetson tilted back on his head and his blue jeans tucked into his black cowboy boots.

It was Saturday, and the race was going to start soon. Dad and the other eight riders drew out of a hat for position on the rail, since it was a lap-and-cap race. Dungo got third position, which was close to the inside rail, giving him an advantage to take the lead.

Mom and we kids sat in the grandstands, cheering Dad on as he rode Dungo proudly around the track, when the announcer named each horse and their jockey. The butterflies were coming back in my stomach as all the horses lined up on the dirt track to start the race. I could see Dad on Dungo, confident and ready to go, when suddenly the trumpet sounded.

To our surprise, Dungo jumped way out ahead of the other horses and ran as fast as he could go around the dirt race track, taking the inside and the lead. "Come on, Dungo!" "Come on, Dad!" Lori, Devan, Mom, Kristi, and I stood up screaming for Dad and Dungo to win. Steve got to be close to the track to help Dad.

The dust was rising as all the other horses tried to keep up with Dungo. They were no match for the juiced-up stallion as Dad urged him on to the finish line. "Yah, Dungo, yah!"

We were all standing up and cheering as Dad and Dungo crossed the finish line and took first place! I've never seen Dad so happy as he rode Dungo proudly in front of the grandstands as they announced Dungo as the winner of the race! Steve held on to Dungo as Dad received his prize of three hundred dollars.

Dad and Mom went with us kids to the carnival that night, and we had a great time riding all the rides together and eating cotton candy.

We went home after the Sunday race, which Dungo took first place in that one, also winning another three-hundred-dollar purse. Dad left the other racers worrying about this newcomer and his fast stallion coming back next year.

Before we left Palmer, Dad said he had a surprise for us kids and pulled into a feed store at the end of town. After getting out of the pickup and opening the door to the camper, Dad said, "You kids come in and help me pick out some baby chicks and a rooster. We're going to raise chickens!"

Lori, Steve, Devan, and I scrambled off the bed in the cabover of the camper, quickly putting our shoes on and jumping out onto the gravel parking lot. Kristi had a great time holding the little yellow baby chicks in her small hands. She put the twelve we had picked into the box with holes the feed store gave us. Dad and Mom picked out a big red-and-blue rooster that he put in a separate box to take home so it would breed the chickens, and we could have more eventually. After Dad paid for them, he put the boxes of baby chicks and the rooster in the camper with us kids all the way home.

On the way home, we stopped at the Tam O'Shanter kennel in Palmer to pick up Meardha, Pete, and all four of Meardha's puppies where Dad had taken them a few days before the fair so they would have a place to stay for a week. Soon we were going to have to let three of the puppies go to their new home except one. We all agreed on the golden male puppy with big floppy ears we had named Shane. Dad didn't want to give any of the papered Irish setter puppies up but made some money selling them to good homes. Uncle Doug took Mickie, and the owner of the father took the little female I had named Devan. The Smiths from church took Lucy. We would get to see her and Mickie often.

It was a loud ride home in the camper with all the puppies, dogs, chicks, and the rooster. When we finally got there, we all piled out of the camper, exhausted from the fun week at the fair.

For the next couple of weeks Mom took us out cranberry picking by the railroad tracks with the Savage rifle across her chest in the sling, and we helped take care of the chicks until they were big enough to be outside. Dad built a chicken coop beside the cowshed with chicken wire. It had roosts for the hens to lay eggs, hatching some for new baby chicks. They were a lot of fun to play with, but the big rooster was kind of mean and liked to chase us around the yard.

One day while Dad was at work and Kristi was in the house taking a nap, Devan and I were outside playing under the big cottonwood tree, and Devan said, "Hey, Dawn, let's go play hide-and-seek in the field."

Dropping the marbles in my hand down into the fall leaves, I said to my twin sister, "I don't know, Devan. You know we're supposed to stay close to the house."

Devan grabbed my hand, pulling me toward the field, yelling, "Mom, Lori and Steve are at the spring getting water. They will be gone for a while!" When we got to the grass that was over our heads, I could see Dungo way out in the field grazing on the high grass that Dad was going to cut and hay again if the rain stopped.

Devan cut through the grass running, making a trail for me behind her, saying, "Hide somewhere, Dawn, and I'll find you. Watch out for grizzly bears!" Remembering what Dad had told us about grizzlies not making much sound in the grass, I didn't really want to play hide-and-seek in the field. I hid as close as I could to the edge of the field by the house. Crouching down in the high grass after Devan got to ten, I was hoping she would find me soon, and she did. Then it was my turn to count to ten while Devan hid in the field. "Don't go too far out!" I told her before she ran back into the high grass.

After I got to ten, I was going to look for Devan, when I heard Dad's pickup drive up into the driveway. My heart started to beat fast as I yelled for Devan, who was hiding in the tall grass somewhere in the field, "Devan, Dad's home!" She didn't say anything, and Dad was getting out of his truck, looking over at me as I walked toward him.

Dad said to me as he walked closer, "I got off work early. Where is everyone?" Looking up at my tall Dad into his stern blue eyes, I said quietly, "Mom, Lori, and Steve are getting water at the spring, and Kristi is taking a nap." He cocked his head and looked into my eyes and said, "What were you doing in the field, and where is Devan?"

Just then Devan came running out of the high grass, gasping for air as she ran over to Dad and me in front of the house. Dad said to her in a stern, serious voice, "What were you two doing in the field,

Devan, when I told you to stay close to the house?" Devan's eyes got big, and so did mine as she said, "We were playing hide-and-seek, Dad!"

We knew we were in trouble, and my heart started to beat fast as Dad took his belt out of his pants and said, "You two are going to get a lickin' for not listening!" Devan cried as Dad gave her the first swats with the belt, and I was crying before I even got mine.

After Dad spanked us, he gave us each a hug and said, "I love you both and don't want you to get hurt, so you need to listen to me."

Mom, Steve, Lori, and the dogs came walking up with the buckets of water right after our lickin', and Dad told them we were playing in the field. Mom said she told us to stay in the yard and keep an eye on Kristi while she napped.

Lori and Steve were glad they weren't home to be responsible for us, or they would have gotten a lickin' too.

That night Devan and I had to do the dishes and go to bed early. Lori and Steve got to hike up to Goose Creek and go salmon fishing with Mom and Dad.

Devan felt bad that it was her idea to play in the field and that we got in trouble and had to stay home alone, so she tickled my back until I fell asleep next to her.

12

DUM DUM!

LORI

Cranberry sauce, cranberry syrup, and cranberry jam were some of the things I helped Mom make in our kitchen one cloudy day in September. Dad and Steve were in the woods with the pickup, cutting down birch trees for firewood. They loaded it into the pickup and stacked it up against the house by the front door. We needed at least twenty cords of wood to last all winter. Dad and Steve stacked most of the firewood under a tarp against some trees next to the blue wood camper.

In late August, Mom had driven the Ford pickup with us kids down the long dirt road to the railroad tracks. Steve and Mom and the twins and I picked the low bush cranberries that were ripe on the green banks by the tracks all day. Kristi's mouth was stained red as she ran to us with cranberries stuffed into her small stained hands to put in our tin cans.

We kids ate our fill of the millions of little bright-red tart berries that grew in the moss on the banks while filling our cans to the brim. On a break we ate peanut butter and cinnamon sandwiches with carrots from our garden this summer and Kool-Aid to drink. The blue-and-gold Alaska train blew its whistle at us as it roared down the tracks east toward Talkeetna.

When our cans were full, we dumped them into a cardboard box in the back of the pickup. Then when we got home, we stored the box of cranberries in the cool garage until we were ready to use them.

Mom boiled the small red berries with water in a cast iron pot on the woodstove in the kitchen. Then she had me add sugar until it dissolved in the boiling dark-red liquid of cooked-down berries. After it cooled, we put the sweet syrup into mason jars to store to use on our pancakes and salmon.

I poured more of the cranberries that the twins had cleaned into the cast iron pot, boiling them with water again. This time we left the berries whole to have for Thanksgiving. Leaving some of the cranberries for my homemade muffins Mom taught me how to make, we used the rest of the berries we had picked this year for cranberry peach jam!

Mom let me help as I boiled more berries in a little amount of water until they were cooked down and thick. Then I mashed into the thick boiling liquid berries a can of smashed peaches and sugar until they were combined. Mom poured into the sweet bubbling jam a box of pectin to help thicken it. She then poured the jam into small pretty mason jars and let me put the gold lids on them that had a round brown seal.

Steve filled Mom's big metal gray pot with spring water out of the reserve drum. He put it on the iron stove to make a boiling bath for the jars of cranberry peach jam. After setting each jar carefully into the boiling water, we watched them get hot in their bath, sealing the lids. Mom said it was called canning, and we would can many other things for winter as well every year.

Combing my straight shoulder-length red hair until it shone was the last thing to do before leaving for my first day of the third grade.

It was the middle of September now, and school was starting at the little red Talkeetna Elementary School for grades one through six. Steve was starting the second grade and would be hiking with me out to the bus every day.

Dad and Mom had discovered a trail that was a shortcut out to the Parks Highway where the school bus stopped, and the county was building a community center.

The warm summer was gone, leaving us with wet and cold autumn days. Mom bought us each two pairs of jeans and long-sleeve shirts to wear under our thick coats. She also got us thick wool socks to wear inside of our snow boots to keep our toes warm.

Dad had to work, so he told Mom to take the rifle that she carried often and hike with us until we get to know the long trail to the highway.

Closing the front door, Mom told the twins to stay inside the house with Kristi and our three dogs until she returned. Steve and I made our sack lunches and then followed Mom down the trail through the woods toward the spring.

A relentless cold breeze jingled the clusters of heart-shaped leaves like many windchimes atop the tall birch. If you listened quietly, the gentle flutter made a lovely swishing sound as if keeping rhythm for a new season. Our feet sunk comfortably into the dark-green carpet-like moss trail that made its way narrowly through the willows and tall grass. Steve and I had not been beyond the road that went down the bank to the spring before now.

After we passed the spring, we hiked deeper into the tall trees with higher brush, grass, and ferns, overwhelming us as we ended up at a small cabin perched on a knoll. The brown cabin made of birch wood was square with a slanted roof and had one chimney stack, one door, and several small windows. There was a small wooden outhouse back in the woods behind the cabin. The cabin was empty, and Mom said the owners rented it out to hunters and fishermen.

Walking over to the edge of the high knoll and looking through the trees, we could see the train tracks below us. As we hiked down the steep bank of the knoll, Mom held the willow branches so they wouldn't hit me in the face, and I did the same for Steve, who was behind me. We snapped off the ones we could to clear the way to the bank next to the tracks. We could hear Goose Creek rushing high from the autumn rain, running east and west close to the trail. Carefully, we walked down the trail on the small bank and onto the gravel next to the steel rails. Mom stopped us and said, catching her breath, "Look for oncoming trains before crossing these tracks!"

Mom's glasses were fogged from the morning dew as she pointed down the tracks to the south, which was to the right of the trail, and continued, "See that part of the tracks where there is darker wood and no bank on the sides? That's the trestle bridge over Goose Creek. Stay off of it!" Mom continued, looking serious, "The bridge is very high up over the rocky creek bed!"

I noticed that beyond the bridge, the steel rails curved to the left, disappearing into the thick forest, and I said to my little brother, "Yeah, and trains could come around that corner really fast!"

We crossed over the thick railroad ties that were bolted down with iron stakes under the rails, then over a small hill and onto an old tractor trail as a bald eagle soared above, then a half mile farther through the eerie tall trees with thick brush and grass on either side before suddenly the Parks Highway lay in front of us.

There were men with hard hats and orange vests at the end of the trail working on building the upcoming community center.

A big yellow school bus pulled into the shoulder of the highway and parked. Mom and Steve and I passed by the men working who were looking at Mom with the shotgun still strapped across her chest with the leather strap. One of them said to Mom, "Are you Shotgun Annie?" Mom pulled her stocking cap off her short wavy red hair and laughed.

The next few times Mom walked us out to the highway, the name stuck and the workers got a kick out of calling her Shotgun Annie.

Mom told us as we stepped up into the bus to have the driver drop us off at the end of our main road after school. She would pick us up there around four o'clock.

As Mom waved to us, Steve and I looked out the small windows of the big bus, watching her turn to walk back down the long trail home. I couldn't help worry about her walking alone through the woods.

It took forty-five minutes to get to Talkeetna since the bus had to stop several more times to pick up more rural kids.

The small red elementary school had twenty-eight kids attending and was a lot of fun. Steve and I got to stay together.

After school Mom picked us up in the blue pickup at the end of the long dirt road.

The next day after school, Mom told us that Mr. McCullough had come by earlier and left their sheep dog, part collie with us at our homestead to take care of. They were going to Hawaii for the winter.

The friendly, shaggy big black-and-white dog came running up to us with Meardha, Pete, and Shane as if he already knew Steve and me. He had patches of brown on his face and black freckles on his white nose. We scratched his black hairy ears that stuck straight up all the time and rubbed his long black wagging tail.

The twins and Kristi had run down off the small porch out of the kitchen right behind the dogs, and Devan yelled as she almost tripped on her untied shoelaces, "His name is Dum Dum!"

Shane jealousy jumped up on me and licked my face with his golden floppy ears swinging side to side. Soon Meardha and Pete were surrounding me also. I had a soft spot for animals and wished we had more.

Steve and I took all four dogs with us to put Dungo in the corral and feed the chickens. Steve walked out to the field to catch Dungo up, and the chickens scurried into their coop after me. I poured chicken scratch onto the ground, shutting the door, closing them in for the night.

Dad usually didn't get home from work from Anchorage until late. It was our job to make sure all the animals were fed and put away first thing when we get home from school.

The twins wanted to help with the animals too, so Dad told them to collect the chicken eggs from the roosts every day. We were all scared of the big red-and-blue rooster that liked to hide behind things and chase us around the yard.

One day the twins were collecting the eggs from the chicken coop and carrying them back to the house. Devan was walking by the pickup where the big rooster was hiding behind, and he ran out and jumped on her leg, spurring her and wouldn't let go. Devan and

Dawn were screaming, eggs were flying, and the dogs were barking at the rooster.

Dum Dum wasn't having it! He grabbed the rooster's body with his big mouth and pulled it off Devan's leg and threw it up into the air!

Mom came running out of the house to the sound of cackling, barking, and screaming as the rooster hit the ground running.

Dum Dum was Devan's best friend after that, and the twins made sure he was with them every time they collected eggs.

We fed the dogs in the garage where their food was kept and then closed the big wooden doors with the latch when they were done eating. When we were inside the dark garage, Steve pointed at a cardboard box that was stuffed under one of the wood shelves and said, "Lori, what's in that box?"

Looking curiously at the dusty box in the corner of the garage, I said, "Dad's not home yet. Let's see what's inside of it."

Getting down on our knees, we pulled the big box out from under the shelf, dusting it off with our hands as we opened it. The whole box was filled with little round and square dark-green tins with lids. We were so curious to what was inside of these tins. Steve opened one of the little round ones to find white round crackers with thin round white wax paper protecting them. I opened one of the square ones to find packets of powdered strawberry milk. Steve opened another round one to find a stack of thin chocolate cookies.

Finding these snacks was so much fun, so we opened a few more to find more crackers and cookies. Knowing Dad would be home any minute, I said to Steve, "Let's put this away for now and not tell anyone it's here, and we'll snack on it sometime." When we closed the box, we saw writing on the top that we had not seen before, and it said in big words, "Army Rations."

We shoved it back where it was before and closed the garage and went in for supper just as Dad drove up in the driveway.

One day the first week of October, Steve and I were getting ready to walk out to the bus when I heard Mom and Dad talking in the kitchen. I heard Mom say she didn't like leaving the twins home by themselves with Kristi for the time it took to hike out to the community center and back.

Dad came into the living room and said to Steve and me, "After you two eat your oatmeal, head on out and catch the bus!"

Steve and I looked at each other apprehensively, and I said to Dad, being the one to talk back, "We know the trail, but what about the bears?"

Dad said, "Stay together and make a lot of noise. They won't bother you. It's getting cold and going to snow soon, so the bears are already hibernating, but watch out for the moose!" He continued as we both listened with our mouths open, "You know how to climb a tree, don't you?"

Steve and I both said yes at the same time, knowing we all climbed several of our big spruce and cottonwood trees on our property this summer to see who could climb the highest. Steve always won, getting more than thirty feet up in a spruce tree that had the most branches.

After eating breakfast and putting on our boots, coats, mittens, and hats, we headed out by ourselves on the long trail as it was barely getting light out. The dry grass was still wet from the morning dew, and we could see our breath in the cold air. Steve and I made it to the cabin on the knoll and took a break overlooking the tracks below and the white-capped waves on Goose Creek.

It rained a lot here in the fall, causing the Susitna River to rise, overflowing the slough and the creeks. The banks became nonexistent, covered in the wide bodies of rushing water.

Both of us dreaded hiking the rest of the way, especially through the dark forest on the other side of the train tracks. We knew we had to get going, and so we slid down the bank off the knoll and onto the train tracks, which was our favorite part of the hike, being it was out in the open.

Steve walked ahead of me through the last thick wooded area and then came to a sudden stop! I almost ran into him and said, "What's wrong, Steve?" He put his finger to his lips and backed up beside me and then whispered, "I heard something in the bushes up ahead."

I whispered back as fear started to set in, "You better not be teasing me!" Just as Steve was getting ready to answer, only yards ahead of us, the bushes to the right of the trail were moving and making a rustling sound.

Out of the brush and through the high dry grass, a huge grizzly bear down on all fours was making its way slowly onto our trail!

Steve and I both gasped at the same time, holding on to each other, frozen with fear!

The big brown grizzly stopped in the middle of the trail! He turned his massive hairy head, looking straight at us with his blood-shot beady brown eyes! He had long light-brown hair all over his body with a big hump on the back of his neck and small round ears on his huge head.

Remembering Dad's words, I looked around to find a tree we could climb, knowing a grizzly couldn't climb very high if at all.

Steve was thinking the same thing and grabbed my shaking hand, pulling me into the woods to a big spruce tree!

The big bear ignored us and put his large head down as he walked across the trail and into the high grass.

Steve gave me a boost up to the first branch with his hands clasped together. I frantically reached for each sharp branch, climbing higher into the big spruce.

Looking down at my little brother as he climbed right below me faster than I've ever seen him climb a tree, I stuttered to get the words out, "Hurry, Steve, hurry!"

As he swung up next to me on a big strong branch, he said, catching his breath, "Let's stop here and wait." We were about twenty feet up in the big tree, away from the huge grizzly, hanging on to each other's shaking bodies.

Steve kept looking down from the big tree into the brush and woods to see if the bear was still around.

After what seemed like a long time, Steve said, "We have to get down and try to catch the bus."

I said to him, still shaking, "Besides, we might get a lickin' if we miss it!"

Steve started to slowly climb down out of the big tree, stepping on each limb. Then he shimmied down the rest of the way with his arms and legs wrapped around the large trunk.

Right behind Steve, I climbed down the tree, and then wrapping my skinny long legs around the trunk, I jumped to the ground. After we looked around again, I said, "Let's run fast and make a lot of noise all the way to the community center."

Steve said, "Let's race! Ready, set, go!"

Steve and I ran as fast as we could down the dark trail through the woods, especially past the part where the big grizzly had crossed.

I said, barely able to breathe, "Maybe we didn't miss the bus!" and then continued, "Thanks, Steve, for saving us from the bear. You're a good brother."

Steve smiled big with his rosy freckled cheeks and his golden eyes shining and then said, "Don't worry. I'll take care of you, Lori. Come on, let's catch the bus."

When Steve and I came running around the community center, the big yellow bus was just pulling out to leave. The driver saw us running and came to a stop and opened the big glass doors as we ran up into the warm bus.

Steve and I had fun telling our grizzly story to the other kids at school after we got over the shock.

That night Dad came home with a black-and-gold Polaris snow machine he had bought new in Palmer using all of Mom and Dad's savings. It was big enough for two people to ride on it, and he also bought a big used dog sled to pull behind it for the rest of us to sit. Dad said we would need it this winter to get out to the highway when the snow was too deep to drive.

He said we could use it to get out to the bus if we needed to when we were old enough to drive a snow machine.

Steve and I could hardly wait to tell Mom and Dad about the grizzly crossing our trail on the way to school.

During supper that night, we told Dad and Mom how we climbed a tree to get away from the grizzly.

Dad said, "You did the right thing, but don't forget, if a bear comes charging at you and you can't get away, get on the ground and roll up into a ball." All of us kids stared at him as he continued, "The important thing is to protect your face and stomach!"

I shivered at the thought of that big grizzly charging at us and suddenly felt scared again, realizing it could have happened that way.

13

LONG, COLD WALK

DENNIS

Snuggled next to Evelyn in our bed in the dining room, I listened to the crackling of the birch wood burning hot in the big barrel stove.

Both woodstoves kept this old shack warm on this below-zero Thanksgiving night as the snow continued to fall outside. Our five kids were all asleep in their beds in the living room, and it was almost ten o'clock. Meardha was curled up in her usual spot in my big easy chair. Pete slept with Steve on the couch, and Dum Dum was on the end of the girls' bed. Shane was curled up on the kitchen floor by the little woodstove, snoring loudly. Evelyn was fast asleep next to me in the kitchen as my mind wandered.

The Lankfords had us over for a nice Thanksgiving dinner, and our kids made me proud, remembering their manners.

We were still able to drive with the Ford pickup down our road in four-wheel drive through the three feet of snow on the ground.

Christmas was coming, and I hadn't seen my parents since we had moved here a year and a half ago. I thought maybe if we had enough money in savings, we could drive to Idaho for Christmas so the kids could see their grandparents again.

I was just falling to sleep when Meardha let out a sharp bark and jumped off the easy chair. Shane started barking and followed Meardha to the kitchen door.

Evelyn woke up as I jumped up, reaching for my twenty-gauge rifle under the bed, still in my long johns.

Pete and Dum Dum joined the loud barking at the kitchen door, and all the kids sat up in bed, awakened by the noise.

Evelyn lit a kerosene lantern as I swung the kitchen door open, feeling the cold snow flurry hitting my face. All four dogs ran outside around my legs, almost knocking me over. I reached for my flashlight on the counter by the door and pointed it at whatever the dogs were bravely barking at.

By now the whole family was standing in the doorway, and to our surprise, there by himself only feet from the porch was one of the biggest black bears I have ever seen!

I could tell he was a male by his size and his big head, and most females were hibernating by now with their cubs. The big black bear with long hair and a sloped brown nose stood four to five feet tall on all fours.

Evelyn called all the dogs into the house as the black bear sauntered off by the garage toward the woods.

I quickly slipped on my cowboy boots and headed out the kitchen door. With my flashlight and rifle, I followed the bear's tracks as he was heading into the woods behind the camper.

The snow covered my body instantly as I realized the only thing I had on was my white T-shirt, my long johns, and my cowboy boots!

The black bear's big tracks were easy to follow in the fresh snow as I stepped into each one, filling my boots with the cold powder.

I had only shot one moose this year and shared it with my brother Doug, who had bought some of the land out here from me and had built a cabin. His cabin was about a mile down at the end of our field.

My thoughts raced as I ran through the dark woods with my dim flashlight, hoping to find the big bear and shoot it without getting too deep into the woods.

I had a shell in the chamber of my old thirty-thirty rifle and one in my teeth since I had no pockets in my now-wet long johns.

I was trying to be as quiet as I could, shivering and crunching through the brush and crisp snow, weaving in and out of the big spruce and birch trees, following the bear's tracks that suddenly disappeared.

I stopped and looked around to see where the black bear that probably weighed five hundred pounds or more had gone. My flashlight was going out, and the woods were so dark I couldn't see my own numb hands.

Not wanting to let fear take over me, I picked my old rifle up into my arms and pulled the big pin back, ready to take aim. I stood there quietly, knee-deep in the snow behind a big spruce, about to give up and go back to the house.

Then I heard a crashing sound in the brush behind me. I whipped my heavy rifle up on my chest as I turned around quickly with my finger on the trigger!

Only yards away, there was the old black bear up on his long hind legs, looking straight at me!

I was worried I would miss my shot in the blinding black night, and he would charge me before I could reload.

Evelyn and the kids would only find some of my clothing ripped to shreds in the woods.

Before the black bear, just yards away, could move, I pulled the gun up and aimed at him, barely able to hold the rifle still with my shaking arms!

He thrust his big head up, opening his mouth with a thundering growl!

I pulled the trigger and fired my one shot straight at his chest, throwing me backward against the large spruce!

My eyes still on him, I watched him fold to the ground, and then he let out a loud shrilling noise that sent a chill into my bones!

Cold, wet, and tired, I slid my back down the rough bark of the tree until I was sitting in the deep wet snow, staring at the black bear in the snow.

I shook violently as my body temperature was dropping rapidly, so I peeled myself up and started back through the woods toward the house. I was barely able to pick my numb legs up to hike through the snow with my icy long johns sticking to them.

Hanging the dead flashlight in some branches on a spruce, I marked the spot where the heavy carcass lay.

Making my way through the dark woods, hoping to not come upon any timber wolves that might smell the dead bear, I hung on to my rifle tightly and picked up the pace.

Finally I saw the light from the kerosene lantern that Evelyn had put in the window, giving me a focus as I trudged on toward the house.

I was never so glad to see the old wooden front door to the shack as I turned the big copper knob and burst into the warm living room.

Evelyn and the kids surrounded me standing there covered in snow. Evelyn threw a wool blanket around my shaking shoulders and said, "Dennis, you're freezing!" She helped me take my cowboy boots off after I sat down by the barrel stove, and she said, "You were gone so long. We were all worried!"

Steve took the rifle out of my frozen hands and propped it up against the wood-paneled wall.

After I warmed up for a few minutes and was able to talk, I said, "I got him! First shot!" Evelyn and the kids wanted to hear the whole story, but I knew I had to get him out of the woods and into the garage tonight. It would mean a lot of meat for the winter that would freeze in our cellar.

I told them the exciting story of how I chased the black bear through the woods would have to wait until breakfast.

Evelyn turned the lanterns down in the living room as the kids climbed into their beds.

After I changed into dry clothes and put my snow boots and coat on, Evelyn did the same, and we went out into the dark night, closing the kitchen door behind us.

I grabbed the spare flashlight and my rifle and saddled Dungo up outside the cowshed, throwing one of my long thick ropes on the saddle horn.

Evelyn put her foot in the stirrup and reached for my hand as I swung her up behind the saddle.

Dungo picked up his legs high, flinging the snow around as I reined him through the thick woods. Evelyn shined the flashlight in the trees and the tracks in the snow, and eventually we found the flashlight I had left in the spruce tree.

The dead bear was still lying in the bloodstained snow where I had left him. I quickly tied the rope to his front feet and then tied the rope onto the front of Dungo as he nervously danced around.

I had Evelyn stay on the saddle as I led Dungo home, hiking in the snow beside them to save the weight. When we got back to the dark and quiet house, I untied the carcass.

Evelyn and I dragged the hairy big black bear into the garage and shut the wood doors, latching them behind us. By now it was the middle of the night, and I was worn out to the bone.

I put Dungo away in the barn, and then Evelyn and I climbed back into bed, giving thanks for the bear and my sure aim.

The next day after I told the whole story at breakfast like I promised, my brother Doug came out and helped me gut and butcher the bear in the garage. Evelyn and the kids wrapped the dark rich meat and put it in the cellar below the kitchen floor.

A couple of weeks later, Evelyn, the kids, and I drove the Bel Air all the way to Idaho on Evelyn's twenty-eighth birthday. I took the back seat out and made a place for the kids to lie down.

When we got there, we drove to Mom and Dad's in Oldtown, Idaho, to their small red house on a large hill with many neighbors. It was on the state line dividing Washington from Idaho.

When I was growing up, we lived four miles out of town on a ranch in the Hoodoo Mountains where we learned to hunt and fish with Dad. It sold a few years ago.

My dad, Austin, was a stern man who wore his gentlemen's hat cocked to one side and was a logger by trade. He was thin these days and stood at only five foot seven.

My Irish mother, Viola, was a grade school teacher. She was pretty, short, and petite, with short red hair always set. Mom would make sure all the grandkids in the neighborhood went to church every Sunday by picking them up and taking them with her.

She had a big Christmas tree up all decorated in the living room, and all five of our kids were standing around it, admiring the beautiful lights. Mom said to them, "I thought we might string popcorn tonight for the tree and have hot cocoa." As she gave each one of them a squeeze, she continued, "I made a lovely supper. I bet you are all hungry."

Lori spoke up and said to her, "Can I help you, Grandma?"

Mom said she would love to have Lori and the twins set the table, and so they followed her into the small kitchen.

My dad was smiling at little Kristi as she held on to Evelyn's hand. He was watching her from his easy chair with soft eyes I had never seen before. Dad was a tough old bird, and most kids stayed clear of him. They seemed to take to each other as Kristi ran over to her grandpa with no fear as he pulled her up onto his lap.

We stayed at Mom and Dad's house for the week in Idaho and went to Evelyn's folks for Christmas Day, which was only a few miles away near Newport, Washington.

They had an even bigger Christmas tree with lots of gifts under it for our five kids and Norman's two kids, Joy and Dougie.

My brother Norman was in a state of shock when his young wife had died, and he moved to Hawaii to go to college.

Kristi and Joy were both two and a half years old and had a great time getting to know each other, except when they opened their Christmas gifts. Evelyn's parents got them each a doll dressed in pretty clothing. Joy was upset that Kristi's doll was bigger even though her own doll was fancier and had lots of hair. Kristi's doll was tall and stood up on its feet and was plastic and moved at the joints with no hair. Joy cried for hours, wanting the doll Kristi had already named Kristine after herself.

Evelyn had a good visit with her family while we were in Idaho, and the kids met a lot of cousins and other relatives. It seemed like the week went by fast, and before we knew it, we were saying good-bye again.

My brother Dave decided to go back with us and look for a place to live in Alaska.

He had four kids in Idaho, but his wife and he were getting a divorce, and Elizabeth, David, Kenny, and Kimberly were staying with her.

My brother Dewey was Dave's twin and had a ranch in Oldtown. I had a nice ride with him while we were there. He had two boys, Kevin and Darren with his wife Judy and she had three girls, Laura, Linda and Leanne.

It was snowing quite a bit when we drove back into Anchorage. I wondered how cold it was at the homestead if Anchorage was below zero.

For some reason, we had not packed our snow boots, gloves, or hats on our trip since it wasn't too cold when we left. All of us had our winter coats on at least.

The Parks Highway from Anchorage had been plowed and left six-foot snowbanks on the sides. It was late and dark, and when we finally got to our road, I wished we had our snow machine. We had been gone only a week, and there must have been five feet of snow on the ground and was still snowing.

Turning the Bel Air packed full with all of us and Dave, I began to try to make it down the two-mile road. Taking it slow as the Bel Air slid around on the ice below the thick snow, we only made it a short distance before the back end of the car slid into the bank. Dave, Evelyn, and I pushed and rocked the car without success and knew we had no choice but to hike in the long road home.

Evelyn got the girls out of the car and zipped their coats up and tied their hoods for the long cold walk home. I was worried about trying to hike the two miles we still had to go with only regular shoes and no mittens for the kids on this below-zero night.

Strapping on my guns and picking Kristi up into my arms, I said as I could see my breath in the freezing air, "Dave, can you carry the twins?"

My brother said as he put Devan on his back and Dawn in his arms, "Let's get these kids home!"

Evelyn took Lori's and Steve's hands, and we headed down the cold dark road surrounded by snow-covered trees. The snow was up to my hips and into my boots, soaking my thin socks and numbing my toes. Kristi's nose was red, and her red curls under her hood were turning into icicles. She was starting to cry and was shaking from the cold. Opening the zipper to my leather coat, I put her inside it, zipping it back up, holding my rifle underneath, bracing her up.

We were only a half mile down the frozen road when all the kids' faces and ears were red and they were starting to cry. Evelyn looked scared and said to me, trembling, "We're not going to make it. We are all freezing!" Dave said, "We could stop at Doug's cabin." I felt like I had to do something quick or we were going to freeze to death.

Quickly I said a prayer for the Lord to get us home. As we kept trudging through the deep snow, I said, "Keep moving! Doug's cabin is about a quarter mile up at this end of our field."

By the time we reached my brother Doug's small cabin, all the kids were screaming, especially Steve and Lori, who had to hike in the snow with the adults. Evelyn was crying, and I felt like crying. It was the most awful sound to hear your kids scream in pain from the inevitable frostbite. I felt horrible and responsible.

We could barely see Doug's cabin through the woods set back from the road at the border of the field. Steve yelled through his tears, "There's a light on in the window!"

I yelled, "Let's get to the cabin quick!"

The chimney on the roof was blowing smoke, meaning Doug was there. Just then a bright light made a path on the white snow as the door burst open. Mickey was barking as Doug came out with his rifle to see what was outside. The kids were crying and screaming as he helped us hurry them into the warm cabin and had them sit by the fire.

I told my brother, "We had to hike in and had no winter boots or gloves. The kids have frostbite!"

He said, "I'm glad I was here to have the fire going, Den. You guys wouldn't have made it all the way home."

As cold as Evelyn, Dave, and I were also, we quickly got the kids' shoes, socks, and coats off, while Doug wrapped blankets around them. Lori and the twins had frostbite on their toes and fingers. Steve had frostbite on his toes, fingers, and ears. Kristi was the only one without frostbite because she was inside my coat but was very cold.

Evelyn heated water on the stove to lukewarm temperature, and we soaked the kids' feet and hands until the pain resided. Feeling bad, I hugged each one of my kids and told them I was sorry this happened to them as the sobbing receded.

Once Evelyn, Dave and I took our boots off, we saw the frostbite on our toes. With no wool socks on inside my cowboy boots, the blisters were pretty bad. Doug made us all warm chicken noodle soup, and after the kids were quiet, we doctored ourselves.

Evelyn made beds on the floor of the small cabin for the kids right by the woodstove. There were two beds that us adults shared, and we stayed the rest of the night in Doug's warm cabin only a mile from the house.

The next morning, Dave and I hiked into the homestead and got the snow machine and sled to pick Evelyn and the kids up in. Dave stayed at the house and got the woodstoves going and fed the animals, while I roared through the deep snow with the big sled behind me to get my family home. I spent the rest of the day shoveling five feet of snow off the roof of the house and the barn. Making sure to dress warm, I put on wool socks in my snow boots and my overalls under my tan leather coat. I put on my warm black wool stocking cap that covered my ears and my warm winter gloves. While I was shoveling the deep snow off the roof of the house, I thought about the cold walk and how I wished we had our winter gear with us.

I thought about how 1968 ended with a hard lesson learned.

14

AURORA BOREALIS

DEVAN

Dawn nudged me, waking me up in the middle of the night on the eve of our fifth birthday. It had to be midnight, and everyone was asleep. Rolling over and facing her, I whispered, "What's wrong, Dawn?" She looked at me with her sleepy eyes and whispered back, "I have to go to the bathroom."

It was the middle of January and forty below zero outside with six feet of snow on the ground. Hiking out to the outhouse sounded dreadful, but I knew I would have to go with her. Dawn tugged on my nightgown sleeve and whispered loudly, "Devan, I can't hold it!" We must have woken Lori up, because suddenly she rolled over toward us and whispered loudly, "Be quiet you two!" I looked up at our big sister and said quietly, "Dawn has to go to the bathroom bad."

Lori whispered back, "Take the flashlight by the door and Dum Dum and go with her."

Dawn and I slipped out of bed and put our knee-high snow boots on that had warm liners and tied at the top to keep the snow out. Quietly we put our coats on by the door, and I grabbed the fat red flashlight.

The worn-out wooden front door creaked when I closed it as we stepped out into the bitter cold night with Dum Dum beside us. He was a good dog and would let us know of any danger. Our black snow boots crunched over the icy snow on the path Dad had made with his wide snow shovel. Dawn hurried into the big wood outhouse and then poked her hooded head out the door and said, "Devan, we forgot the toilet seat!"

Dad had put a handle on the porcelain toilet seat that was removable to take into the house and put by the woodstove to keep it warm. We were supposed to bring it with us, but we had forgotten it.

I climbed into the dark outhouse and helped Dawn sit over the big open hole so she wouldn't fall into the lime-covered frozen tower of poop below. After Dawn was finished, we put more lime out of the bag into the hole and then closed the door to the outhouse that faced the dark woods.

Dawn and I held each other's cold hands as Dum Dum led us down the trail back to the house. Peering up over my tightly closed furry hood to look at the millions of stars in the big sky, I saw something words cannot describe! "Dawn, look up!" I could see my breath as I squeezed my twin sister's hand trying not to yell. Both fear and excitement came over me and Dawn as our mouths dropped open at the breathtaking colorful curtain of light covering the sky.

Stopping in the trail halfway to the house, I could see the flashing pink, green, and yellow colors bursting up from behind Mount McKinley and spreading over the stars and the whole sky above us!

Dawn shivered and said, "Maybe the Rapture is coming. We better go tell dad!" Dawn wasn't the only one scared this time, but I couldn't get myself to look down from the bright array of colors that snuck in on this quiet cold winter night. Dawn tugged on my hand, pulling me down the trail as I thought about how I would wake Dad up to tell him what we had seen.

The scratched wood door creaked open as we quietly slipped inside the dark living room. After Dawn and I took off our boots and our winter coats and laid them on the floor below the red-hot barrel stove, Dawn took Dum Dum back over to our bed.

I tiptoed by the couch where Steve and Pete were stirring around and quietly made my way into the kitchen. Mom and Dad were sleeping in the big bed by the black woodstove, and Shane was on the floor curled up next to Dad's side of the bed.

As soon as I got close to the bed, Dad opened his eyes, jerking up, looking straight at me! "What are you doing up, Devan?" he said, quietly trying not to wake Mom up.

Whispering back, I said, "Dawn had to use the outhouse so I went with her."

Dad said more sternly, "Why are you waking me up then?"

Bold like I was, I whispered to Dad, "Something's happening outside in the sky!" Trying to catch my breath from the fear of getting in trouble, I continued, "A big bright curtain of colors is coming up over the mountains!" My dad's blue eyes lit up as he seemed to know what I was trying to describe.

As Shane sat up panting, Dad climbed out of bed and said, "Get everyone up and let's go look at the northern lights!" He reached over and shook Mom, waking her up as I ran into the living room, yelling, "Wake up, everyone! Come see the northern lights!"

Steve and Pete jumped off the couch, and Lori climbed out of bed half asleep. Dawn, who was already motherly, had picked Kristi up out of her wood bunk and was putting her coat on while I put mine back on.

After we all got our winter gear on, Dad led us outside through the kitchen door and off the small covered porch into the crisp winter night.

My whole family just stood there in complete amazement at the starry sky that was lit up with long luminous and colorful lights. There was pink, green, and yellow colors of the rainbow with hues of gold!

I felt like I was inside of heaven as my eyes followed the beams of color from behind the field stretching across the whole sky. Even the dogs sat still in awe of the breathtaking natural phenomenon happening that only few people ever see with their naked eye.

We all walked down to the edge of the field while the luminous colors danced off our shiny smiling faces.

Mom's loud voice broke the beautiful silence, "Aurora borealis is what a French scientist called these magical lights. They glow after earth's magnetic field forms them into beams of light rays!" Our smart mom continued, "The light rays hit gases in the atmosphere, creating different colors."

Straight ahead over the high mountains, I could see the big dipper through the array of color.

Lori had heard something from one of the native girls at school and said, "The village people believe that if you whistle during the northern lights, the demons that steal children in the night will take you!"

We stayed warm by dancing around under the beautiful lit-up sky that painted subtle colors onto the white snow. Wearing ourselves out and being probably two in the morning, Dad told us to go back to bed, and he let us sleep in an hour later than usual.

Dawn and I must have been sleeping soundly, because Mom was already making breakfast and Steve was outside doing the chores with Dad. I thought I heard Lori tell us to get up, and then Kristi ran over to our bed where we were snuggled together. She jumped up on us, bouncing around. "Happy birthday to the twins!" she said over and over in her cute little jumpsuit as her red curls bobbed up and down.

Dawn and I climbed out of bed and put on the same jeans and long-sleeve white cotton shirts we had been wearing for several days now.

The only way out of our road was to hike or take the snow machine, so Mom wasn't able to get to the Laundromat and we were running out of clean clothes. She still had the washboard Dad had made the first year we were here and used it to wash towels and a little bit of clothes.

"Happy birthday, girls!" Mom said as she told us to set the table.

Dad and Steve brought the icy cold air in with them as they came in the kitchen door, stomping off their boots. Dad gave Dawn and me a hug and told us, "Happy birthday to my big twin girls. How many swats?" Lori and Steve giggled, and Mom laughed as Dad took Dawn and me over his knee and gave us each five light swats for our birthday.

We knew it was tradition to get birthday swats, so Dawn and I went along with the fun. Kristi started crying, not wanting us to get spanked on our birthday. Dad gave her two light swats and tickled her until she giggled. Before we all sat down at the small table to eat the pancakes and moose sausage Mom had made, Dad said, "Lori and Steve, hike down to the spring after breakfast and bring up some more water. We are almost out, and tonight is bath night."

"I'm going to take your mom and all the laundry on the snow machine sled and try to get into Talkeetna with the pickup at the end of the road." He continued talking as we all sat down to eat, "The twins can do the dishes and watch Kristi."

Along with my brothers and sisters, I said, "Yes, Dad," and bowed my head for prayer. Breakfast was delicious, and as always, I rubbed elbows with Dawn while we quickly ate. I was the only kid in our family that was left handed, and nobody wanted to sit next to me around the tight table.

Dad struck up a conversation about the northern lights we had seen last night, and that was all we could talk about. I saw the snow start to fall again out the kitchen window as we girls picked up the perfectly cleaned plates and stacked them on the counter next to the sink.

Mom put all the boxes of dirty clothes on the kitchen floor for Steve to carry out to the big sled. Dad put his overalls and his leather fringe coat on with his snow boots and gloves. Then he put his black stocking cap on that folded down on the sides and covered his ears. Mom put on thick black snow pants and her blue winter coat.

Grandma Viola taught Lori to knit while we were in Idaho for Christmas. Mom wore her teal knitted hat Lori had made her for her birthday, and her brown gloves and snow boots.

Dad was heading out the kitchen door with the dogs to warm up the snow machine so Steve could load the boxes. He didn't even make it off the porch when he came running back in and slammed the door!

We all went running into the kitchen, and Mom said, acting startled, "What's wrong, Dennis?" He let out a loud laugh, looking surprised at the same time, and said, "There's a whole herd of moose in our yard playing in the snow!"

I saw Steve and Lori look at each other as if they thought maybe Dad was teasing, but we could all hear the dogs barking. At the same time, Mom and we kids ran for the kitchen door to look out the framed window. Dawn and I got crowded out and barely got a glimpse of all the moose in the yard.

I got the step stool, and we climbed up on the kitchen sink next to the dirty plates. We watched the hairy black moose play in the snow out the small framed window. Mom said, "I have never seen such a thing! They are right next to the house, and they don't even care about the dogs chasing them!"

There must have been eight or more large moose stirring up the snow, looking for food and running from the dogs.

Steve said, "I think there's more moose around the other side of the house!" He ran into the living room, and getting on his tippy-toes, he was able to look out the old framed window on the front door. He yelled into the kitchen, "There's big moose over here too!"

I jumped down off the kitchen sink and ran with Lori into the living room to try to see out the door window with Steve. After numerous attempts at jumping up to see, I gave up.

I picked Kristi up and took her to the kitchen window while she screamed with excitement.

Mom grabbed the video camera Grandma Gloria gave her for Christmas and headed out the front door to catch this amazing sight on film.

Dad yelled at Mom as he picked up his thirty-thirty rifle, "Evelyn, don't go out with that herd unless I'm with you!" She waited on the porch as Dad headed out the door closing it behind him, telling us, "You kids stay in the house!"

Steve kept running from door to door, steaming up the windows to count how many moose were in our yard. He counted two bulls, six cow moose, and four calves that were almost fully grown. The big animals were running at the dogs in the snow with their heads down and their flapping bell under their chin swaying side to side. Their long scraggly manes stood straight up showing a defense mode.

Dum Dum was trying to get close enough to their heads to nip at them, while Meardha and Pete stood back and barked. Shane's big shiny ears were flopping around as he sprang into the air right next to the big moose, trying to play with them.

Dad and Mom were standing in the circular driveway, filming the big herd of moose, trying to stay out of their way.

Remembering the moose at our door last year, I said to Dawn, who was still up on the sink, "There's something about our house the moose really like!"

Lori heard me and said, "It's probably the dog food we have in the garage!"

The dogs eventually chased the herd of moose out of our yard and into the woods behind the blue camper, and Mom came back into the house. Dad pulled up the black-and-gold snow machine with the big sled hitched on the back. Steve loaded the cardboard boxes of dirty clothes while Dad strapped his scabbard onto the snow machine with his rifle in it. He also took his big red flashlight and a spare can of gasoline.

The rest of us watched him and Mom drive away on the snow machine down the long road out to the highway, making a windy trail through five feet of snow.

Steve and Lori put on their winter gear and got the big white buckets from the garage and headed down the trail to the spring.

After Dawn and I dried the last dish and put them away in the cupboards, we lay down with Kristi in our bed to get her to take a nap. She was worn out from the excitement and fell asleep quickly.

Dawn and I quietly crawled out of the two twin beds put together in the living room and started to straighten up the house, when I said to her, "Hey, Dawn, we should go see what else is in the garage the moose might want."

My twin looked at me as if she was afraid I would get her into mischief and said quietly, "Lori and Steve will be back any minute, and they will tell Dad!"

My mouth dropped as I looked at my sister with disbelief. "They are not going to be back any minute!" I put my hands on my hips and kept arguing, "Come on, Dawn, let's go!"

Slipping on my snow boots loosely, I looked behind me to see if she was going with me. Dawn slowly walked over to her snow boots and put them on, tying the vinyl strings. We hurried up with our coats, and closing the front door behind us, we walked down the short narrow path to the garage.

I pulled the big wooden handles up from their metal bracket.

Dawn helped me open the creaky big wood doors, shutting them most of the way behind us. It was dark inside the garage, but the rays from the small windows above the shelves sent enough light for us to see what was inside. Dad had a lot of tools on the shelves and fishing poles propped up against the wall. There were boxes of canning jars and cans of oil and gasoline under the shelves. Dawn noticed a big cardboard box that was closed under one of the long shelves on the left and said, "I wonder what's in that box, Devan." I walked over to where she was pointing and began pulling the large box out from under the wood shelf. She came over and helped me, and when we pulled it out, I saw writing on the top of the box that I couldn't read since we hadn't started school yet.

Mom and Lori read books to us and taught us our letters and how to sound them out. Dawn was staring at the first word and then blurted out, "Army!" The second word was much harder, and Dawn and I both were trying to sound it out when suddenly more light came into the garage as the big doors opened wide!

"Rations!" Lori said loudly as she and Steve came bursting through the big doors. Dawn and I both jumped up startled, and I said, "We just wanted to see what was in here!"

Lori said, "You two are supposed to be in the house with Kristi!"

Dawn looked scared and said nervously, "Please don't tell Dad, Lori!"

Lori and Steve laughed as if they were in control.

I wasn't falling for it and suddenly wondered how Lori knew what the top of the box had said when she wasn't close enough to read it.

"How did you know what the box said, Lori?" I blurted out boldly with my hands on my hips, "You and Steve have been in here getting into things, haven't you?"

Steve and Lori looked at each other suspiciously, and Steve said as he walked over to the box behind us, "Well, since it's your birthday, we won't tell Dad, and we'll show you what's inside our box!"

Dawn and I looked at each other and smiled with relief as Steve opened the box and Lori pulled out some of its contents. Curiosity was overwhelming me, and I said, "What's in those tins, Lori?"

She looked up at me grinning and said, "Snacks!" All four of us eagerly opened the lids to the dark-green tins as we felt like we were opening a present with each one. We sat around the box and sampled crackers, cookies, and stuck our fingers into the powdered strawberry quick.

Lori looked up from her tin with chocolate on her lips and said, "We had better put this away for now. Nobody better tell Dad or Mom that we got into it!"

Lori, Steve, Dawn, and I all swore we wouldn't tell by crossing our hearts and hoping to die. Then we put the big box away under the shelf and left the garage exactly like we had found it.

When we walked back into the living room and took our boots off, I noticed Lori and Steve came back from the spring with empty five-gallon buckets. I asked Steve, "Where's the water you guys were supposed to get?"

Steve looked worried as he said, "Dad's going to be mad, but the spring was frozen solid, and we couldn't break the ice!" My brother continued talking as he took his coat off, "Dad told me to heat up water on the stove and make sure we all took our baths before they got home!"

Lori spoke up and said, "Hey, Steve, why don't we use the clean snow outside and melt it for bathwater?" Steve thought that was a great idea and put his coat and boots back on.

After Lori and Steve packed the metal bucket with snow, they put it on the barrel stove in the living room to melt it and get it hot. Then carefully they carried it into the kitchen and poured it into our round tub on the floor, which took several buckets to fill.

Lori took the first bath with Kristi, who had woken up from her nap from the noise of us talking. Dawn and I took the next bath one at a time since the tub was so small, and then Steve got in last. After he was done with his bath, he and Lori carried the dirty water outside through the kitchen door and tipped it off the porch to empty it.

Steve put on his coat and boots again and carried in more firewood from outside the living room door under the eve. After stoking the fires, he said, "Let's play Monopoly!" We all agreed that sounded like fun, and so we sat there for what seemed like hours, playing together on the card table in the kitchen.

Suddenly the dogs started barking, and all of us looked up from the game, hearing the roar of the snow machine pulling up into the circular driveway. A few minutes later, Mom and Dad came in the kitchen door, each of them carrying paper bags. Dad must have looked in the water drum outside before he came in and looked at Steve and said, "How come there's no water in the drum?"

Lori spoke up, "The spring was completely frozen, Dad. We tried to break it!"

Steve said, "Lori and I melted clean snow on the barrel stove for our baths!"

Dad looked upset about the frozen spring and said, "I'm going to have to build a spring house around it to keep our only water supply from freezing."

It was our birthday, and I wanted to look on the bright side of it, so I said, "At least we have clean snow to melt!"

Dad looked pleased as he said, "That was smart thinking to melt the snow, and it looks like you kids are all bathed and ready for the twin's birthday supper!"

Steve and Lori helped unload the clean laundry out of the sled and into the house while Dad fed the animals. Mom told Dawn and me to unpack the frozen bags of groceries. To our surprise, inside the bags were hot dogs, buns, chips, Jolly Rancher sticks, and store-bought vanilla ice cream!

Mom laughed as Dawn and I held hands with Kristi and danced around the kitchen, squealing with delight. After Dad came back into the house, Mom boiled the hot dogs, and then we stuffed the treat we rarely had into our mouths after putting ketchup on them. Our mouths were stained with Kool-Aid as we crunched down the last potato chip.

Then Mom pulled out a small square box from the cellar under the kitchen floor and opened it on the table in front of us. She pulled out a beautiful two-layer white frosted strawberry birthday cake she had made to go with our ice cream!

Dawn and I thought this was the best birthday ever while we blew out our five candles at the same time and enjoyed every bite of the cake and ice cream afterward.

Lori jumped up and said loudly, "Now for your gifts!" She walked into the living room and came back proudly with the two presents in her hand that she had neatly wrapped in paper sacks with pretty red ribbon.

Eagerly, Dawn and I pulled the ribbon off, saving it, and then we tore the paper sacks open. Inside were new matching dresses Mom had made for our birthday with her sewing machine. They were so beautiful we both wanted to cry as we hugged Mom, thanking her.

Dad told us to try them on and see if they fit so we could wear them to church tomorrow. Then he handed each one of us kids a watermelon Jolly Rancher stick he had bought in Talkeetna.

Dawn and I felt like princesses as we put on our new pretty white lace dresses that had a fluffy slip Mom had sewn in to make the skirt flow out. They had white lace around the collars and around the bottom of the skirt. The pure white dresses had a shiny wide ribbon sash around the small waist, each one a different color to tell us apart. Mine was yellow, and Dawn's was pink.

The rest of the family smiled and clapped as we pranced into the living room with a sparkle in our big blue eyes, flipping our short strawberry-blond hair back as Dad said, "There's my beautiful twin girls!"

15

BUBBLE AND SQUEAK

EVELYN

The hot iron stove in the kitchen barely had enough room for the big cast iron skillet. It was sizzling hot with melted butter and black bear steaks. Wishing I had a bigger stove, I flipped the steaks over with a fork.

As I opened the small oven and checked on my Irish soda bread, my mind wandered. Memories of temperatures reaching forty below zero this winter. We were barely able to keep the house warm and the spring froze up, so we had to melt snow for months.

I shivered as I remembered the long cold walk in our everyday shoes and the frostbite we'll never forget.

Lori and Steve had to hike the bus trail almost every day that was under six feet of snow. They had to wear the ski masks Dennis bought them to keep their faces warm in the bitter cold. Dennis and I both took them out on the snow machine when we could, and some days they just had to miss school. I even hiked in the snow next to Lori and Steve on Dungo, fighting the winter storms to get them to the bus.

One day Dum Dum had followed Lori and Steve as they were hiking out to catch the school bus. Instead of going back to the house, he went up the highway to some people's house and got in a fight with their dog.

After we realized Dum Dum was missing, Dennis took the snow machine out to the highway to look for him. He found our large playful dog at the Beckers', who had him chained up outside their house in a snowbank. Mrs. Becker came out of the house and told Dennis, "Keep your stinking dog away from here!" After they exchanged harsh words, Dennis brought Dum Dum home and told us to stay away from them.

The bear steaks were golden brown and cooked to perfection. I put them on a plate and then put a big metal pot with a small amount of water on the stove to make my bubble and squeak. It was Saint Patrick's Day, and since we were all very Irish, it always felt like a special day. Besides, it also meant spring was here even though there was still three feet of snow on the ground, and Kristi was turning three tomorrow on Sunday.

Dennis would be home any minute from his new job contracting for Bureau of Land Management as a welder working on their fire equipment. He still had to commute to the BLM shop that was southeast of Anchorage on the Seward Highway. He got his brother Doug a job with BLM as well. This winter money was scarce, and our food supply got very low. Thank God Dennis got a moose and a bear, and he also shot several ptarmigan that tasted like chicken. We also ate some of our hens that spent most of their time in the chicken coop this winter not producing eggs.

We still had a lot of projects to do on the homestead, and we were always running low on money. Dennis and I had talked about me getting a part-time job since the twins would be going to school this fall.

The front door creaked open, and Lori and Steve knocked the snow off their boots and came in the warm house. I yelled from the kitchen, "How was school and your hike home?"

Lori answered, "School was fun, and on the hike home, we saw some moose by the tracks!"

That worried me and I said, "The cow moose are having their calves now, so be careful. They are very protective!"

As Lori took off her coat and hung it up by the stove, she said, "If we need to, we'll climb a tree again!"

Steve came into the kitchen and sniffed the black bear steaks as if he could hardly wait to gulp them down. While he watched me cut cabbage on the cutting board at the counter, he looked up at me, smiling, and said, "Mom, are you making bubble and squeak?" He was so cute with his short red hair, his freckles, and golden eyes that sparkled. It seemed like he was always hungry!

Taking his face in my hands affectionately, I said, "Yes, I'm making bubble and squeak! Now you had better go feed the animals and put Dungo up before your dad gets home." Being the good boy he was, Steve always did what he was told and ran into the living room to get his coat.

The twins went with Steve outside to feed, and Lori came into the kitchen to help with supper. She had made bubble and squeak with me before, and at almost eight years old, Lori was becoming quite the cook.

She got out the ingredients for a white sauce using powdered milk for the cream as we rarely had regular milk.

After the cabbage was boiled soft, I drained the water from it and set it on the counter on a pot holder. Lori put a small cast iron pot on the woodstove and began melting butter while whisking flour into it, make a rue. Then she slowly added the milk she had made until the white sauce became thick and creamy. I grated a small block of cheddar cheese and added it to her white sauce while she stirred until the cheese melted. I had cooked ground pork sausage in a skillet earlier today and had Lori add it to the white sauce also. Then we added the sauce to the cabbage in the big metal pot and mixed it all together, making bubble and squeak.

Kristi wanted to help with supper, so I let her set the small table as best as she could.

Just as Steve and the twins were coming in the house from feeding the animals, Dennis roared up into the driveway with the snow machine. With the new community building at the end of the trail to the highway, we could safely leave our vehicle if we were snowed in and leave the snow machine there as well.

As Dennis came in the front door and took off his leather coat, he yelled, "Happy Saint Patrick's Day! I smell bubble and squeak!"

We all sat down after plating up at the counter as the table was too small to put the food on. As the kids were dishing themselves up, Dennis said, "Only take what you can eat! You can always get seconds." We were strict about wasting food and wanted our kids to have good manners, especially when we were at someone else's house.

Crowded together at the small card table next to our bed in the kitchen, I said to Dennis, "We have to do something about this crowded kitchen, and this table isn't even near big enough for all seven of us!"

He laughed and said, "Well, we'll stay close this way! I plan to add on to the house sometime this year so we can bring our big picnic table in that I made."

He continued as he winked at me, "Besides, we need our privacy so we can add on to our family." All five of our kids started giggling as I felt my face flushing. With everyone bedding down in the living room and kitchen for two years now, there was no such thing as going to your bedroom. After the bubble and squeak was completely gone and most of the bear steak and Irish soda bread, we had lime Jell-O for dessert with fresh whip cream. The bear meat was good but had a strong rich flavor, and you could eat only so much. Dennis said he might make a smokehouse to use for bear meat and salmon this summer.

We spent the rest of our evening taking our baths one at a time in our little round tub by the glow of the kerosene lanterns. Kristi was able to take her own bath now but needed someone to wash her long curly red hair.

The bubble and squeak earned its name that night as the whole family giggled in the dark every time someone bubbled and squeaked!

The next morning Dennis got out of bed his usual early time and woke everyone up. The kids all jumped out of bed except Kristi, who was already up and playing with Shane on the living room floor. She was an early riser like her dad and was up before us often.

Dennis went over to her sitting by the barrel stove in her flannel nightgown petting Shane, and crouching down beside her, he said, "Happy birthday, sweetie." She grinned and looked up at him as he continued, "How many birthday swats do you get?" As we all gathered around, I saw her face turn to a pout, and she said through tears, "I already got my swats on the twins' birthday!" She surprised us all when she then got up and ran to the built-in bunk beds, jumping on the bottom bunk, and then she hid under the covers! The kids and I all felt bad for her as we listened to her cry on her birthday and just knew Dennis was going to spank her for real.

I could tell Dennis's heart was melting as he went over to the bunk bed and pulled Kristi out of the covers. He hugged her as he wiped her tears away and told her she didn't have to have birthday swats this year.

Lori and I made biscuits and moose sausage gravy with fried potatoes for breakfast, and then we all got dressed for church.

Dennis pulled the snow machine up in the circular driveway with the big dog sled hitched to the back. After the kids were bundled up in their winter gear, Steve put Meardha, Pete, Shane, and Dum Dum in the house and closed the door. Devan and Dawn sat down in the back of the sled with Kristi snuggled between them. Lori and Steve sat in front of the twins, and they all held on to the metal rails on each side of the big sled.

I straddled the wide seat behind Dennis on the snow machine, resting my boots on the runners. The big sled that had long metal skis to cut through the snow easily also had a small flat runner on the very back to stand on with a bar to hold on to.

Dennis started the snow machine, and we took off on the snowy trail past the spring and then to the empty cabin. The main two-mile road was a smoother ride, but we had to leave the pickup at the community center so the only way out in the winter was the bus trail.

Looking back at the kids to see if they were all right, I realized we had to take the snow machine with the sled down the steep bank by the cabin. Dennis drove the snow machine to the very edge of the bank and yelled so the kids could hear, "Lean back and hold on tight!" I leaned back on the snow machine and held on to the bar on the back, as Dennis took us straight down the snow-covered fifteen-foot bank. About halfway down, I turned to look at the kids to see if they were hanging on. They had all laid back against each other, hanging on to the rails with both hands. I could barely see

Kristi's hood poking out from in between the twins, as she was buried under her protective siblings. The big sled came down almost at a ninety-degree angle as it slid down the bank with the snow machine.

Dennis stopped and looked back at the kids before he headed down the wooded trail after train tracks. Once we got over the tracks, there was a small hill that caused us to go off the ground, sled and all. I could hear the kids laughing as they bounced up in the sled as if it was a carnival ride.

A short distance later, we were at the community center loading up into the pickup to go to Talkeetna Bible Church. While we were snowed in, we rarely made it to church this winter.

We had heard from Betty Lankford that Pastor Dean had retired and moved to Anchorage with his wife, Ruth. We were all excited to meet the new pastor named Gary Calhoun, his wife, Shirley, and their three kids, Patsy, John, and Casey.

The kids had a great time at church meeting new friends and playing Ping-Pong afterward. Dennis took us to the Fairview for an early supper of hamburgers and french fries for Kristi's birthday. Before we left Talkeetna, we stopped at B&K Trading Post, where Dennis and I grabbed a few supplies and groceries.

Later that evening, we had the chocolate cake I had made with three candles to celebrate Kristi's birthday. She tore into her birthday presents eagerly, sitting on the floor in the living room, while we all watched. She ran and gave Lori a hug for knitting her a pink dress for her big doll Kristine. The next gift was a pretty blue Easter dress with a blue bonnet I had made on my sewing machine for her. The final gift was from Dennis, and it was a set of ten matchbox cars.

I think Dennis wanted his little Kristi to be a tomboy since he had mostly girls. She loved all the gifts and had a great night playing cars with her brothers and sisters after all the chores were done.

Easter soon came upon us as well as an early spring breakup in the middle of April. Spring breakup caused the roads and trails to be full of big puddles, thick mud, and deep ruts. We could barely get the Ford pickup through it in four-wheel drive. With the temperatures still down, there was quite a bit of snow left on the ground.

Dennis had towed the Bel Air with the pickup out to the highway and to the community center so that I could use it to get to town if I needed to, since he had the pickup most of the time for work.

With Easter Sunday five days away, I needed to get to Palmer for a small amount of groceries and to make a few dishes for the potluck after church. Dennis was at work, and Lori and Steve were at school when I decided to hike out to the car at the community center.

It was a sunny midmorning, and the twins were playing quietly with Kristi and her new matchbox cars on the living room floor. I put on my snow boots that went up above my calves and were open at the top and my heavy coat and gloves. Then I strapped the holster around my waist with Dennis's .41 pistol in it.

The girls were so busy playing they didn't even notice I was leaving until I said, "Devan and Dawn, I'm going to hike out to the car on the bus trail and go get some groceries in Palmer." The twins both looked up at me as I grabbed my purse heading for the door and said, "I'll be back in a couple hours, so stay in the house with the dogs and watch Kristi."

Our twins were so cute looking at me as Devan said, "Okay, Mom, we will."

Dawn said, looking a little scared, "Be careful and hurry back!"

As I was closing the door, I said, "I won't be long."

The trail out was wet from the recent rain, leaving huge puddles and thick slippery mud. I made it out to the Bel Air without any problems and drove to Palmer, which is sixty miles toward Anchorage.

Finally getting back to the community center and parking the car, I realized I had bought more groceries than I could carry a mile and a half back into the homestead through the mud.

I decided to hike back into the house and get Dungo and the big saddle bags to put the groceries in. Besides, it had been a couple of hours already, and I was worried about the twins being home alone with Kristi.

After locking the groceries into the car and strapping the .41 back around my waist, I headed back to the house. Along the way there were several moose with their calves quite a ways from me next to the tracks, eating from the willows. I quietly kept walking and made it home to find the girls making peanut butter and cinnamon sandwiches.

After telling them that I was taking Dungo out to the highway, I went out to the wet field to catch him up.

Dungo slipped around on the trail but never lost his footing as he took me back out to the community center. The big leather saddle was comfortable as I rocked back and forth with his smooth muscular stride. When we arrived, I ground tied Dungo behind the community center. After I unloaded the groceries from the Bel Air, it was hard to find a spot where there wasn't thick mud or deep puddles to set them down. Then I took all the cans and cartons of our food out of the paper bags and neatly organized them into the saddle packs that were hanging on each side of the back of the saddle.

Grabbing Dungo's thick lead rope, I pulled him forward from the low grass he was nibbling on and out of the mud where I could get up in the saddle. After tying the lead rope up onto the saddle horn, I went to lift my left foot up into the stirrup, and then I realized I couldn't lift my booted foot out of the thick mud! I pulled on it and then tried lifting my right foot up out of the mud, and I was sinking further into it!

Suddenly I fell backward into the wet slimy, thick mud flat on my back with my booted feet still stuck! I had fallen right next to Dungo, who was still standing there right over me, craning his neck, looking down at me. I could feel the mud and water seeping into my shoulder-length red hair and into my boots and pants as I lay there in the mud.

As wet and cold as I was, I couldn't help but laugh at Dungo staring down at me with his big brown eyes. He was snorting at me as if he was getting a kick out of it!

I finally was able to get out of the mud and got into the saddle wet and dirty, to get home and take a bath! Saturday night or not!

16

SMOKEY THE BEAR!

DAWN

*B*ang! Bang! Bang! Thinking I was dreaming about someone pounding on the front door of the house, I rolled over next to my twin under the warm covers and went back to sleep.

I heard the banging again, and then Dad's loud voice startled me awake. "Time to roll out, girls!" Devan and I sat straight up in bed and yelled in unison, "We're up, Dad!" I had forgotten where I was for a minute until the loud sound on the wooden door made me realize Dad had let Devan and me sleep in the camper for the past week.

It was the end of May and warm enough at night for us to sleep outside in the camper. Lori had just turned eight years old on the second.

She got two brand-new books for her birthday, one of which was a Harlequin Romance. Mom bought her two new pairs of jeans to wear to school, which, according to Lori, was the style now.

Lori was the oldest, so she was in charge when Mom and Dad were away, and she was becoming quite bossy. Devan and I liked sleeping in the camper by ourselves because we could stay up late at night and talk. Sometimes it was scary being outside of the house at night when we heard the wolves howling and other noises.

When we went outside the camper, there was a strange dog playing with our other four dogs by the garage. The dog was big and black with long hair and a white patch on his chest.

Devan called the stray dog over, "Come here, dog!" It seemed to be friendly as it ran over to us, almost knocking us over, licking our faces. I thought he was a nice dog but wondered where he came from. Just then Dad came around the side of the garage from feeding and saw us petting the strange dog. He said as he came over to us, "That's the dog I have seen running by the highway from time to time."

Devan and I unintentionally said at the same time, "Can we keep him?"

Dad smiled at us and said, "We already have to feed four dogs!" He bent down and pet the friendly dog and said, "We can keep him for a while until we find his owner." After we took him into the house, we all agreed to call him Smokey because he looked like a bear.

Mom and Dad were going to Anchorage today to meet with Grandma and Grandpa Stanton to lead them up to our place. They were coming for a few weeks to visit and look for property as they were wanting to move to Alaska. My grandpa Vern loved to hunt and fish just like Dad and had always dreamed of living in Alaska. Uncle Dave also bought some property in a small town called Houston about forty miles south of us.

After breakfast all five of us kids stood in the driveway and waved goodbye to Mom and Dad as they left in the Bel Air down the wet, muddy road full of ruts.

Right after they left, Lori put her hands on her hips and said to Devan and me, "You guys have to do what I tell you. I'm in charge!"

My twin sister was braver than I was, and she said back to Lori, "You're too young to be in charge!"

Steve piped in and said to us, "Lori and I are the oldest, so Dad put us in charge of you two and Kristi!"

Lori smiled and said, "If you twins get your dishes done and sweep the kitchen, we'll let you hang out with us."

I finally and rarely got up the nerve to speak up and said to Lori, "What are you two going to do?"

Steve smiled and pointed at the field. "We're going to make a fort in that windrow!"

Even though I knew Dad wouldn't approve of us going out to the windrows, the thought of making a fort sounded like fun. So Devan and I ran into the kitchen to do our chores with Kristi right behind us. She followed us everywhere, and we took care of her most of the time. Dad bought a little portable radio that we kept on the large open ledge that separated the kitchen from the living room. Devan started to heat water for the dishes, while I reached up and turned on a country music station. Both of us were excited about going out to the windrow to make a fort with Lori and Steve, so we did the dishes as fast as we could.

We didn't ask them if it was okay with Dad since they were the ones that came up with the idea. For the past three years, we were only allowed to go out in the field if Mom or Dad were home.

When Devan and I were finished with our chores, I helped Kristi tie her tennis shoes so we could all go out to the windrow. She insisted on carrying her big doll Kristine and her blankie with her.

The wind was softly blowing my hair, and I could feel the warmth in the air as we ran over to the chicken coop where Lori and Steve were cleaning it out. We watched the big red rooster as he pecked the ground by the cowshed to make sure he didn't chase us as we walked by. Devan asked Lori and Steve, "Are you guys done yet?"

Steve was putting the shovels away that they used to scoop the chicken poop out with and said, "Yeah, let's look in the dump for some old wood for the fort!"

The dump was in between the house and the field in the back toward the woods. Dad put a fence around the dump and used his tractor to bury the trash when it got too full.

All five of us kids climbed through the fence to look for anything to build a fort with.

Meardha, Shane, Dum Dum, Pete, and Smokey followed us all into the field as we carried little pieces of rope, an old broom Mom had thrown away, and a piece of rotted plywood.

The windrow was out in the middle of the field and was like an island of trees and brush. There were other windrows farther out in the large field but were too far from the house. Steve led the way through the waist-high grass as we sang "Billy boy, Billy boy, where have you been charming, Billy?..." The bears were coming out of hibernation and had cubs, so we sang a lot this time of year.

When we got to the windrow, Steve went in and checked for wild animals and then yelled for us, "Come in, you guys. This is neat!"

As I held on to Kristi's hand, I followed Lori and Devan into the island of trees. It was like being in a whole other world with its cave-like darkness, created by the large spruce trees that had grown over time. Like a house, it had two big rooms that were separated by willow vines and old rotted logs on the ground.

After Devan and Lori argued about who got what room, we all went to work sweeping the dirt floors and clearing the brush. Our wild imaginations created a house-like fort for only us kids to know about.

After our big fort in the windrow was ready, we played house for what seemed like hours. We made a little table with the piece of plywood Steve carried out and used the empty soup cans to catch the rainwater for us to drink.

Before we knew it, the cold dusk was settling in, and we were still in our fort playing, when Lori said, "It's starting to get dark, you guys. We better go in before Mom and Dad get home."

As we left the fort and hiked across the large field toward the house, Steve said, "I'm going to catch Dungo up and put him in the corral for the night. You twins need to feed the chickens and the dogs!"

When we got back to our house, Devan and I threw chicken scratch into the coop and stood back while the rooster and hens ran in one by one. After all the animals were fed and we were all back in the house, it was getting dark outside.

I was starting to worry about Mom and Dad as I helped Kristi take her shoes off. Lori lit the mantles in our two kerosene lanterns to light up the darkening house and said, "I wonder where Mom and Dad are. They should have been home by now."

Steve carried in some firewood from outside the living room door to start a fire in the iron stove in the kitchen. He said, "What if they don't come home tonight?" Devan and I listened as Lori answered, "I can make us something to eat, and then we'll go to bed." I felt an emptiness in my stomach as I let all five dogs in the house.

Just as Lori was opening the cellar door to look for something to cook, two sets of headlights lit up the kitchen and the dogs started barking loudly. Steve ran to the door and yelled, "Its Mom and Dad!"

I know I was relieved not wanting to be home alone at night in this dark house in the woods. Grandma and Grandpa and Aunt Wendy (Mom's younger sister) came in the door right behind Mom, giving us all hugs and looking around our small house, glad to see us.

Mom said they had decided to go to the food warehouse and get some groceries and seed for the garden. It was late and they had eaten already, so Mom made us kids tuna fish sandwiches with pickles.

The next two weeks flew by as our relatives explored our place, Talkeetna, and more of Alaska. They even went to church with us and met all of our new friends. Grandpa had a new camper on his brown pickup, and that was where they slept when they were at our homestead.

A couple of days before Grandma and Grandpa went back to Washington, they came out to the homestead to spend the day.

It was a warm day in the middle of June. The temperatures were in the sixties, and to us kids, that meant shorts weather.

After eating breakfast and doing our chores, Devan, Kristi, and I asked Mom if we could go outside and play. Grandma and Grandpa were sitting at the card table in the kitchen, visiting with Mom and Lori.

Dad and Steve were building a bookshelf in the living room out of plywood.

Mom told us, "Go ahead and go play, but stay close to the house."

I helped Kristi get her shoes on, and then all three of us ran out the kitchen door with only T-shirts, shorts, and tennis shoes on. After playing cars under the big birch tree that was in the front of the house, we got bored and decided to collect ladybugs.

Devan ran in the house and got three empty pickle jars from Mom. We found a nail and poked holes in the lids so the ladybugs could breathe. Then we put blades of grass in the jars for them to climb on just like they do outside.

After our jars were ready, we headed for the edge of the field and looked for cute little red and black ladybugs that bathed in the sun on the blades of high grass. It was fun to see who could collect the most, so we decided to spread out.

The dogs followed Devan as she went over by the cowshed to find some in the grass that grew around it. Kristi stayed on the edge of the field where we could see her, and I walked over to the house.

There was a lot of high green grass growing around the fence that closed in the big dump behind the house.

Since the big trash area was up against the woods, I decided to stay at the end of the fence closest to the house.

The delicate friendly ladybugs liked to be held and slipped into the jar with ease, as if I was making new friends. I looked over at the field to see Kristi laughing as she scooped the colorful bugs off the blades of grass into her tiny hands.

I turned around with my back up against the fence to the dump to see if there were more ladybugs in the thick grass. Then suddenly, while I was concentrating on my collection, I heard a deep growl behind me! My heart skipped a beat as I whipped around to see what had growled at me across the fence.

I was so relieved to see Smokey, our new big black dog, in the dump, nosing around in the trash only a few feet from me. He was big on all four legs and close to the fence where I was standing, so I reached over the top wire to pet him and said, "Hey, boy, you're not supposed to be in here!" Then fear and horror sent chills down my spine as Smokey took a few steps toward me and then stood up on his hind legs! He growled like a bear with his big paws up and his mouth wide open, exposing long sharp teeth!

Realizing the big black bear was not Smokey, my body froze with fear and my jar of ladybugs hit the ground! As the black bear stood growling, towering above me only a few feet away, I knew I had to run!

Fear and adrenaline set in with a rush, and my feet suddenly started to run toward the house like a streak! I screamed at the top of my lungs the whole way to the kitchen door! "Bear! Bear! Bear!"

Devan and Kristi heard me screaming and saw me running into the house. In only a few seconds, they were right behind me, wondering what had scared me so bad.

Everyone in the house had heard me screaming and could see me running past the window in the kitchen that was behind the iron stove.

Dad had already grabbed his rifle and slipped his boots on when he heard me scream "Bear in the dump!" He was headed out the kitchen door to the dump with Grandpa Verne right behind him, carrying Dad's twelve-gauge shotgun. The black bear had left the dump and sauntered off into the thick woods behind the house.

I was still shaking and crying from my close encounter with death while Devan and Grandma Gloria sat with me on the couch, trying to calm me down. Everyone else was excited about the bear I had thought was Smokey and were looking out the kitchen window to see if it was still there. Mom had just brought all the dogs in the house when I heard a loud bang from Dad's rifle, which was what killed the big black bear that day.

Dad and Grandpa gutted and skinned it, keeping the hide, and then cut the meat into quarters. They took the raw meat into the kitchen, where Mom cut them up into steaks and roasts and then wrapped them with paper.

Grandpa Verne was so excited to be a part of tracking and killing the black bear before he had to go home and couldn't wait to move to Alaska. Turns out the curious black bear poked his face through some forked branches on a large birch, and when Dad shot him, he hung right there.

Bear meat was very rich and hard to digest, so Dad decided to make a smokehouse to smoke the bear meat after brining it in salt, making jerky. Grandpa Verne, Steve, and Dad used an old refrigerator that was behind the house when we moved in. The small white but rusty old rounded Frigidaire model made a perfect smokehouse for fish and bear meat.

Dad cut a round hole on one side and put a smoke stack through it into the fridge, creating a tight seal. We all watched as he then hooked the smoke stack to a small old woodstove that was also out of commission. Then he lit a fire inside it with poplar wood that burned for several hours, sending smoke inside the closed refrigerator that was set up next to the blue camper.

Later that day, the McCulloughs drove up into our circular driveway and parked in front of the house. They had left Dum Dum with us for the whole winter and spring and were coming to get him.

They came over to us at the smokehouse where all the dogs were. Devan and I looked at each other while our eyes started to water, knowing Dum Dum was leaving.

Even though he had gotten into some trouble with the Beckers, Dum Dum was like part of our family and a lot of fun to play with. He loved running around the property with our other four dogs and lying in the warm house at night.

After Dad introduced George and Delores McCullough to Grandma and Grandpa, he called Dum Dum over to him.

Mr. McCullough also called for Dum Dum, but he ran over to us kids, standing several feet from them.

Mrs. McCullough tried whistling for him to come to her also, but Dum Dum just sat there against my leg next to all of us kids and didn't seem to want to go to them.

I couldn't help but think that Dum Dum knew they were going to take him from his new family and he wasn't about to leave us or this homestead.

To our surprise, the McCulloughs knew Dum Dum was happy right where he was and decided to give him to us as our very own dog.

A few days later, Grandma and Grandpa had left, and Mom and Dad went to Palmer for the day.

Devan teased me after they left about the black bear coming to get me, and I hid behind the couch and cried.

Later that day, we kids took all our dogs, including Dum Dum, and walked single file through the chest-high grass, singing, "If you're happy and you know it, clap your hands," as we clapped our hands and stomped our feet out to our secret fort in the windrow.

17

THE KINGS ARE COMING

DENNIS

S ummer in Alaska was the best time of year, but the warm sun and
long days seemed to leave us too soon. I felt a sense of accomplishment this year and more prepared for the cold winter ahead.

A few weeks ago, Steve and I built a springhouse out of plywood
and fiberglass to hopefully keep the spring water from freezing. The
winters were dark, and with few windows in the house, the kerosene
lanterns only provided little light.

With my winnings from the horse races this year, I decided to
use the money to put in propane lights in the house.

After installing copper tubing along the walls of the kitchen,
I connected the tubing to two glass propane light fixtures and then
attached the lights to the wood-paneled wall.

The two twenty-four-gallon propane tanks fit right up against
the outside of the house below the kitchen window. It was nice not
having to depend on the kerosene lanterns alone for light.

The house was quiet with the warm August sun bursting through
the slightly curtained windows in the kitchen. I looked around the
inside of our crowded but cozy dark home.

Last year I had built a gun cabinet out of birch wood and
attached it to the end of the built-in bunks at the entryway to the
kitchen. It was big enough for six rifles to stand upright and secure.

Our neatly made bed continued to crowd the kitchen and remind me we had no room in this old shack.

My brother Doug worked for a fellow named Bob Watkins, who had a trailer he was giving away. We decided to go have a look at it to see if it was something I could add to the house to give us more room.

Evelyn had hiked with the kids and the dogs down our main dirt road toward the train tracks to find cranberries on the banks in the moss.

This year they had picked an abundance of blueberries in the woods and raspberries that grew thick along the trail to Goose Creek.

I could hear my brother Doug drive up in his Chevy pickup, so I grabbed my cowboy hat and shut the kitchen door on my way out.

When we got to the train tracks, Evelyn waved to us, smiling with the twelve-gauge shotgun across her back in the leather sling. Lori, Steve, Devan, Dawn, and Kristi were all busy picking and eating the tart wild cranberries, enjoying the warm day. Shane, Pete, Smokey, and Dum Dum were chasing each other in and out of the thick wall of spruce trees. I didn't see Meardha but knew she had to be close by.

By the time we got to Petersville Road, which was on Parks Highway, north of the Talkeetna cutoff, the sun was starting to get blocked by clouds, and it was going to rain.

Bob came out of his log cabin, which was small but well built, when he saw us in the driveway. He stretched out his large hand to shake mine as Doug introduced us to each other. Bob was a big man with short dark hair and a deep voice, "The old trailer's yours if you want it. I'll even haul it for you!" The nineteen fifties model trailer was eight feet wide and twenty feet long and had a round dome roof.

It was dark blue and white and looked like it had seen its years. Inside it had wood-paneled walls with three potential bedrooms.

What a blessing the trailer was and my new friend Bob as he hauled it with his big two-ton truck all the way to our homestead as we followed behind him.

Using my hands, I directed Bob as he backed the long trailer behind the house, getting it right up against the back wall so we could attach it to the house.

After Bob had left my brother, Dave showed up and helped Doug and me cut a large hole the shape of a door in the wall behind our bed in the kitchen. As we were cutting through the wall, a huge swarm of flies came out of the hollow wall that was poorly insulated with sawdust. After removing the big metal door from the trailer, we used a come-along with a long chain to pull the trailer in tight, creating a seal, aligning the two doorways together to make one. Using concrete blocks and tie-downs Bob had given me, Dave, Doug, and I set and secured the trailer to the ground. The whole family pitched in and got to work cleaning the trailer out and moving furniture to create new bedrooms.

The front of the trailer was attached to our kitchen and had enough room for mine and Evelyn's queen-size bed.

Now we could bring in the large wood picnic table I had built with benches and two end chairs and actually have a dining room.

The small room that was at the back of the trailer had a built-in dresser and enough room for one of our twin beds. There was a door to the outside with a small window that faced the backwoods where the outhouse stood. Lori, who was eight years old and the oldest of our kids, got to have that room all to herself.

The middle of the trailer had varnished wood walls and had a fold-down table to make a bed for the twins.

Kristi was getting taller and would now sleep in the twin bed left in the separate part of the living room. Steve had to keep sleeping on the couch. It seemed like it took hours to finish setting up the new addition to our house, and we were all exhausted.

Evelyn cooked a moose roast with mashed potatoes and cooked carrots, and after we all ate our fill, my brothers went home for the evening.

Steve and I went outside to feed the animals, and suddenly I realized I still hadn't seen Meardha. I asked Steve, "Where is Meardha? I haven't seen her all day."

Steve was petting Shane as he said, "I don't know where she is. I thought she was with us."

After we fed the chickens and put Dungo in his corral for the night, the whole family walked around outside, calling for Meardha, who had disappeared quietly.

My heart sank and I felt a knot in my stomach as I knew something had happened to her, or she had run off chasing or hunting something. I loved Meardha and knew the whole family did also and hoped and prayed she would return.

One day I decided to take Dungo to my secret king salmon hole about three miles away. Last year I caught several king salmons there at the mouth of Sheep Creek, where Goose Creek branches off. In the nineteen forties someone built a dam on Sheep Creek to make another creek, which is Goose Creek, that runs behind our property.

With a little can of grain, I caught Dungo up from the field and led him to the cowshed where I kept my tack. The big leather saddle was heavy as I swung it up on Dungo's sway back after putting my Indian print blanket on first. Dungo put his head down to take the large bit in his mouth as I threw the thick leather reins up over his head.

The two large saddlebags on the back of the saddle flopped around as Dungo started into a graceful trot in the direction I wanted him to go. The shortcut to Goose Creek was around the electric wire behind the house by the outhouse and through the thick woods.

My metal spur hit against my twelve-gauge shotgun in the scabbard under my right leg as Dungo crossed the rocky bed of Goose Creek. Breaking into a lope through the willow brush and fiddlehead ferns, we made good time the long three miles to Sheep Creek.

After tying Dungo to a poplar tree near the fishing hole, I took my fishing pole out of the saddle bag and assembled it.

The salmon roe was fresh and thick on the big hook attached to my thirty-pound fishing line. The first large salmon took the bait, and I reeled him in after a good fight and then pulled him in with my long-handled metal hook to the shore.

It was midmorning, and not another soul was around besides the two bald eagles circling above the tall white birch trees in the clear blue sky.

These were the times I enjoyed the most, listening to the splash of the rushing creek and the excitement of my line becoming suddenly heavy with a large salmon on the other end.

Very few people in these parts knew the kings gathered together at the mouth of Sheep Creek or were able to get in except on horseback. Dungo grazed on the fiddleheads around the poplar trees taking up the four-foot slack on the lead rope. My fourth king salmon that had found its way onto my large hook was at least thirty pounds and four feet long. I knew the limit was one, and with still more salmon roe left, I pulled in three more large kings and laid them in the grass next to the others.

Looking at my huge score in the grass, I thought I heard a vehicle close by. I quickly folded up my fishing pole and started stuffing the large kings into the two large canvas saddle bags that were strapped to the back of the saddle.

My fear was confirmed when I got a glimpse of the dark-green fish and game jeep. It was making its way from the south on the other side of Sheep Creek to where I was fishing. He must have been watching me with binoculars, I thought, as I quickly untied Dungo and tightened the cinch. Cramming my shotgun into the scabbard, I jumped up into the saddle, nudging Dungo into a lope through the thick poplar trees away from the creek.

Two large kings wouldn't fit in the saddle bags, so I laid the heavy fish across my lap on the saddle. Suddenly, I realized there were two fish and game jeeps, and they were gaining ground fast on the other side of the creek. I ran Dungo even harder, cutting up the steep bank toward Goose Creek, hanging on tight to the slimy fish flopping around on the front of the saddle. The jeeps would have to go north to the only way to cross both creeks, which was up by the slough.

Being on horseback and knowing all the trails around the property, I was hoping to make it back to the homestead before the fish and game.

Dungo was breathing hard and lathering up when we crossed the rocky bed of Goose Creek. I was hanging on to the months' worth of fish for my family for dear life and the reins in one hand. Dungo sprinted up another bank and then through the thick woods that came up behind the house. About a hundred yards from the house, I stopped Dungo and threw the two large salmon I had on the saddle onto the thick willow brush. Reaching behind me on the saddle, I untied the saddled bags with the other four king salmon and threw the whole thing in the brush.

It didn't take much to get Dungo into another full run right up to the cowshed, where I jumped off him and unstrapped the saddle as fast as I could. After I pulled the bridle off his head, I swatted his butt to get him onto the field.

I could hear the roar of the two jeeps getting closer, and my heart began to beat fast as I threw the tack into the barn and ran for the house.

Steve came out of the house as I ran across the driveway, and he yelled, "Is everything okay, Dad?" As I ran past him, I said, "Get in the house! Fish and game are on my trail!"

Evelyn was putting a plate of tuna fish sandwiches on the large wood table in the kitchen, and the girls were sitting down to eat when I flung the door open with Steve behind me.

I quickly kicked my boots off and hung my hat by the stove and sat down at the big wood table.

I heard the two fish and game jeeps come roaring up into the driveway while Evelyn and the kids were all staring at me, wondering what was going on.

I grabbed a half of a tuna fish sandwich and put my finger to my lips as to keep everyone quiet while shoving a bite into my mouth.

I recognized one of the three fish and game wardens that came walking up to the kitchen door, knocking loudly. His name was Bob Miller, and he was short and skinny with red hair. He was a friendly man who had been out to the property before to make sure I wasn't letting people fish illegally on the slough.

Steve let them into the house, and Bob spoke up first. "Hi, Dennis. We could have sworn we saw you up at Sheep Creek pulling in king salmon."

I thought carefully before answering, "I think you have mistaken me for someone else."

One of the other game wardens said, "I bet you have king salmon hanging in your barn." Bob looked over at me and said, "If we look and you have over the limit, we'll have to arrest you."

Sitting there with my wife and five kids having lunch, I knew I couldn't confess and risk not only going to jail but also losing months' worth of meals. So I casually said, knowing the six huge salmon were far enough away from the house, "Go ahead and search the barn and any part of the property you want!"

Bob and the other game wardens looked at each other, and then the one that hadn't spoken yet said, "That's okay, Mr. Clark. We aren't going to search this time, but when you do go fishing for kings, stay within the limit!"

As they were leaving, I said, "Thanks for stopping by. Have a good day!" As soon as we knew they were completely gone, Steve, Evelyn, and I carried the huge kings from the woods to the garage to gut and clean them.

The next day after church, we went to the Valentines for lunch, and after I told Glenn my story of how I outran the fish and game, he offered to let me store the numerous packages of king salmon steaks in their freezer. I was glad to share the salmon with the Valentines and other friends and invited Glenn to come fish with me next year.

18

AIN'T NO BULL

STEVE

E ven though we still had four dogs, Shane, Pete, Dum Dum, and
Smokey, the whole family missed our Irish setter Meardha.

Dad said she must have gotten out to the highway where someone probably picked her up and stole her. She had been gone since
August, and now it was almost Christmas. Even if she wasn't picked
up, she wouldn't survive the now-below-zero-degree weather with
five feet of snow on the ground, not to mention the wild animals.

Lori and the twins and me had to hike out to the bus early in
the morning by ourselves through the deep snow and bitter cold. We
wore ski mask over our heads and faces that were made of wool and
had holes for our eyes and mouth. Ice balls formed and clung to the
outside of the ski masks from the snow still coming down that hit our
faces as the wind whirled it with great speed.

The big branches on the trees on our trail were weighed down
with snow and would sometimes dump their heavy load, covering us
as we brushed by and under them.

When we hiked down the steep bank by the empty cabin, the
snow was so deep all four of us sunk down up to our armpits in the
cold wet snow.

Often we saw moose along the way, eating from the bare skinny
branches of all the trees and willow brush. They were usually in the

woods, and we were able to walk by quietly without disturbing the large hairy animals with big racks.

If the weather was severe, we either stayed home from school or Mom took us out on the snow machine and sled.

Dad took a job working on the North Slope as a welder in the wintertime and still worked for BLM in the summer. He was gone for weeks at a time now in the winter, so I was the man of the house with lots of responsibility.

I was almost eight years old now and able to keep the woodstoves going and take care of all the animals, including Dungo, who stayed in the small barn most of the time in the winter.

Every day after school, Lori and I stacked large pieces of birch and poplar on each other's arms and carried them into the house.

I used Dad's hatchet to cut kindling to start the fires if they went out. We stacked the kindling neatly next to the barrel stove in the living room.

Uncle Doug had met a lady friend named Kathy, who was going to college to be a schoolteacher and lived in Talkeetna. Uncle Doug quit his job at BLM and started to pan for gold on the many creeks and riverbeds that veined their way all over the southwestern part of Alaska. Kathy joined him when she could, and eventually they moved in together in Talkeetna. Mom got a job with the school district driving the school bus in the afternoons just by showing the local trooper she could shift the gears and drive the bus.

Mom took Kristi with her and picked us up at the highway where our main road ended if her route allowed. Sometimes on the few days she drove the bus, she would be done much later. She would park the bus at the community center and drive the snow machine into the homestead while we had hiked in already. I would have the woodstoves going by then, and my sisters would start making supper if Mom was late getting home.

Riding the school bus was certainly a test of one's tolerance for bad behavior. The Becker boys lived across the Parks Highway across from our main road where Mom would pick us up sometimes. Bruce and Bob were older than us by a few years and started out as our friends.

Then this year after the Dum Dum incident, they began harassing us kids on the bus. They were big boys who were loud and obnoxious, making fun of us and other kids. They threw spit wads made out of paper balled up in their mouths and saturated with saliva. That made the spit wads fly long and hard to the target intended.

Lori and I sat together in one of the smooth large green highback seats, while Devan and Dawn sat in the one in front of us where we could protect them from the bus bullies. We kids sat in our seats quietly like Dad had taught us and knew only to fight if in self-defense.

After we were dropped off at the end of our road one day, the Becker boys called us a few names and then started across the highway to their house.

Mom told us to wait for her at the end of our main road until she finished her route and made it there to pick us up. Then we would ride in her bus to the community center to take the snow machine into the homestead.

As I watched the taillights of the big bus disappear into the flurry of cold snow blowing in the high winds, I shivered under my thick winter coat.

We all had snow pants on that were like overalls under our coats. Mom sewed our mittens to long strings of yarn that stayed inside the arms of the coat so we wouldn't lose them.

Lori and the twins were starting to get cold also, so we all danced around, stomping our feet to keep warm while watching for Mom's bus to arrive. Suddenly to the right of us in the woods came a crashing sound in the crunchy snow and dry brush. My heart began to beat fast as I whipped around toward the noise that broke the sound of the cold wind.

Expecting moose, we were all surprised when we locked our eyes on a huge bull charging toward us. His enormous body was all white, and he had large thick horns on top of his head that curved up and had sharp points on the ends.

The twins started screaming, and Lori screeched, "Where did that come from?" The large animal stopped in the thick white snow not far from us, with his head down, blowing puffs of cold air out of his large nostrils.

I was frozen in my tracks, staring the bull down, thinking fast, wondering where this bull had come from and how we would get away from it.

The twins were clinging on to Lori as I said quietly, shaking in my shoes, "When I say go, everyone run across the highway!" The big white bull scraped his hoofs in the snow and put his head down, shaking it from side to side as if he was going to charge at us again.

I quickly looked both ways and then told Lori, "Take the twins and run across now!" Lori looked at me with concern but did what I said and took off running, holding Devan's and Dawn's hands. The bull snorted again as I whipped my head around to face him.

By now sweat was starting to pour down my face even though it was below zero. The big animal started running at me with his horns down to my level as I tried to get my feet to move.

"Steve, run, run!" Lori's yell made me leap forward as my feet began to fly through the deep snow to get across the highway. I could see my sisters on the other side and could hear the bull charging behind me as I yelled, "Go up to the Beckers!" The Beckers' house was up on a hill overlooking the highway only a few yards away.

As I scampered as fast as I could across the highway, I could practically feel the hot breath from the bull on my neck. When I finally made it to the other side of the highway, I quickly looked back. The big white bull had run back to our bus stop where he just stood there as to dare us to come back across.

Lori and the twins were knocking on the Beckers' door when I raced up behind them out of breath. As much as I hated to ask for help from the two biggest bullies on the bus, I felt like we had no choice, and I knew Lori felt the same way.

Dad had told us to stay away from the Beckers because he was still feuding with them over Dum Dum, but Mom was late, and that big bull was going nowhere.

The dark-green door at the front of the big white house creaked open, and Bruce Becker stood there with his mouth full of some kind of cookie we could see through his sheepish grin. Pieces of cookie crumbs flew out of his mouth as he turned his baseball hat around on his thick brown hair and said, "What do you Clark kids want?"

His mom came walking up behind him, looking at us four kids standing in the doorway as if to hear the answer. Lori spoke up, knowing I didn't want to ask them for anything, and said, "There's a big white bull across the highway that charged us and is still there!" Bruce's mom told us to come into the house and had all four of us sit on the big brown couch in the living room.

She put her hands on her hips while Bruce and Bob stood next to her, giving us dirty looks, and said, "That bull belongs to the Lankfords, and where is your mom?" Mrs. Becker was a heavy woman with short curly brown hair who wore men's clothing.

Wishing Mom or Dad were there, I decided to speak up and said to her, "Mom should be here any minute with the school bus to pick us up."

Devan and Dawn were still sobbing as they sat in between Lori and me on the couch while Mrs. Becker mumbled something and went into the kitchen.

Bruce and Bob sat in the two easy chairs across from us, staring us down as if they had us right where they wanted us.

Just as I was feeling really uncomfortable, Mrs. Becker came back into the living room and kindly handed each one of us a home-made chocolate chip cookie. Never forgetting our manners, we all thanked her after accepting the warm cookies that smelled so good.

As we were gobbling the cookies down, Bruce and Bob started to make fun of us. "Haha! You guys are scared of a bull charging at you!"

I was thinking in my now-getting-angry mind, *Who wouldn't be scared of a bull charging?*

Just then Mrs. Becker said as she was looking out their tattered white curtains, "Your mom's bus is out on the highway!"

To our relief, a few seconds later, there was a knock on the door. Bob, who was the oldest, opened it to Mom standing there with a worried look on her face. Mom could see us sitting on the couch as Mrs. Becker walked over to let her in and said, "The Lankfords' bull was chasing your kids, so I let them stay here."

Glad to be leaving the Beckers, we all jumped up from the couch and joined Mom at the door as she introduced herself to Mrs. Becker and said, "Thank you for helping our kids, and sorry I was so late."

After we left the Beckers and loaded into the big school bus with Mom and Kristi, who was sleeping in one of the seats, we all talked at once about the white bull that kept charging at us that was now gone.

Just a ways up the highway was the community center where Mom pulled the large bus into the plowed turnabout.

It was starting to get dark as Lori helped the twins get into the big sled that was hitched to the snow machine and then got in herself with Kristi on her lap.

I grabbed the twelve-gauge shotgun Mom had hid under the snow machine and held on to it while I rode behind her on the seat of our Polaris snow machine.

The house was dark and cold when we got home, so I started a fire quickly in both woodstoves while Lori lit the propane lights in the kitchen and then helped me feed the animals.

School was out now for the holidays, and Dad was going to be home in a few days from the North Slope.

One day after eating breakfast, I got my snow gear on and grabbed my .22 rifle out of the gun cabinet. Dad had made it home finally, and we were going ptarmigan hunting.

As I stepped out of the front door, the high cold wind stung my face with ice balls we called snow on this freezing winter day right before Christmas. Dad was out at the small barn checking on the chickens because when he got home from the slope, two of them had frozen to death in the roost.

We still had plenty of moose steaks and sausage and salmon in our root cellar, along with the canned goods Mom stored every year for winter. Almost every month one of us kids got to go with Mom and Dad to Anchorage to the big discount warehouse grocery store. In the wintertime, Dad used the snow machine and sled to get the groceries into the homestead. Most of the time the youngest kids like the twins got to go, so Lori and I could stay at the homestead and look out for things.

The willow ptarmigans were in abundance and liked to nest down into the snow where they dug for willow buds and twigs. The usual white-winged black-speckled birds with beady eyes and colorful heads turned completely white in the winter to match the snow.

I held on to my .22 rifle as I sat behind Dad on the Polaris snow machine with extra bullets in my coat pocket. The loud snow machine stirred up the flocks of ptarmigan nesting in the snow where you could only see their beady black eyes and black beak on their all-white bodies.

Dad and I got off the snow machine and took aim at the white ptarmigan flying around and diving back into the deep snow. I pulled the lever back on my rifle, loading a bullet, and pulled the trigger on one of the birds, laying it on the ground.

Dad shot several to my few, but it sure felt good to shoot my gun and help bring in more food for the family.

When we got back to the house, Dad and I cleaned and plucked all fifteen of the ptarmigan we shot and stored them in the root cellar for Christmas Day.

The next day we all hiked out into the woods behind the house and cut down the top of a spruce tree. The whole family helped decorate the six-foot tree that stood up against the wall in the living room, with bulbs, tinsel, strung popcorn, and candy canes. The youngsters, including me and Lori, were all hoping Santa would fill our stockings and bring us each a gift Christmas Eve.

Christmas morning I woke up early to find Lori looking in her sock and whispered to her, "There's even presents under the tree."

The twins came tiptoeing into the living room from the trailer and then ran over to get their stockings also.

Mine and theirs were filled with walnuts, tangerines, candy, and yo-yos. When I dug down deep into the bottom of my stocking, I found a silver pocketknife. Lori got a new hair brush, and the twins found new headbands.

Kristi was awake and crawling out of her bunk with her eyes as big as saucers, looking at the presents under the tree as we handed her her stocking.

Lori and I had counted the presents, and there were more than one a piece, not including what we had made for Mom and Dad.

Lori and I didn't really believe in Santa Claus because we had seen Mom fill the socks in the middle of the night the last two years since we had been sleeping in the living room.

Besides, I had seen Dad carry in a large box and put it in their bedroom in the trailer when he got home from the North Slope.

Lori and I played along for the twins and Kristi, who still believed in Santa. The snow fell hard and thick outside our steamy windows with white frosted frames while the woodstoves worked hard to keep the drafty shack warm.

The Christmas wrapping paper flew around the living room, as we opened matchbox cars, the Candyland board game, books, clothes, and dolls.

Then we filled our stomachs with roasted ptarmigan, mashed potatoes, green beans, candied yams, cranberries, and pumpkin pie on an unforgettable Christmas Day.

19

LITTLE LAMB

KRISTI

My twin sisters had just turned six the end of January 1970, and it was almost Valentine's Day.

I wasn't sure what that meant, but my sisters and brother exchanged store-bought Valentine cards with their friends at school.

I rode with Mom on the big yellow school bus when she drove it a few days a week and got to sit in the front with Devan and Dawn. Steve and Lori sat across the aisle in their own big seat.

One afternoon Mom parked the bus in the big lot beside the small red schoolhouse in Talkeetna. Like usual, lots of kids came out of the schoolhouse, laughing and talking. One by one they got onto the bus and found a seat. Some of the kids were big and looked at me as if I was in the way as they found a seat in the back of the bus. My brother Steve and my three sisters would eventually come out of the school and sit next to me behind Mom.

One day the Carlson boys, who were twins and stood at six feet tall like their dad, who was a pilot in Talkeetna, sat in the back seat of the bus. They both started spitting wads of wet paper through their milk straws at everyone in the front of them.

Steve had told us kids that they were bullies and to watch out for them and motioned for us to stoop down in our seats.

One of the wet spit wads hit Mom in the back of her curly red head as she was putting the big bus into gear to leave the school. Many more of them stuck to the inside walls of the bus just missing our heads as a couple other kids joined in the fun.

Mom slammed the big bus into neutral and turned around to see who was throwing spit wads as another big wet one made out of lined school paper hit her right on the forehead!

I pulled my long curly red hair out of the way as I struggled in my snow pants to get up on my knees. I wanted to look over the high back of the seat to see who was in trouble.

The twins and Steve and Lori peered around their seats and down the aisle.

Mom looked furious, and her face was red as she scraped the wet spit wad off her forehead and demanded, "Who is responsible for the spit wads?"

The Carlson boys sat back in their seats and shrugged their shoulders as if innocent, and the other high school kids did the same. Mom looked around at the balls of wet paper stuck to the inside of the bus.

She had to help keep the bus clean, and sometimes I helped her.

Mom told the boys loudly, "All of the high school boys are going to the principal's office!" That's exactly what happened as she marched behind the Carlson twins and a few other high school boys right out of the bus to the principal's office, which was in the back of the red schoolhouse.

The rest of us kids stayed on the bus and sat quietly, secretly hoping the boys would get in trouble and stop being mean.

I was proud of my mom for standing up to them, and that was the last time they threw spit wads on her bus.

Since we did our laundry in Talkeetna, Mom took advantage of the time she had to wait in town with the bus. It was still dark outside on a hurried morning in March when Steve was loading the two big boxes of dirty clothes into the snow machine sled. He came in and out of the house, letting the angry wind in through the living room door as I climbed out of my bottom bunk that was warm and cozy. I rubbed my blue eyes and stepped over our dogs lying by the barrel stove and began putting on the same cotton pants and long-sleeve striped shirt I had worn yesterday. Mom told us we had to wear our clothes over and over if they weren't dirty.

Dad had left again for the North Slope several days ago and had promised he would be back in time for my fourth birthday.

Mom was making oatmeal on the black iron stove in the kitchen, and my sisters were getting ready for school, dressing in winter gear as the snow was still deep.

It was forty below zero at night, and our firewood was getting low. Mom took the chainsaw last weekend and cut down a couple of birch trees. We kids carried the pieces and stacked them against the house under the tarp.

The spring had frozen again even with the new springhouse, and our water reserve was frozen. Every afternoon I helped pack snow into the five-gallon buckets to melt on top of the stove for drinking, baths, and the animals.

Most of our chickens had frozen to death this winter, and Dungo had to stay in the small cowshed to survive the almost unbearable high cold winds during the snowstorms.

Devan and Dawn ate their oatmeal, put on their winter coats, masks, and mittens, and went to the outhouse and out to feed the dogs. I forced down the hot mushy cereal that I knew was good for me and would fill my small stomach even though I didn't like it.

Lori helped me find my winter coat and my blue snow boots that were in a messy pile of boots and liners by the stove.

Mom turned the drafts on the stove pipes down and shut the propane lights off as we all stepped out into the dark morning, leaving the dogs in the house.

I saw Steve grab Dad's rifle that was in the gun cabinet before we went outside and then suddenly realized after feeling the urge to pee that I hadn't used the outhouse yet. I yelled through the whistling sound of the high wind that took my breath away, "Mom, I have to pee!"

Lori heard me and said something in Mom's ear as she was starting the Polaris snow machine. My big sister then walked over to me, grabbed me by my mittened hand, and pulled me toward the outhouse.

Lori was tall and took big steps, making it hard to keep up without running, as we hiked down the trail behind the house on the edge of the dark woods.

Lori was left in charge a lot and felt more like a second mom to me than an older sister. Sometimes she even spanked us when Mom and Dad were gone. We quickly learned to stuff our pants to soften the blow of her hairbrush swats. No matter what though, I knew she would take care of me, and she did like to brush my long hair that I left tangled most of the time.

We walked through the dark, but knew the trail well, and Lori had our big flashlight to light the way.

I struggled to take off my coat and snow pant suspenders to pee quickly after I climbed up on the big wooden seat.

After we got back, Lori, the twins, and I were all sitting close together in the snow machine sled. We sat behind the boxes of laundry with me down in the middle of the twins.

Mom drove the snow machine down the trail to the community center with Steve riding behind her, holding the big rifle. I hung on to the twins as they hung on to the metal rail to keep us on the big sled.

We bounced around as the big sled came up off the packed snow and slid straight down steep snowbanks as we passed the cabin, through the woods, and then crossed the railroad tracks.

The red morning sunrise started to peek up over Mount McKinley as Mom pulled the bus away from the community center.

After picking up the twenty-one kids along our route to Talkeetna, we pulled into the empty lot beside the red schoolhouse.

All the kids got off the bus except me, and then Mom drove us to the Laundromat on Main Street across from B&K Trading Post.

After she unloaded the boxes of dirty clothes, I helped her sort the eight loads and throw them into the empty washers.

There were a few other women but no kids in the log building with the big window facing the main street. One of the other women was a small elderly lady who Mom said was a retired schoolteacher.

The elderly lady flowed around in her green cotton dress, smoothing her gray hair that was in a neat bun on top of her small head. She waved at me as she was busy talking to Mom and the other two women. She told them about how she had heard a streaker was going to run down Main Street.

I couldn't help but overhear the gossip and wondered what a streaker was and hoped to hear more about it.

Mom seemed horrified and told me to cover my eyes as the little schoolteacher said loudly as she looked out the big glass window that faced the road, "Here he comes!"

I half covered my eyes and could see Mom hiding her face in her hands so to not see something I knew nothing about but must be horrible!

I got closer to the wood bench that was under the big window and peeked through my little bony fingers to see who was streaking and what it looked like.

I couldn't believe my eyes and suddenly realized why Mom didn't want to look! A tall thin naked man came running around the corner by the welcome sign and then down Main Street. He ran right by the big window in the middle of winter with only his cowboy boots on! I looked over at the little elderly teacher who was standing close to me. I saw her looking straight at the streaker as he ran by the Laundromat with a big smile on her face. Stunned at what I had seen, I squeezed my eyes shut, hoping to forget it, and then sat down on the wood bench under the window.

All the women including Mom laughed about the obviously drunk streaker the rest of the day until school let out, while I tried to erase the vision in my head.

Turns out the naked man was Mr. Carlson, the father of the rowdy twin boys who lived on the outskirts of town. His wife had left him, and he had been drinking too much whiskey.

Dad finally made it home from the slope just in time for my birthday and brought me something really special.

When he came in the kitchen door as Mom was baking my cake, his coat was zipped up with something squirming inside.

All of us kids saw it and ran up to Dad as he slowly unzipped his coat and said, "Happy birthday, Kristi. This is for you!" Dad tipped his cowboy hat back and knelt down in front of me.

A white fluffy head with black eyes poked out of his coat and said, "Baa!" It was a beautiful little lamb with tiny ears and fluffy white fleece! What a great birthday, I thought to myself as I couldn't believe she was all mine!

As I reached out for the four-legged baby lamb with tiny hoofs, I swallowed hard and struggled to speak to Dad as I asked him, "Do I get to keep her, Dad?"

Dad laid her in my arms as I sat Indian-style on the kitchen floor and said, "The Lankfords have sheep, and one of the mother sheep gave birth to this little lamb a few days ago."

The soft, cuddly lamb lay in my lap and licked my fingers as Dad continued talking, "The mother sheep wouldn't let her baby lamb nurse, and the Lankfords had to lay her down to let the lamb eat. So they gave the mother and the lamb to us!"

"Your job is to get the mother to lie down so the lamb can nurse, Kristi, since she is your lamb!"

Steve, Lori, Devan, and Dawn sat around me as I held the baby lamb while she licked my face.

Devan said to me as tears filled my eyes with joy, and my stomach flipped with excitement, "What are you going to name her?"

Dad and Mom were watching us as I let the lamb up from my lap to see her walk on her wobbly legs. I said, wiping my tears away, "Little Lamb!"

They all laughed, and Mom said, "That's not a name." I liked it though, and that is what we called her.

The dogs were all curious about the baby lamb and circled her, sniffing at her thick white fleece coat. Dad said, "You can make her and the ewe a bed in the small barn away from Dungo."

After breakfast the twins and I took my little white lamb out to the barn and had a lot of fun making a place for her and the big ewe that Dad had put in the barn already to sleep.

The short plywood wall on the left side in the barn Dad had put up for a stall was tall enough to protect them from other animals, and the loose hay made a perfect warm bed to lay in.

I played with my little lamb by the kerosene lantern in the barn until I heard Lori call my name for supper. Mom made my favorite food, which was potatoes cut into french fries. She made moose burgers using our big silver meat grinder that sat on the kitchen counter.

I told everyone thank you, especially Dad, for the little lamb and the paper dolls I got for my birthday as I wolfed down another piece of my chocolate birthday cake Mom had made.

After supper Steve went with me out to the barn to check on Little Lamb and helped me lay the ewe down so her baby could nurse. Her mother didn't seem to mind too much when Steve and I gently pulled her down to the loose hay.

Every day after that I couldn't wait to get home to see Little Lamb, who ran behind me as I played and did my chores.

20

VOICES OF THE MIDNIGHT SUN

LORI

D ad had built a new barn this summer with the help of Uncle Norman, who was staying with us for a while. He was Dad's younger brother and watched us sometimes when Mom and Dad were gone. It never failed that some mishap or excitement would occur when Uncle Norman was at the homestead. His brain was too full of book knowledge, leaving little room for direction.

One time he drew a line with masking tape across the living room and made us stay on one side. If we crossed the line, he would throw us on the couch and try to suffocate us with a pillow.

We all had fun egging him on by getting too close to the line, as much as he did catching us and holding us down. We yelled "uncle" in a muffled cry until he finally let us go.

Uncle Norman was a little shorter than Dad and balding already and liked to look in the mirror, talking to himself as he combed his hair and then finished it with "Yabba dabba do!"

Glenn Valentine, a railroad worker, and a new friend Dad had met at the Sheep Creek Lodge named Dennis Miller came and helped with the barn also. He went by the name Denny and was a short stocky man with brown hair and brown eyes. His wife, Jean, and their two small boys moved from Iowa with him here, where they bought a house off the Parks Highway about eight miles from us.

The Millers had come over for Easter dinner in April, and Mom and Jean hit it off right away. Kristi was a few years older than their son Jason, and they became instant friends since Kristi was quite the tomboy.

In June the Lankfords decided they had too many cows, and so they asked Dad if he wanted to raise his own beef.

Staying far away from the big white bull, Steve and I went with Dad to the Lankfords to pick out four milk cows from their large herd of Herefords and black angus cows. The black and white cows were big but friendly; we helped load them onto Mr. Lankford's trailer to take them home. They roamed the property, staying within the electric wire, and grazed on the field with Dungo.

Dad taught us kids how to milk the heifers, but Mom was the only one that could get a sufficient amount of milk for us to drink. She enjoyed sitting on the small bucket, milking the cows and singing her favorite hymns. To get a good stream, Mom had to lean in and rest her head on the flank of the cows.

One morning after milking Shorty, Mom noticed her head was itching something awful. She had lice from milking the cows! Mom soaked her head and all of our linens in vinegar water until the lice was finally gone. Then Dad cut Mom's long thick red hair to above her shoulders as we all watched it fall to the kitchen floor. I just wanted to reach down and take some of my mom's fallen hair and put it in my keepsake box as if it were a treasure.

The big barn was next to the field and across the main road from the cowshed. Dad used skinned birch trees to make the high pole walls that held up the slanted roof. Large sheets of plywood were nailed to the outside to keep the cold weather out. Then they covered the slanted roof that reached the ground on one side with sheet metal. The huge pole rafters that were on the inside of the barn and went from one side to the other helped to hold the whole barn up.

The large shocks of hay we covered in the field would be stored inside the big barn to protect it from the winter weather. Dungo ran free around the property within the electric wire that was strung up every spring but had to stay in the cowshed in the winter, which made him restless. He could now find a spacious refuge from the angry storms in the big barn.

Dad built a lean-to out of plywood with walls on the front of the barn. It was on the side facing the house for the other sheep we got from the Lankfords a couple of weeks ago.

We already had the mother ewe of the lamb Kristi got, and now we had two more ewes and a ram.

The white ram was big with enormous horns that curled around and up with sharp tips. Us kids noticed he was always watching us, and he would hide around corners waiting so he could ram us. It hadn't happened yet, but there were a few close calls. The ewes were fat with thick, fluffy white fleece that Dad and Uncle Norman had shaved off for the summer.

While Dad and the other men along with Steve were building our new barn on an unusually hot day in July, Dungo was eating his grain Dad had poured in the grass for him at the edge of the field.

All the sheep and the ram were grazing on the grass near Dungo except Little Lamb, who was running around the yard with Kristi.

Devan and Dawn were helping Mom make lunch in the kitchen, and I was helping by handing Dad nails and boards.

I stood next to the barn in construction and listened to the sound of the horned owl in the distance. I noticed the sheep were starting to roam closer to our big stallion. He was eagerly picking up the grain with his large lips off the freshly cut grass. One of the ewes bravely wandered off from her herd and trotted right over to Dungo. She put her lips down next to his and ate some of his sweet feed.

Steve was on top of the lean-to, nailing some boards down, when I yelled up to him, "Steve, look at that ewe eating with Dungo!" My younger brother stood up and shaded his eyes as he looked over toward the field. He yelled back to me, "Oh boy, she's in trouble!"

Just as he had said that, the ewe looked up at Dungo as if she had made a friend. The giant muscled stallion had his ears laid straight back.

My hand slapped straight across my pale face, covering my eyes as I peeked through my long fingers, not wanting to see what I knew was going to happen next!

Dungo did not like to be messed with while he ate, much less share his food.

Dad and the other guys were inside the big barn when the incident happened, and Steve and I could do nothing to stop it.

As the ewe gazed up at Dungo, he put his head down and looked her square on. Then he whirled around, and with a mighty force and in a split second, his left back leg sprung into the air! Dungo kicked the brave ewe right between the eyes! The poor ewe took a high flight way over the other sheep, tumbling into the field! She rolled a few times and then got right up and shook her head! Steve and I were laughing so hard I almost peed my pants and he nearly fell off the roof!

Dad and the other men came running out of the nearly finished barn after they heard the ewe bleating loudly from humiliation and pain. Steve told them what had happened, and everyone got a good laugh outside while enjoying fresh watermelon.

Dad built us a big wooden bookcase in the living room in June that stood six feet tall and had four-foot wide shelves. I already had quite a collection of books to put on the bookcase, mostly Harlequin Romances that I had picked from the church book box.

I liked to read in my room at night by candlelight in the dark winters, and I just opened my curtains this time of year to let in the midnight sun.

My small bedroom was at the end of the long trailer that was hooked on to our house with a door that opened to the outside. The walls and rounded ceiling had wood paneling, and there was a built-in dresser also made out of wood. Dad and Steve moved one of our twin beds from the living room to my room. Mom put cotton sheets and plenty of blankets on it for me.

The end of the trailer didn't get any heat in the winter, making it almost unbearably cold, for the twins also, who slept in the middle of the trailer in their built-in bed.

Most of the time in the winter, we girls climbed into the twin bed that was up against the far wall in the living room and Kristi had to curl up in the bunk.

I snapped out of my thoughts, hearing Mom calling my name from the kitchen. I was thumbing through the books Mom had recently put in the bookcase.

Then I really woke up when I heard Dad say sharply, "Lori, your mom is calling you!" Sweeping my long red hair back as I ran for the kitchen, the book I had selected dropped to the floor.

Mom was making egg foo yung and wanted me to cut sprouts and onions. Washing my hands and then getting right to work while the twins set the table, Mom said, "Your dad and Norm and I are going to Anchorage tomorrow morning to pick up supplies and groceries. We are going to visit the Seales and the Loks while we're there, so there's a chance we might not make it back tomorrow night."

Even though I knew Dad would leave us plenty of work to do, the thought of Mom and Dad being gone all day tomorrow got me excited.

Dad was back to work for BLM and was home early most days. Between picking berries, haying, stacking wood, cleaning house, feeding animals, cooking, and watching my siblings, there wasn't much time for me to have fun.

I loved riding horses, and Dad finally let me ride Dungo this summer, which was both scary and exhilarating. My arms would ache for days from holding him back as we cut through the grass.

At school the teacher had us do some art one day, and she and I realized I was good at it just like Dad. She gave me a small sketchbook to take home and some charcoal pencils to draw with. I kept it in my room where my creations would come to life as I drew pictures of horses and other animals long into the night. I loved animals and hoped to be a veterinarian someday.

Early the next day on Friday, Dad, Mom, and Uncle Norman took our Bel Air and left for Anchorage. They left a trail of dust as they drove down our main dirt road.

After the twins and Kristi cleaned up the dishes from breakfast, I told them to put on their shoes and head outside to stack wood.

Steve and I had to clean out the chicken coop and scoop the manure out of the two barns like Dad told us to do before he left. We only had a few hens left, as well as the rooster who had survived the long cold winters.

My freckle-less white face and arms soaked up the warm sun on this late July day as I scooped horse and sheep manure out of the big barn.

Steve was working next to me and said as he wiped the beads of sweat off his forehead, "We should go swimming in the creek today!"

Shocked that he would suggest us going up to the creek to swim with Mom and Dad gone, I said, "That sounds like fun, but if we get caught, we'll get a whooping for sure."

The usual mischievous grin appeared on Steve's freckled face as he mocked me, "Are you a chicken? Bock, bock, bock!" I felt my face turn red as I continued to shovel manure and said, "All right, we'll go as soon as the chores are done!"

It seemed like hours before we were done cleaning the barns and the chicken coop, which included the lean-to. Steve and I put the shovels and rakes away in the cowshed and walked back to the house.

The twins were nowhere to be seen, and Kristi was by herself running around with the dogs and her little lamb by the garage. I asked her, "Where's Devan and Dawn?"

Kristi stopped running, which was unusual, and looked up at me and smiled, "We're all done. They're in the house!"

Steve and I inspected the fairly neat stack of birch wood by the front door as we went into the house. Our three younger sisters screamed with excitement as I told them to put shorts on to go swim in the creek.

Steve carried the single-shot rifle and led us all the way down the bus trail to the Trestle Creek Bridge that stood over Goose Creek.

Shane, Dum Dum, Smokey, and Pete came along to take a dip in the clear creek water. We all sang "Billy Boy, Billy Boy" as we made our way down the long trail, watching the brush and grass for charging bears.

I felt so fortunate to live in such a beautiful place where God did his best artwork! Tall fireweed made purple blankets that spread on top of the grass as far as you could see. Big butterflies in all the different yellows and orange colors flew from tip to tip of each flower. Birds of many species sang from the tall white birch and cottonwood trees as huge bald eagles soared above in the blue heavens.

Tiny wild orange blossoms, yellow and white daffodils, and bluebells swayed in the warm breeze. Dandelions lost their yellow luster and turned to featherlike substance. We kids liked to pick them and blow until the tiny star-like feathers blew with the breeze. Beautiful wild red roses were my favorite wildflower. They provided vitamin C, with the sweet and dry seed like rose hips that were left behind after the roses fell off.

Pesky bees and large mosquitos were always a problem in the summer, requiring lots of tolerance and tons of bug spray.

By the time we got to the train tracks, all of us were hot and ready to dunk into the crystal clear creek. The pristine water sparkled in the sun under the big bridge.

As I floated on my back and enjoyed the cool water, I kept one eye on Kristi and the twins. They held hands and then sat down on the rocky creek bed under the water, making bubbles. It was eighty-some degrees outside, which to us felt like the Sahara Desert.

I tried not to let the silver-dollar-size mosquitoes ruin my day as they continued to land on my pale skin, leaving huge red welts that itched horribly as they continued to find a way to bite me.

Steve was diving under the currents, trying to catch a humpy with his bare hands while I practiced my backstroke.

A couple of hours went by, and we were all shivering and soaked, including the dogs. Steve suggested we dry out in the sun while we play on the bridge.

Reluctantly, I took Kristi by the hand as Steve led us up to the trestle bridge where we stood a few feet down the tracks, looking at it.

The Alaska train came often and fast, crossing the only bridge over Goose Creek. The high bridge was made out of railroad ties bolted to tall posts that held it up over the water. The steel rails ran over the top of the railroad ties that went across the bridge to hold the heavy load of a train. Our crossing that the Alaska Railroad company had put in for us was only one hundred yards from the bridge that we weren't allowed to play on. Before going any farther, Steve pulled some pennies out of his jeans pocket and handed each of us one. He said to us, "Put your penny on the track somewhere close, and when a train comes by, you will see what happens!" Kristi put hers on the steel rail, and so did the twins.

I said to Steve before putting my penny anywhere, "Where did you hear this from?"

Steve laughed and said, "I heard it from Chad. He does it in Talkeetna. His dad works for the railroad." I still wondered how we would know if a train was coming around the sharp corner while we played on the bridge by putting a penny on the tracks and said, "I don't think we should play on the bridge. We might not have time to get off the bridge if a train comes!"

Devan and Dawn looked at Steve as if waiting for an answer, and Kristi stood by his side, just knowing he had one.

Steve grinned and said to us as he held on to Dad's big rifle, "I'll show you how to tell if a train is close." He then put the rifle down on the gravel next to the rail and got down on his knees. Steve put his left ear on the steel rail and listened. He got up and said, "I can't hear a train coming right now! Let's walk on the bridge. I'll keep checking."

Steve held Kristi's hand, and I held on to the twins' hands one on each side of me as we walked carefully onto the trestle bridge.

As we slowly stepped from one railroad tie to another, careful not to fall into the wide gaps between them, Steve stopped us in the middle of the bridge that had no rails. I looked down at the creek, which was a long ways down, and felt a little dizzy.

Steve put his ear to the rail again to check for trains while the twins and Kristi were admiring the tall purple fireweed that was growing up the sides of the bridge. He turned to me and said, "I'm not sure. Why don't you try, Lori? Listen for a humming sound and vibration." My heart skipped a beat as I looked down the tracks and then bent down to put my ear on the rail.

As soon as my big ear hit the rail, I heard a humming sound so clear it made me jump up and yell, "Get off the bridge! A train is coming!"

Steve picked Kristi up and started off the bridge, skipping railroad ties as he ran. I grabbed Devan's and Dawn's hands, and we quickly made our way off the bridge.

I turned around after we jumped off the tracks completely onto the steep bank below and saw the light from the big Alaska engine coming around the corner, with a long train following.

Steve and I stared at each other in silence like we knew that was too close and needed to be more careful next time. The twins and Kristi were so scared they just stood there watching the train go by as the engineer saw us and waved, sounding his horn.

After the loud vibrating train went by, we all ran up to the tracks again to see what happened to our pennies. To our amazement, the pennies were as flat as pancakes and as big as a silver dollar!

After another quick dip into the creek and swearing everyone to secrecy, we headed back to the house, picking blueberries and wildflowers along the way.

By the time we got back to the house, it was already time for supper. Not expecting Mom and Dad to get home, I heated up the moose stew Mom had left for us, along with homemade biscuits she had made.

Steve and Kristi went out to feed the animals while the twins set the table for us. After we all ate, Steve started a fire in the small woodstove in the kitchen. The twins and Steve and I sat around the table and played Monopoly for what seemed like hours. Kristi sat in the living room and played with her paper dolls until she eventually took her blankie and crawled into her bunk. Before we knew it, the wind-up clock on the partition showed midnight and it was time to go to bed.

Steve turned the propane lights off, while Devan and Dawn went into the trailer to go to bed. I grabbed the book I had picked out a few days ago that was still on the floor and said good night to my brother.

With my flashlight, I went into the dark trailer and past the twins to my room at the end. I shut the door and opened the curtains so I could read for a while after putting on my cotton nightgown.

As I lay there reading in silence, that eerie feeling came back again like I wasn't alone. I knew my siblings were asleep by now as I glanced at the wind-up clock next to my bed that said two o'clock.

I was just getting ready to close my book and snuggle down into the blankets when I heard a voice calling me from outside the trailer!

I thought I heard Mom say, "Lori, help me!" Springing up out of bed, I stood perfectly still and listened quietly. Then I heard the voice again loud and clear. "Lori, help me! Lori, help me!"

Not wanting to wake everyone up but worried Mom and Dad were in trouble, I slipped on my tennis shoes and turned on the flashlight.

The door to the trailer creaked loudly as it opened up to the thick dark woods behind the house. It was fairly light outside, and I didn't see anything as I stepped out of the trailer.

As I walked around the garage to the front of the house, I heard the voice again that seemed to come from down our road!

For some reason, I felt compelled to keep following the now muffled sound and kept walking past the barn and cowshed down our dirt road until I stopped and looked back. I couldn't see the house anymore, and Mom and Dad were nowhere in sight.

Suddenly I got scared and felt confused about the voice I had heard calling me for help. "Could I be crazy?" I thought to myself as I practically ran back to the house, looking behind me the whole way as if someone was following me.

I stepped back up into my bedroom from the outside of the trailer and latched the door. Then I woke the twins and Steve up and told them about the voice that called me outside to help and nothing was there. Their eyes got big as I told them what the voice had said and that I walked down the road looking for Mom and Dad.

After that, none of us could sleep alone, especially in the trailer, so the rest of the night we snuggled together in the small bed in the living room.

Hay Barn
Fiske
Del

21

PHANTOM BEAR

DENNIS

Dungo pulled through again this year at the races in Palmer, leaving the other horses in the dust. He seemed to live for the track and the win! Having the fastest racehorse made me proud as I sat on Dungo and showed off my training skills as he did everything as I commanded.

Soon all the locals knew me and often asked me about helping them with their unruly horses. I had a large family and could use the extra money, so I took most of them up on it.

Cecil was a friend at the races, and with my winnings and savings, I bought two of his black fillies that had been born in the spring.

I'd bring them home in the spring of next year when they were yearlings and then break and train them at about three years old.

The completely black thoroughbred colts were love at first sight for me, and I couldn't wait to get them home. At this present time, though, I was thinking about taking on an older mare whom Cecil had for sale also. Her name was Jude, a fifteen-year-old gentle registered quarter horse.

It was a cold, foggy morning in late September. The wet ground was packed with autumn leaves hardened by the frost. Dungo was blowing steam out of his nostrils as he spun around by the big barn.

Touching him with my right spur and reining him forward, we took off down the spring trail to Goose Creek to go hunting.

There was an abundance of moose that hung out by the railroad tracks and the creek where they found vegetation and water. The large cow moose I hoped to get would have enough meat for part of the winter as our supply was getting low.

As I trotted Dungo past the empty cabin on the knoll, and off the trail into the tall grass, the fog began to thicken. The wide blades of grass had grown all the way to the top of the saddle from the plentiful rain this year. My leather coat and my wool socks kept me warm, but my jeans were starting to get soaked from the dew on the grass.

Dungo stopped suddenly, as if nervous about the thick fog. Urging him forward, I pulled my thirty-thirty Savage rifle out of the scabbard and rested it on the saddle in front of me, loaded. I knew we couldn't see ahead and relied on Dungo's sharp ears and keen smell. Finally, I made it to the community center and stopped for a break before heading down to the creek bottom.

While hoping for the fog to lift, I dismounted and tightened up the leather cinch under Dungo's belly as he stood ground tied. I put my foot in the stirrup and climbed back up into the leather saddle.

Heading Dungo down the bank toward the creek bed, I was backtracking to get behind the moose so as not to chase them farther from home.

Someday Steve would be old enough to come with me on my hunting trips as he was already shooting my rifles at eight years old.

Dungo walked through the thick fog cautiously with his head up and his nerves high. I had a tight grip on his reins with my left leather gloved hand and the other on my loaded rifle across my lap in the saddle.

Riding here in the bush, the creeks, and the homestead for four years now, I knew every mile and how to get there.

The trestle bridge stood out above the fog, guiding the way as Dungo trudged on through the grass and willow brush. I could hear the sound of the creek rushing under the bridge as we crossed the train tracks.

Cold and soaking wet, I was thinking about getting back on the trail and getting out of the thick fog. Dungo threw his big head up and suddenly stopped in his tracks as if he smelled something. His long legs were shaking, and he began to snort and back up. I pulled back on his bit as his strong thick neck fought against me as if he wanted to run!

Urging him forward with my spurs, Dungo walked ahead into the fog a few more steps and then planted his feet. I knew my well-broke stallion had a strong sense of danger ahead. My heart began to race as I lifted my Savage rifle up and pulled the hammer back, ready to shoot.

Dungo was dancing around, trying to turn back, when the thick fog in front of us moved and parted, as if curtains had opened to a theater stage! That's when I saw it but couldn't believe it! Right in our path, about thirty yards ahead was the biggest brown bear I have ever seen with my own two eyes!

His ears and mane came up to the top of the tall grass on all fours as he stared at me with his beady brown eyes through the blades.

Struggling to hold my large stallion still and keep the rifle from falling, I kept my eyes on the enormous bear. He was staring at me as if he was waiting for the show to start. His body was at least thirteen feet long nose to tail!

The huge brown bear kept his large head down in the grass, facing me off. Dungo kept trying to turn away from him, and it took all my strength to hold him still. I pulled back hard on the reins and brought Dungo's head down to face the danger as his legs shook and my arms ached.

Keeping a tight hold on the rifle and saying a quick prayer, I gripped my wet knees against the saddle and stood my ground. There was no way I was turning my back on this huge bear!

I felt frozen with shock in the saddle, seeing such a large coastal bear so far from the ocean. The fog had lifted completely, and the sun was poking through the clouds as the hair stood up on the back of my neck. I only had one shot loaded and one chance if this enormous bear were to charge. Large spruce stood on either side of my strong but intimidated stallion, making our getaway a challenge as I scoped around for a quick escape.

Then to my relief, the brown bear that looked to be around twelve hundred pounds suddenly turned on his hind legs and was gone into the tall grass like a phantom.

Dungo had lathered up from the standoff, dancing around nervously. I was shaking uncontrollably as the dampness set into my bones. My heartbeat hadn't slowed down yet from the adrenaline rush that anticipated my possible demise.

By now I was so cold and shook up home was the only option, and I knew the bear had headed back down to the creek where I needed to go. Even though the thought of his huge hide on my wall and a great story to tell was tempting, I still hoped he had gone south back to his home.

Dungo started to calm down as I poked him forward, indicating the huge animal was already far from us. With my rifle still laid across my lap, I reined Dungo down the bank and up the creek bed towards home.

I knew that massive coastal bear had pulled the curtains on my hopes of killing a moose that day. He was the star of the show.

One week later my friend Dean Bunker shot one of the biggest brown bears ever seen in a long time up Sheep Creek. After I saw it stretched eight feet across his ceiling, and Sheep Creek only a few miles away, I was sure it was the same brown bear I had my encounter. Coastal brown bears were known to travel up the river, sometimes more than seventy-five miles from the inlet, following the spawning salmon.

I finally got the mare Jude home in October, giving my stallion company for the winter. All the kids wanted to ride her, and they did as much as they could before the snow on the ground was too deep.

Winter set in with a vengeance, and I still hadn't shot my moose yet.

Steve and I set out one early morning with Dungo and Jude, whom he handled with ease. Taking the same route as I did that morning I saw my bear, I told Steve the whole story, reliving every moment, although this time, we packed home big moose quarters to cut and freeze in the root cellar for the long winter.

22

MOOSE GONE MAD

STEVE

It was the eve of 1971 when I awoke to a wet bed and the chills. Wrapping the wool blanket around me as I sat up on the couch in the living room, I realized it was still night and the house was quiet.

The big barrel stove by the front door put off plenty of heat, but I still shook as I looked out the framed door window. Maybe I had cabin fever from the ongoing blizzards that prevented us from going to school or even outside the house.

Dad had made it home for Christmas from the North Slope bringing gifts and a large ham to cook for supper. Mom and I rode Dungo and Jude through the high drifts of snow out to the community center to get him into the homestead. The horses struggled in the white powder that reached their bellies. The high winds froze ice pellets to their lean bodies.

I had my ski mask on and could barely breathe through the relentless cold wind hitting my face as I rode behind Dad on Dungo.

While he was gone to the slope, we had temperatures forty below zero. I was the only one that bundled up and went out to the barns to feed the animals. Our four dogs didn't even want to go outside, except for Shane, who was loyal to me since Meardha had disappeared two years ago.

My chest felt tight and congested, causing me to cough several times as I climbed back onto the couch, pulling the blankets up over my head.

The next time I woke up, Mom was standing over me in her cotton nightgown, feeling my forehead as beads of sweat soaked into my feather-filled pillow.

I could hear Kristi coughing from her twin bed as Mom said quietly, "You have pneumonia, Steve, and so do all of your sisters."

My head felt fuzzy, and the room was spinning as Mom propped me up and gave me a cup of hot Jell-O to sip. We were never sure why Mom always gave us hot Jell-O when we were sick. It seemed to make us feel better. It tasted really good on our fingers when we kids dipped them into the dry boxes we found one day hidden in the trailer.

It was already morning, and Dad was stoking the fire in the barrel stove with the birch pieces I had stacked the night before. He was melting snow on top of the barrel stove, and Mom was making oatmeal in the kitchen. Lori and the twins came into the living room with their nightgowns still on carrying blankets and pillows. Kristi was sitting beside me on the couch now and sipping her own hot Jell-O with her doll and blanket.

Lori and the twins put sheets on the twin bed Dad had carried into the living room from the trailer that was pushed up against the other one. We would keep them that way as it was too cold to sleep in the trailer, and the girls slept in the living room most of the winter anyhow.

Then he and Mom took more blankets and made a tent over all of us kids as all five of us lay on the beds and covered up. Mom and Dad used big books from our bookcase to create a tight seal.

Mom brought us each a hot bowl of oatmeal, which felt warm in our empty stomachs, and aspirin for the fever.

Mom and Dad looked concerned as they filled the large metal pot in the tent with boiling water and Vicks, letting the tent fill with steam.

Mom kept the hot water coming as us kids coughed and tried to sweat out the pneumonia, while Dad did the chores and kept the fire going.

During the night we coughed so bad Mom stayed up and boiled water every hour to keep the steam going.

The snow outside was too deep, and the cold blizzards made it almost impossible to get us out to the highway. None of our vehicles would start, and we didn't have a phone like most people. I had heard people can die from pneumonia and prayed silently for my sisters to get well.

Bowls of chicken noodle soup and days later, to Mom and Dad's relief, one by one my sisters and I got over the pneumonia and were allowed outside the tent.

This was one of the coldest winters I remember at seventy below zero where no one was allowed to go outside except Dad.

There was a hole in the trailer floor where a toilet would normally belong. Dad dug under it into the ground to make a large hole where we could go to the bathroom.

Lori, the twins, and Mom and Dad couldn't sleep in the freezing trailer. After we all had pneumonia, Dad closed it off with a removable board, and everyone slept in the living room. Lori and I moved the mattresses from the beds in the trailer to the floor by the barrel stove so everyone had a place to sleep. I have to admit, it was kind of fun being so close to my family playing board games and cards into the night.

The severe cold wind was seeping through our shack walls, making it almost impossible to keep the house warm. Turns out one night the cows got out of the barn and ate all the Visqueen off the outside of our house. Dad and I bundled up the next morning, the day before the twins' seventh birthday, and went out into the snow to find as much tar paper as we could to nail to the outside of the house. We found several large pieces that were leftover from the big barn and nailed them to the weather boards on the northern walls.

Dad had his black furry hat on with ear muffs and his overalls under his leather coat, and I had my ski mask on with the knitted cap Lori made me and all my snow gear, but I still felt the bitter cold under it all. Dad handed me the hammer and told me, "Keep nailing this down. I'm going to start the snow machine."

Even though I wondered why Dad was starting the snow machine, I kept on working like I was told. I could hear the Rupp model snow machine struggling to start in the garage. Someone had given it to Dad, and he had worked on it and got it running again. It had a faded red color and was old and worn out. Dad came roaring up to the front of the house and yelled for me.

I set the hammer and can of nails inside the kitchen on the counter, closed the dogs in, and then ran out to the snow machine and hopped on behind Dad. He yelled back at me in the wind, "Some of the sheep are missing!"

My face was shielded by Dad's back as I hung on tightly around his waist. The old snow machine blazed through the deep snow, throwing it up around us as Dad drove it past the big barn and down our main road.

Early afternoon and a complete whiteout with flurries still blowing in, it was hard to see ahead or around us as we scanned the woods on the right side of us for sheep.

The snow machine made hills as we rode on top of the several feet of snow on the road and got stuck a few times. Dad and I would get off and pull on the large blades until they pulled free from the snowdrift.

I yelled for Dad to stop, when I suddenly saw one of our ewes in the snowbank to the left of the road by the field. He stopped the snow machine, and we both got off, leaving it running.

We could barely hike over to her, sinking down up to our chests into the deep snowdrifts on the road. I thought I heard Dad laugh as he looked at the ewe frozen in the deep snow up to her neck, bleating loudly.

Dad and I removed the snow around her with our gloved hands, and then he got out his big knife that was in its holster on his belt. He began cutting the sheep's wool from the frozen bank to free her with the big knife.

It was snowing hard again, and the icy wind worked against Dad as he finally freed the ewe from the bank and set her on her way back to the house. She ran down the road, bleating and lucky we found her when we did in the unbearable temperature.

I looked at Dad as we got back on the snow machine covered in snow already but still running. He yelled above the loud motor, "There's one more!" As I got behind Dad I looked over to where he was pointing in the woods and saw a large herd of moose digging in the snow for twigs.

The snow machine faithfully ran slowly but surely through the blowing snow and drifts until we spotted another ewe frozen solid right in the middle of our road! The big timber wolves we had seen many times would have had a feast if only a few more hours, or the sheep would already be dead from the angry winter.

Dad and I were off the Polaris and cutting the ewe free within minutes as we were ready to get out of the cold. She took off running toward the house as Dad and I were turning the snow machine around to head back.

I was numb now and had learned a few winters ago to keep moving everything, and after a while, you just adjust to the loss of feeling.

We were about a half mile from the house rounding the corner at the edge of the field when Dad slowed down and raised his right hand up. I looked ahead of us and saw a bull moose running in the road in front of us about a hundred yards, kicking up snow. The bull moose have no antlers in the winter and are larger than a cow moose. His big hairy black body was covered in snow and ice as the hair on his bony back stood straight up. Dad kept making his way over the deep snow when the moose stopped, turned, and started trotting toward us.

Dad stopped the snow machine and grabbed his rifle when that moose came charging at us at a full run!

Dad grabbed my arm and practically dragged me off the snow machine as he jumped off too, aiming the rifle at the charging moose who had suddenly stopped. The large animal looked uninterested in us and turned around, walking back down the road in our path again.

We just stood there watching this long-legged moose get down the road a ways so we could get home. The Rupp was starting to sputter out from the extreme cold weather, and so were we.

Dad motioned for me to get back on the snow machine, and after a few more attempts at keeping it running, we took off down our road again.

A short distance later as the winds picked up, I could see through the flurries the same moose running ahead of us in the middle of the road. Dad saw him too and stopped the snow machine once again as that moose turned around and came charging at us!

The deep snow slowed him down enough to give us time to get off the Rupp and run into the woods. Dad would have a hard time getting a good shot in the flurries of snow.

As soon as we found a tree to climb, the moose looked at us again and ran down the road. Dad threw his hands in the air and said, "What did I ever do to that mad moose?"

We had been out in the cold now for at least two hours, and I was hungry as always. Dad wanted to wait longer this time, and while we stood there in the woods, he pulled out of his overalls a small bag of smoked bear jerky. He must have read my mind as he handed me a big chunk of black bear that he had killed and smoked this last fall.

My dad was strong and a survivor, and I felt safe when he was around me. Sometimes when he was gone, I was scared something bad was going to happen. Life in the bush with no conveniences was a daily struggle that we all shared, bringing us closer together, especially when us kids stayed home alone.

The short summers were the best time at the homestead. The midnight sun kept everything scary in the light as we made forts and played hide-and-seek in the woods.

Last summer Mom and Dad were away for a couple of days in Fairbanks, visiting friends. Lori and I got the twins and Kristi to play hide-and-seek in the thick woods behind the house. Dawn was afraid of everything, and we knew it! Lori and I plotted to have her be the one to count to ten and then leave her in the woods by herself.

We all hiked into the dim forest of birch and cottonwood until we could barely see the house. Devan and Kristi played along reluctantly as Dawn agreed to stand behind a thick white cottonwood and count to ten. Then the rest of us ran for the house as fast as we could, leaving Dawn in the woods looking for us. Lori, Devan, Kristi, and I hid around the garage and watched her get closer to the house, still trying to seek us out.

Then she began to cry when the fear of being alone in the woods set in, knowing we were gone. Devan and Kristi ran out to the woods and got her, and we all felt bad.

Dawn told on us when Mom and Dad got back, and all of us kids including her had to line up. We got a lickin' for playing in the woods with a willow Dad made me cut with his pocketknife.

Dad and I loaded back up onto the snow machine and headed down the road again for home on a day I thought would never end.

That mad moose came out of the woods as the Rupp was running hard over the drifts and got in front of us again! This time looking straight at us with a vengeance! I knew the drill and jumped up off the snow machine and ran straight for the woods a few yards away as Dad did the same. The big black moose, who seemed to have it out for us and was stopping us from getting home, put his head down; and with his withers up, he charged right for the snow machine.

Dad and I watched with our mouths opened wide in disbelief when the huge animal dove right in the middle of the snow machine with the whole front of his body! Then the angry moose pounced down with his front hooves several times, literally beating the old Rupp up!

Dad had a sick look on his face as picked up his rifle to shoot the mad moose but couldn't see through the blowing snow. The moose took off running down the road again, and Dad and I hiked over to the snow machine to assess the damage. Dad shook his head and said a few choice words as he looked down at our snow machine badly bent down in the center. Both skis were broke, along with the running boards and cowling. There was no way we were going to drive it home, and we had a half mile to go.

Dad said, shaking from the cold, "Let's move it off the road and hike home." It took some strength to shimmy the heavy snow machine off the road. Then Dad and I hiked home on our road by ourselves with no moose in sight. We were glad to see the lit-up windows of the house as our numb bodies hiked the last few yards in the deep snow.

23

ICE PALACES

DEVAN

T he brilliant moonlight reflected off the slough that had frozen solid this winter. The only light on a dark early afternoon was above us, shining off the white snow.

It was almost spring and still below zero, and we had cabin fever. Dawn and I each got a pair of ice skates for our seventh birthday that were white and had single blades. Then Mom found some second-hand skates for the rest of the family to use, even a double-blade small pair for Kristi to wear. After a few spills on the ice, I finally started to get my balance and could skate a few feet.

Dawn and I held Kristi's hands while all three of us held each other up. The thick ice was shining like glass under the moonlight, inviting even Dad to join the fun. Lori and Steve skated like they always knew how, up and down the frozen slough where we normally fished.

Mom had to sit on the snowbank and listen to the laughter on this beautiful still winter night. She sat us all down in the living room one night in February and told us that she was going to have another baby. We siblings were all excited about having another brother or sister.

After a while Dad sat with Mom after he built a small fire on the bank. I felt moist under my heavy coat even though it was cold outside. Skating right up with Lori and Steve as they did laps around the ice took a lot of work on my blades. Dawn held Kristi's hand as they slowly made their way around the brightly lit rink. It felt like a little bit of heaven had been exposed only to us as we skated into the late hours of the night.

Then Dad told us all to come in and get ready to hike back to the house.

With my hands on my hips, I was skating back to the bank so gracefully next to Lori. Then a notch in the ice caught the ridges on the front of my right blade! Down I went unprepared for the speedy descent onto the hard, thick ice! All I could hear was laughter as my siblings found my destiny to be too funny to contain themselves. I couldn't release my hands from my hips before my chin broke the inevitable crash on the concrete like surface.

Feeling humiliated, I lifted my face up off the ice and felt my chin. Blood saturated my hand, and I began to cry as I felt the sting from the fresh wound. Lori and Steve got on each side of me and helped me get up off the slick ice and onto the bank. Mom put snow in her scarf and had me hold it on my chin until the bleeding stopped while I sat by the fire Dad was putting out. Wounded and worn out, I couldn't wait to get back to the house into our warm bed.

I lay there that night remembering how much fun we all had on our own ice rink on the slough. I knew there were many more nights of skating under the light of the big round moon.

A couple of days later, Dad took Mom to see a doctor in Palmer, and then they were going to drive to Anchorage to get groceries.

Dad told us to stay close to the house as they wouldn't be home until the next night. They took Kristi with them, who was almost five, and left on a Friday morning on the Polaris. The rest of us kids piled into the sled and got a ride out to the bus with them as the pickup was out at the highway.

After school we got off the bus at the community center as usual and hiked our trail home. The snow was still deep, held captive by the freezing temperature. The wind was breathing ice, stinging our faces as we pushed against it.

We got to the train tracks next to the overfull frozen Goose Creek and stopped to walk across Trestle Creek Bridge one time as it was already getting dark.

Several moose were far enough down the tracks east of us to cause us no worry. Soon the bears would be out of hibernation, often with cubs. Steve would have to pack the single-shot rifle and hide it in the woods behind the community center. Oftentimes he would go to school with extra ammunition in his pockets, unnoticed by the teachers.

Dawn and I held hands as we followed Steve and Lori across the ice-covered Trestle Creek Bridge. As my boots were slipping around on the frozen railroad ties and Dawn was looking down starting to get frightened, I said to Lori and Steve, "The bridge is too slick, and we're getting off of it!" We took one last look at Goose Creek frozen in time as dusk came upon it and carefully started to walk off the bridge to go home.

I was looking down at my feet to make sure I didn't slip into the gaps between the railroad ties. I smacked right into Lori, who was right in front of me and Dawn. Steve, who was in the lead, had suddenly stopped us all on the bridge only a few yards from the end to the tracks.

"Oh no!" Lori blurted out in a startled tone. There right in front of us, blocking our way off the bridge, were the moose we had seen earlier. The three large dark-brown bulls and one cow moose just stood there in a pack, trapping us on the icy bridge between them and a possible oncoming train. I was thinking fast, as I'm sure we all were, and said quietly, tugging on the back of Lori's shirt, as we were all backing up slowly, "Let's go to the other side." Dawn, who had not said a word, was sobbing quietly as to not upset the moose, with her hand trembling in mine.

Steve said loud enough for us to hear as he continued backing us up on the bridge, "Keep going until we get to the other end, and go faster if you can!" My short legs took careful quick steps backward until we got to the middle of the bridge, then we all turned our backs on the moose, who were not budging, and stepped the rest of the way off the bridge onto the gravel bank.

Then to our amazement, the crazy animals started to cross the bridge after us! We knew they were too big and clumsy to step on each railroad tie carefully like we did, to not fall into the wide gaps where you could see the creek below. However, we kids also knew not to challenge nature, and we took off running into the snowbank to the woods below us.

The trees by the creek were skinnier, and it was hard to find a good birch or spruce to climb. Steve pushed Dawn and me up into a thin but strong spruce with large branches and told us to climb up higher. Dawn's face was streaked with tears, and I was about ready to cry also as I pulled her up higher into the strong tree next to me. Lori and Steve walked back over to the tracks to see if the moose were still blocking our way back across the tracks to our trail home.

I was starting to get scared as the darkness was coming upon the late afternoon. We only had one choice if the large moose didn't leave, and that was to cross over the thick ice on the wide creek to get to the trail. Even then, the dangerous moose would be on that side also and could easily charge at us as they sometimes did.

Steve and Lori had disappeared out of sight as the woods were getting darker. Dawn and I held on to each other perched on a frosted branch in the spruce tree when she said in a quivering voice, "Are they going to leave us here, Devan?" I knew my twin was scared to death, and I had to be brave for her sake. I wiped the few tears that were starting to freeze on my cold face and squeezed Dawn's mittened hand.

Just as I was trying to think of something comforting to say to my scared twin sister, Lori and Steve came walking up to our tree out of nowhere. "Climb down, you two. The moose are gone. We need to get home!" Steve said, looking up at us. I held on to Dawn's hand as she started down the tree first, hanging on to each branch until Steve caught her at the bottom as she jumped to the ground.

Barely able to see now in the almost-dark woods, I climbed down the spruce as fast as I could and then jumped down to the ground, also into the snow. Turns out the moose only came a few feet onto the bridge before they backed off and went on their way. Lori and Steve made sure they were clear out of sight before coming to get us out of the tree.

After we crossed the bridge again, all four of us were silent as we made our way home in the dark at a faster pace than usual, cold and hungry.

Steve and Lori started fires quickly in both stoves and lit the propane lights in the kitchen.

Mom hadn't told us what to cook for supper, so Lori and Dawn decided to make chocolate chip pancakes with cranberry syrup. All of us scarfed it down, not worrying about table manners and talking out of turn.

Steve and I took the flashlight and the dogs and went out to the barns to feed the animals. Dungo and Jude were in the big barn with the cows, and the sheep were in the cowshed. After a few harsh winters, we lost all our chickens, leaving the coop empty and covered in snow.

We decided to stay up late and play Candyland on the kitchen table and drink homemade hot cocoa. The trailer was still cold, so that night we slept in the living room with Steve. He had Dad's big rifle propped up against the wall next to the couch where he slept. Dawn and I and Lori slept on the twin beds next to the wall. We lay there in the dark telling scary stories, some of which were true, until one by one we fell asleep.

It was still dark outside when I opened my eyes after I heard wood being shoved into the barrel stove next to us. Dawn was curled up against me, still asleep, as I rolled out of bed. Lori's side of the bed was made and empty.

We kids were used to getting up early. Dad was an early riser, and so was Mom, making us kids get out of bed also. Dad would yell "Rise and shine!" or "Roll 'em out!" Even though water was a precious commodity, it was thrown on us if we didn't get out of bed when told to.

I rubbed the sleep out of my eyes and saw Steve stoking the fire. Lori was in the kitchen making oatmeal for us as I put my boots on to go to the outhouse. She said, "Devan, wake Dawn up to go with you." Dawn was already crawling out of bed as I was putting my coat on, barely able to hold it.

After we got back from the outhouse and ate our oatmeal, Steve said to all of us, "Let's hike down to the creek behind the house. I've never been that way, and I know there is a trail behind the dump."

We all knew Mom and Dad wouldn't be home until this afternoon and also were curious about the closer access to the creek. So after daylight, which was late morning, we all put on our winter gear and headed out of the kitchen door. Steve carried the Savage rifle, and all four dogs ran in front of us as we hiked around the house and past the dump. The so-called trail was still covered with two feet of packed snow that had deep holes where Dad had taken Dungo to moose hunt.

It was about a quarter mile hike through the woods to the bed of the creek. Goose Creek ran east and west and was wide and deep. We all loved to dip into the icy cold water on warm summer days even though we didn't know how to swim. The extreme cold water caused cramping in our feet and legs. We would dare each other to wade in the cold water with our shorts on and see who could go in the farthest.

We stopped to look at a bald eagle sitting on a moose carcass, dominating his find from the large ravens in the woods.

Finally we made the last stretch through a willow thick bank overlooking the wide creek. The poplars were bare but thick surrounding the deep rushing water that was frozen in time.

The ice surface on the creek reflected the sun that was poking out of the clouds. It was shining through the trees in long beautiful rays as if we had found a treasure.

Steve, Lori, Dawn, and I just stood there for a moment on the bank. We were in awe of yet another piece of heaven right on our homestead, as if God was revealing himself to us.

Then as we walked closer to the wide body of water, we noticed the creek was frozen in layers. I couldn't take my eyes off the glasslike formations illuminating all the colors of the rainbow. Lori said as she stared at the large layers of transparent ice that seemed to be held in midair, "It looks like the ice is frozen enough for us to walk on it."

Steve tiptoed onto the ice that reached the bank a few feet from where the sharp peaks were. Lori, Dawn, and I carefully walked behind Steve until we all reached the breathtaking formations on the creek.

We all got down on our knees and crawled inside of the layers of ice that sparkled in the sun. I thought it was the most splendid thing, besides the northern lights, that I have ever seen!

As I lay there on my stomach on the thick transparent ice inside the rainbow lit tunnel of opulent icicles, I looked at the barely moving creek below and said out loud, "These are like ice palaces!" Everyone agreed, and we stayed and explored for what seemed like hours.

Soon it would be spring, and our newly found secret would have to wait until next winter as the ice would melt off the creek. I took one more look back at the pretty palaces in the sun before we hiked back to the house.

We got back in time to do our chores before Mom and Dad came home on the snow machine. All of us ran outside to greet them as Dad parked the Polaris in front of the garage. Along with lots of sacks of groceries, Dad pulled a well-worn medium-size bike out of the big sled and set it up on its kickstand in the soft snow. It was orange with a white seat and white plastic handles. The wide white wheels with wire spokes looked durable, and the thick chain was tight and in place. He said, "This two-speed bike is for all of you kids to ride for being respectful and obeying." As we all admired it, he said, "The Seales gave it to us as a gift."

Lori, Steve, Dawn, and I thanked Dad as we all looked solemnly at each other, hoping he wouldn't see the sparkle from the ice palaces in our eyes.

During spring breakup, Mom went to Anchorage to get groceries with Dawn, Kristi, and me in the Bel Air. On the way back on the Glenn Highway near Palmer, Kristi was crying in the back seat, causing Mom to turn around and look at her. Next thing you know, Mom drove the car straight into a ditch. Some nice man stopped and pulled us out of the deep wet snow, and then Mom drove us home, madder than a hornet.

24

SAVING STEVE

LORI

My body started to develop slowly as I hit double digits this year on my tenth birthday. Tall and thin still earned me the nickname Wrigley, after the flat piece of gum.

Mom and Dad were gone a lot, and I was left in charge of my siblings more often. I would miss Mom so much that sometimes at night I would go in their bedroom in the trailer and smell her pillow.

Summer was here, putting an end to the fifth grade and the long hikes home from the highway. Wildflowers of all kinds bloomed everywhere, painting pretty colors from the field to the woods. The green grass on the field was growing tall, and it was almost haying season. The cows, sheep, and horses loved grazing in the warm sun and wandering freely around the property.

It was the end of June, and Mom was getting big at almost seven months pregnant. Our baby was due the end of September, and Dad was hoping with four girls it would be another boy.

Grandma Gloria and Grandpa Verne were moving here next week from Washington with Aunt Wendy and our cousins Joy and Dougie. They had bought a house near Talkeetna off the Parks Highway from the Smiths. It was a white A-frame with an orange door back off the highway surrounded by tall birch trees.

I didn't have many friends besides Farrah and was excited about Aunt Wendy moving here. Wendy is Mom's little sister and is only four years older than me. She has red hair like Mom and me, looks like Grandpa Verne, and is tall and outgoing. She and Steve and I hung out together and had become like the Three Musketeers. We even had our own nicknames, just the three of us. Wendy was Brains, I was Beauty, and my brother Steve was Brawn.

Joy is Kristi's age, and Dougie is three years old now. They also are bringing Wendy's horses, Pepper and Chico, and their collie, Lad.

We had more horses now, and Steve and I got to ride by ourselves bareback. The two black fillies Dad had bought were too young to ride and mostly ran around the property, kicking up their legs with their black manes flowing in the wind.

Mr. Milton from the races sold Dad a strawberry roan registered quarter horse mare named Babe. She was thirteen years old and was from New Mexico, where she won a lot of races. Between owners, Babe didn't want to run anymore and was clumsy around the track.

Dad brought her home and broke her again sometimes using the long black whip. When he was a young boy, his dad taught him how to whip break a horse without actually whipping them. My grandpa Austin told him, "Any discipline more than you need to get what you want is abuse." Babe was riding good now, and Dad was thinking about putting her in the horse races in August.

All of us kids including Kristi were allowed to ride Jude, who was gentle as a lamb, ridden with just a lead rope around her neck.

Right after my birthday, Steve and I went for a ride through the field heading north and quite a ways from the house. He rode Dungo and I rode Jude, both of us bareback. All four dogs followed us, and when we rode back a couple of hours later, our golden setter Shane wasn't with us anymore.

Steve and I rode back a ways, calling his name, but he never showed up again. We thought we were going to be in trouble, but Dad just frowned and said, "Maybe he'll find his way home."

I know Steve was heartbroken when Shane didn't come home after several days because I heard him cry in his sleep. After that happened, Dad decided to give Smokey to some people in Palmer, who were looking for a nice dog. Now we just had our sheltie Pete and Dum Dum.

Grandma and Grandpa Stanton pulled into our homestead on the fourth of July, while we were all out haying the field. The sky was blue, and the sun was evaporating the puddles.

The railroad company let us tap into their phone line, and we now had a black dial phone, but you could only call out. We had no way of knowing when they were coming but knew it would be any day.

A brand-new red-and-black Ford pickup with a white camper pulling a white horse trailer came driving up into our driveway. Aunt Wendy jumped out of the pickup and ran over to us in the field. She hugged all of us, with their collie, Lad, trailing behind her.

Grandma and Grandpa got out of the truck by the time we all walked over to greet them. The back door of the camper opened, and Joy and Dougie climbed out. They were both so cute and shy. Joy was tiny for five and had brown hair and big sky-blue eyes. Dougie was pale with the same eyes and had the blondest hair I've ever seen.

Dad and Grandpa Verne unloaded twenty-seven-year-old Pepper, the gray dapple gelding that was Mom's when she was a teenager. Then they backed Wendy's paint Chico, who was a gelding also, out of the horse trailer with ease. Wendy said when they left Washington Grandpa had a struggle loading him. Dad handed me Pepper's lead rope and told Wendy and me, "Take them out to the field with the rest of the horses."

The two geldings were excited to see green grass and the other horses. When we got close to Dungo and his brood in the middle of the field, all the horses started whinnying to each other as if introducing themselves. Pepper and Chico ran to the other horses with their tails up in the air as we walked back to the house.

Wendy said, "So, I heard you like to ride."

I noticed we both had long dark-red hair that was blowing in the breeze, and we looked quite a bit alike. I looked up at her as we hiked through the grass and said, "We should ride together sometime!"

When we got back to the house, Mom was making peanut butter and raspberry jam sandwiches for a picnic lunch. Dad and

Grandpa were gearing up to go fishing at the slough. Mom said as Grandma helped her pack radishes and carrot sticks from our garden, "You kids get ready to go swimming in Goose Creek!"

All I had to hear was swimming and no chores! I ran to the back of the trailer to put my swim shorts on and my tattered tank top. What a beautiful warm summer day at the homestead.

Before we left, Uncle Dave showed up with his new wife, Noreta. She was a fancy lady with her stiffly sprayed fluffy hair and her face painted thick with makeup. Noreta had a little blond-haired daughter, who had chubby cheeks and wore horn-rimmed glasses. She was seven like the twins, and her name was Raylene.

After closing all the dogs in the house, we all took off hiking up our road next to the cut field to the creek.

Steve and I led the way to the slough where Dad, Uncle Dave, and Grandpa left us to fish for salmon and dollies.

Mom had Dad's pistol on her hip, and Steve carried the Savage rifle as they led the way on up to the creek. Wendy and I walked with Grandma and Noreta. The twins and Kristi walked with our cousins and Raylene in the middle of us.

This was grizzly season, for them I mean! They liked to lie in the tall grass that bordered our narrow trail, ignoring us as if they were used to the sound of our singing. We siblings knew to always be looking around for bears that were too large to not see if you are alert. If cubs were present, you had better make a quick plan, most of the time involving climbing the biggest tree you could find. The first thing to do is create a distance between you and the large carnivore without causing a ruckus. We often passed their mounds of dead moose carcass or other animals covered in dirt and bear poop. The grizzly saves his kill until it ferments. Then he comes back unburying it to share with his family. We knew the large smelly mounds meant a grizzly was nearby, and they were usually right at the top of our hill leading down to the spring. Hopefully, you remembered your rifle and your prayers!

Mom told Grandma that we should all sing, and then Grandma led us in a chorus of "I'll Fly Away!"

Goose Creek was running high and deep over the rocky bed, thrusting its translucent water downstream. The poplars were brilliantly green, stretching their thick leafy branches, bordering each side of the wide cold water. Silvers were spawning in thick groups, looking for dark holes to lay their eggs.

I loved our homestead and hoped we would live here forever. We didn't have much money. In fact, some people considered us poor, even though Mom and Dad worked for every dime we had. I felt like we were rich with our endless emerald-green fields, thick forests, streams, animals, and family. Like our own piece of paradise in the bush of Alaska.

Looking across the creek, I saw Stephanie, who was a lady we had met last summer, bathing in the sun on the bank by herself. She and her husband were camping in a tent near our property and various empty cabins in the winter. Mom and Dad had gotten to know them and said they had two kids, a boy and girl twins. They were from Georgia, where Stephanie's husband was an uptight bigwig for a car company. One day he came home a changed man for some reason and wanted to give it all up and move to the bush of Alaska. His once-clean-cut look turned into long hair and a beard. Stephanie was Greek with long straight black hair, pale skin, and a slender shapely body. Unlike her husband who referred to their kids as boy and girl, she was sweet and friendly.

Once again we all sprayed mosquito dope on our white bodies to ward off the huge bugs that were swarming and biting us.

Grandma wore a blue silk scarf over her head and tied it under her chin. She sat on the bank with Mom and Noreta and watched us kids stick our toes into the cold water to warn our bodies before plunging in.

Wendy and Steve walked into the shallow water first, adventuring out farther into the rushing creek. Steve stopped and bobbed with the current when it reached his chest as he didn't know how to swim.

The twins took Kristi and Raylene and waded into the clear cold water, staying in a shallow spot. I waded in, slowly letting my body get used to the freezing water. I watched Joy hold Dougie's hand as they stepped in up to their knees, looking scared and lost.

I couldn't imagine losing my mom at such a young age and not seeing my dad very often. It had been two years since Mom's little sister Joyce had gone to heaven, but you could still see the pain on Joy's face as she clung to her little brother.

Protecting my eyes from the bright sun, I could only see Wendy's head as she yelled to us from the middle of the creek, "Go farther up. It's too deep out here! I'm swimming across!"

Mom, Grandma, and Noreta stood up from the bank where they were sitting and motioned for us kids to wade farther north up the creek. I walked over to Joy and Dougie and held their hands as we followed Mom and Grandma up the narrow bank, looking for shallow water.

Fourteen-year-old Wendy was a good swimmer and made it to the other side of the creek. I could see her walking on the bank opposite of us.

Suddenly the sound of the girls' laughter behind me was broken as we all heard Wendy scream, "Steve!" I whipped my head around to the terrifying sound in Wendy's voice, and so did everyone else!

Walking with Joy and Dougie, I was behind Mom quite a ways and saw the top of Steve's red head bobbing up and down like a cork into the deep hole in the middle of the creek!

Wendy screamed again as she jumped back into the water, making her way against the current toward my drowning brother, "Steve's drowning! Steve's drowning!"

Mom, who was pregnant, and Noreta turned toward me, running down the bank to get back to where Steve was.

Tears ran down my cheeks as I left Joy and Dougie on the bank and waded back into the water to help, but I didn't know how to swim!

Aunt Wendy was closest to him on the other side of the creek but was having a hard time against the current, as if she were in deep sand. Stephanie had heard the screams and jumped off the bank into the water, making her way to Steve also.

I felt helpless as I watched Steve's head disappear under the water and not come up this time. It felt like it was happening in slow motion as my little brother was fighting for his life under the water, slowly drowning. *I couldn't lose my best friend!* I thought to myself as I waded deeper. Stephanie was upstream and reached Steve before Wendy was able to get to him. She grabbed him and pulled him up far enough to get his head out of the water. Then they both went under the water as Steve was panicking and pulling her down with him into the deep hole!

Mom, who barely knew how to swim, was running into the creek to try and reach him, screaming, "Save him! Save him!"

Wendy finally reached the hole where Steve was drowning as Stephanie came up from under the water, her face as white as a sheet. She looked at Aunt Wendy and then peeled Steve off her and swam for shore!

By now everyone was screaming from the shore, even Grandma, who looked terrified as precious Steve was may be going to die!

Wendy dove under the clear water, grabbed Steve by his legs, and then turned him with his back to her. Then she heroically put her arms around his chest, pinning his arms to his sides and began swimming side stroke to shore. Steve's red head was barely out of the water as Wendy swam with him quickly to the other side of the creek.

We all held our breath as she pulled him up on the bank. I could see his face as white as snow with his freckles standing out like red measles. Aunt Wendy sat him up and shook him. "Steve!"

My heart sunk as I thought he was dead as his face had no expression and his body went limp. Aunt Wendy quickly slapped his back, and then he coughed and took in a big breath.

We were all partway into the creek, watching as Steve opened his eyes and said, "What happened?" Aunt Wendy yelled to Mom and us, "He's fine!" and then she lay on her back, gasping for air.

Grandma said loudly as she raised her arms into the air, "Praise the Lord!"

Wendy and Steve lay on the bank until they got their strength back while we packed up to head home. None of us felt like swimming after the accident, so we hiked home, feeling exhausted and thankful.

25

HOME ALONE

DEVAN

It was August and fair week again! My siblings and I looked forward to the whole family going somewhere once a year together to have fun.

Dad was running both Dungo and Babe this year in the races and spent hours working with them racing across the long and wide cut fields.

He had Steve running them too, and he watched as Steve and Dungo leaped over a windrow with ease and kept running on the other side.

This year Dad was going to have Steve jockey on Babe even though he had just turned nine and the age limit was twelve. My brother was a good rider and was both excited and nervous about racing.

All of us kids rode our horses almost daily in the summer except Dawn, who rode with us rarely.

Kristi, our little tomboy, would go out by herself at five and get on the lean-to roof by the big barn and jump on Jude with just a lead rope.

After church one day on Steve's birthday, we stopped by the A-frame house Grandma and Grandpa had moved into with Aunt Wendy and our double cousins Joy and Dougie. It was only four miles south from Talkeetna going toward our homestead, which was another sixteen miles. The A-frame was small compared to the house they had in Washington. The orange door opened up to a small kitchen that led to a living room with a master bedroom attached. There were wide wooden folding stairs that went up to a small loft where Wendy, Joy, and Dougie slept.

Wendy's horses were still at our homestead as she and Grandpa were in the process of building fences and an A-frame barn.

Grandma made us all fried chicken, homemade bread, and corn on the cob for lunch. Then we all sat in their living room and watched the Waltons on their large TV and ate vanilla ice cream.

We all talked about how, with her long red braids and freckles, Kristi looked just like Elizabeth Walton. Sometimes at night we would imitate the Waltons by saying good night to each other, echoing the walls of our shack.

Our long two-mile dirt road was full of ruts and holes as I pedaled our orange bike past the barns with Dawn sitting on the handlebars. Our short bob-style, fine blond hair blew in our sun-absorbed faces.

Mom, Lori, and Kristi were at the train tracks picking low bush cranberries. Dad and Steve were in the woods cutting down birch trees for firewood and stacking them into the bed of the truck.

Dawn and I were sent back to the house to get the mosquito dope Mom had forgot to pack, which was unusual.

After we rode all the way back to the house by ourselves, Dawn and I talked loudly on the way back about the carnival rides and cotton candy, unnoticed by Dad and Steve in the woods using the loud chainsaw. Dawn hung on to the handlebar as I took a wide turn around the cottonwood at the end of the field. It was a sharp corner on our dirt road where we often saw grizzlies.

Mom was bending down, picking low bush cranberries with Dad's big pistol strapped around her waist when we got back to the tracks. Her eight-month belly stuck out of her too small maternity top over her polyester pants.

I stopped the bike, and Dawn and I started picking cranberries and eating a few as well of the tart red fruit.

The big, loud blue-and-gold train came whizzing by, blowing our hair all around us as we were close to the tracks. The engineer blew his horn when we pumped our flexed arms, motioning for him to do so like Dad showed us.

After filling our tin cans with tons of cranberries, which weren't my favorite by the way, Lori wanted to ride the bike back. So she pedaled, with Kristi on the handlebars, down the dirt road not far in front of the rest of us hiking. My favorite berries were the raspberries that grew wild by the creek.

The big red velvety berries were plump, soft, and sweet squirting in your mouth when you ate them. They were ripe right now too, and we picked several cans of them while swimming at the creek. Mom was making jam with blueberries also and entering her jams in the fair this year.

When we finally made it back before dusk, Mom and Lori started supper. Dad and Steve came in the house worn out from cutting wood and ready for a hot meal.

Dawn, Kristi, and I were going outside to ride the bike again, and Dad looked at us sternly and said as he took his cowboy hat off, "You girls make yourselves useful and stack all that wood Steve and I cut."

It was starting to get cold, and my stomach was growling as my sisters and I stacked wood for the next hour. Then Lori called us in for dinner—humpies, rice, homemade bread, and green beans.

Dad let Steve and Lori join the 4-H club in Talkeetna, and Lori learned to make bread. I watched her this morning after breakfast knead the dough and cover it to rise with dish towels on the counter in the kitchen. Lori told me next time she would show Dawn and me how to make bread with her. Before supper she put the loaves into the new porcelain stove Dad had brought home from Anchorage.

It was hooked to the propane lines and sat on four strong legs next to the black iron stove in the kitchen. The ivory-white stove had a high back behind four burners on the top flat surface. The oven was small but big enough for a moose roast. Mom loved it and put it to good use after struggling to use the small iron woodstove for the past four years.

I sat to the right of my twin sister at our long wooden table as she was the only one that could put up with me being left handed. There were seven of us and soon to be eight counting Mom and Dad, and it was crowded on the benches. Dad had his own seat at the end of the table that he made special for himself.

All of us kids had our hands in our laps as Dad said a prayer before supper and bowed our heads with our eyes closed.

Sometimes I would peek up and see if anyone had their eyes open while the prayer was being said and felt guilty when I realized God was watching me.

With my right hand in my lap, my left hand was busy shoveling in pink salmon and homemade bread by the light of the propane lamps. Dad took a drink of some of Shorty's milk and looked straight at me and said, "Did you girls finish stacking the firewood?" Dawn put her head down, and Kristi had a mouthful of food.

Looking straight into Dad's blue eyes as mine got wider, I said to him, "Almost all of it!" Knowing we might get a lickin', I continued making my case, "Supper was ready, and it was getting dark!"

Dad pushed his chair back from the table and set his fork on his plate as all of us kids stopped eating and waited. He said, looking right at Dawn, Kristi, and me sitting next to each other on the same side of the table, "Well, you can go out and finish stacking the wood under the moonlight!"

My sisters followed close behind as I jumped up from the table and headed for the front door, putting my boots and coat on. Mom said as we were getting up, "Can't they just finish their dinner, Dennis?" We knew the answer even though Dad was silent and headed for our coats.

For the next two hours we stacked pieces of birch until our hands were ice cold and embedded with splinters. Steve came out and made sure we stacked the wood right so we wouldn't have to redo it, and then Dawn and Kristi and I headed into the house for bed.

Fair morning seemed like a blur when I climbed out of bed and put my clothes on. My head was spinning, and I felt worn out from stacking wood last night, as I felt the stinging blisters on my small hands.

Dad and Steve were already outside loading Dungo and Babe into the horse trailer. Mom had cinnamon rolls in the oven to take for breakfast on the ride to Palmer. Dad wanted to set out early to get a good spot at the fairgrounds to park the camper. It was Tuesday, and we were going to stay at the fairgrounds until Sunday afternoon after the big race.

Still dark outside, Dawn and I took Kristi out to the outhouse. I had to pee real bad and couldn't find my coat, so Lori loaned me hers.

When we got back, Dad was in the house and ready to go. Everyone put their coats on and mittens as the late summers were already cold early in the morning.

I looked around frantically for my coat that I had on last night and thought I put it by the door.

Dad seemed cross this morning and impatient as he said to everyone, "Load up!"

Dawn was helping me look for my blue parka all around the living room when I looked up at Dad and said, "I can't find my coat, Dad!" Mom and the others had gone out already and were loading up into the pickup and camper.

Dad's face was red, and his eyes were squinting as he said to me, "Stay home if you can't find your coat!" Tears started to well up in my blue eyes as I hoped Dad wasn't really going to leave me behind.

Dawn slipped out the kitchen door, looking back at me like she was never going to see me again. Dad grabbed his rifle and followed Dawn out to the driveway, shutting the kitchen door behind him.

Getting down on my hands and knees, I continued looking for my coat, hoping to find it before they all left me.

Suddenly, fear and loneliness gripped me as I heard the pickup drive away, leaving me home alone! I got up from the floor with tears running down my face and ran to the kitchen door, flinging it open!

It was barely light out, but I could see through my wet blurry eyes that my family was gone to the fair without me!

Feeling like no one cared about me and not knowing what to do next, I shut the door and went back into the dark house. Pete and

Dum Dum were left with me and lay on the floor with sad eyes like they knew.

All I wanted to do was cry, and that's what I did for the next few hours as I lay on the couch in the living room, thinking about the fun I was going to miss.

I must have cried myself to sleep because I woke up to the sound of heavy rain on the roof and forgot where I was. *Maybe it was a bad dream,* I thought.

I got off the couch and looked around to find an empty dark house just like it was when I fell asleep. It was raining hard, and the house was starting to get cold since Dad had put the fires out in the woodstove. Opening the front door, I let the dogs out and felt the chill in the air as the rain continued to fall. I was only seven and had not started a fire by myself yet and would probably get in trouble if I did.

It was close to noon, and I was hungry thinking about the cinnamon rolls Mom had made for the ride to Palmer. I knew how to make oatmeal and began heating water on the stove in a small pot.

It felt strange and lonely in the house by myself, something I had never experienced before. Our small house was always full of noise and voices with a big family in tight quarters. My twin was with me all the time, and my stomach felt anxious without her.

I sat down at the empty table all by myself and swallowed hard as I ate my lumpy oatmeal. Looking up at the propane lights on the kitchen wall next to the table, I wished I would have paid attention all the times I had seen Mom light them.

Slight rays of light streamed into the open curtains of our small windows with streaks of water running into the wood panes. Heavy rain continued to pound on the roof, and the wind was beginning to blow, causing the old cabin to creak as if talking to me.

Even though it was in the middle of the day, I was too afraid to go outside by myself even to go to the bathroom. *Slam!* My bowl dropped into the single sink as I jerked around in the direction of the opening to the trailer! "What was that noise?" I said out loud to the open air while my knees started to tremble.

I picked up the large flashlight and walked across the kitchen, slowly looking behind me every step of the way. Passing the large table and turning the flashlight on, I stepped up into Mom and Dad's bedroom, which was just a bed and dresser.

The dark hallway leading to Lori's room at the back end of the trailer suddenly seemed like a horror film that I had only heard about. The big alkaline battery flashlight was heavy and shone bright in front of me as I tiptoed down the hall.

I passed mine and Dawn's small built-in bed on the left of me across from a tall narrow closet with the door closed.

Lori's round crystal doorknob was rattling as I shone the light right on it! Was someone in the trailer? I knew I had to be brave and find out! Holding the flashlight like a weapon up in the air above my four-foot body, I grabbed the diamond-shaped knob to Lori's bedroom door and flung it open as hard as I could. Then scaring me worse, it came back at me harder as it slammed shut again! The trailer was shaking in the wind, and so was I as I jumped back into the dark hall, fearing for my life!

Once again I reached forward and opened the bedroom door and then slowly poked my head inside, looking for strangers. The door to the outside was open and swinging in the wind, slamming as it swung back and forth. Lori's neatly made bed was intact, and the small room was empty.

Like solving a mystery in the Trixie Belden books I had read, I figured out that the outside door slamming shut was making the loud noise and causing the doorknob to rattle.

One of our cows was wandering around behind the house, grazing, as I reached out and grabbed the heavy silver door, closing it tight.

Speaking of books, Lori had Harlequin Romances in her room that I was dying to read. Flopping down on her bed on my stomach, I thumbed through the stack of worn paperback books on her nightstand.

Still shaking, I took one that had a cowboy on the front holding a red-haired woman and closed the door to Lori's bedroom. It was called *The Ranch Hand*.

Before leaving the trailer, I squatted over the emergency toilet hole that was under a board in the hall and then covered it with lime powder that was in a bag next to it.

As I was squatting down, I spotted my blue parka wadded up under our bed! I must have taken it to bed with me last night and forgotten that I had.

Snuggling into the wool blanket on the long couch in the living room, I used the flashlight and began to forget everything as I entered the world of romance. A long time went by as I struggled with some of the adult words in the book.

Looking up, I noticed it was almost completely dark outside through the small living room door window. My stomach started to growl, and the house was freezing cold. I could see my breath as I peeled myself up off the couch. I still couldn't believe Mom and Dad had left me home alone. *What about the night?* I thought to myself.

I put my coat on and stepped up into the kitchen to look for food. Then I remembered the army rations in the garage!

Wanting to beat the total darkness, I quickly put my boots on and headed out the front door. The big wooden doors creaked open to the garage where Dad kept everything. I shone the flashlight on the cardboard box under the wood tool shelf in the corner of the garage that was labeled Army Rations.

As I stuffed my coat pockets with the little flat dark-green cans, I noticed Lori and Steve had been into them. Just as I was closing the box and getting up off the dirt floor, I heard something that made me stop in my tracks. "Meow, meow." My ears perked up as I thought I heard a meow! The sound was coming from the other side of the garage as I heard it again. "Meow, meow." I followed the sound, shining the light in all the dark corners.

Dad's new used welder, called a power plant, was blocking some boxes under one of his shelves. I peeked around the big blue square machine and shone the light. There behind the boxes I saw a skinny brown and black Siamese cat looking up at me and meowing like it was starving!

Not even wondering where it came from, I scooped the scared kitty cat up into my arms as she struggled to get down.

Holding her in one arm, I was able to shut the two heavy doors and latch them. Petting her and talking to her quietly calmed her down as I carried her into the house.

The long-haired cat was beautiful, and I decided to name her Missy as she slurped down the bowl of canned milk I poured her and ate the smoked salmon Dad had in the cellar. I opened my rations and ate cookies and crackers with strawberry quick mixed into the powdered milk I had made. Hoping Dad would let us keep Missy, I was thankful she was there to keep me company along with the dogs who were keeping their distance. The night set in, the rain had stopped, and the house was quiet, except for a few meows.

My heart sunk remembering Dad telling me to stay home and that he had really meant it. I broke the cold silence as I said to myself out loud, "Are they going to leave me here all week?"

Tired of reading and feeling left out, I put my pajamas on and gathered more blankets to put on the couch. Shivering from the cold house, I put my parka back on and snuggled under the three heavy blankets. Missy jumped up and curled up into a ball next to me on the couch, purring loudly.

As I lay there in the dark, quiet house, listening to the sound of howling wolves, thoughts of my family made me start crying again until I fell asleep for the first time without Dawn and my other siblings.

My swollen eyes opened to see the kitty kneading my chest with her claws to the morning light shining through the door window.

Overexhaustion had caused me to sleep into midmorning, waking to the empty house once again. Petting Missy didn't make me feel any better, so I decided to get dressed and go outside.

Just as I was putting my coat back on to step out into the clear day, I heard the sound of a vehicle coming up our road. Slipping my boots on, I ran to the kitchen door to see who could be coming to our house with me all alone. I decided I would hide if it was a stranger.

Peeking through the kitchen window out at the driveway, I was surprised and relieved to see our blue pickup drive up and park!

Practically breaking the kitchen door as I burst through it and onto the porch, I saw Mom get out of the pickup. Dawn was in the passenger seat and got out also.

"Devan!" she yelled to me as we embraced, both of us crying. Mom gave me a hug and said, "I was really worried about you!"

Dawn said through her tears, "I hope you found your coat." She and I laughed as she could see I was wearing it.

I told Mom how cold and scared I was and then showed her and Dawn the kitty I had found. Mom told me to put her back in the garage until we got back and were able to tell Dad.

The rides at the fair were so much fun, and Dad felt bad about me staying alone at the homestead. He let Dawn and me stay on the rides past dark every night with Lori and Steve. Aunt Wendy rode the rides too, and Grandma and Grandpa were there with Joy and Dougie.

Dad put Steve on Babe in the big race on Sunday for the first time. She was running against one of her foals named Julie.

The big metal gates were new this year, and all the horses had to get used to loading into the tight closed metal chutes.

We all watched from the grandstands as Steve sat up on the ledge of the metal gate, waiting to mount Babe. I looked up at Mom, who was worried about nine-year-old Steve racing with the older jockeys.

Dad had to lay the big black whip behind her, pushing her forward into the chute. Babe was shaking and quivering as Steve mounted onto the race saddle on her back and took the reins.

The trumpet sounded, and the twelve gates opened with a bang all at once, releasing racehorses as they jumped out of the chutes. We all gasped as Babe planted her feet, not moving from the chute, and was left behind in the dust. I watched intensely as Dad took his hand and slapped her ass!

Steve hung on as Babe leaped out of the metal chute, and with the crowd cheering, she ran like a blur! Catching up to the other horses and then passing every one of them except her foal Julie, Babe took second place in the race! A couple of weeks later, Dad ended up selling Babe to a lady in Palmer. Babe slipped out of her horse trailer one day and messed up her tendons in both back legs that got caught under the trailer and never ran again.

Mom won first place for her raspberry jam and got a blue ribbon, and then the fair was over and we were packing up to go home.

As I zipped up my parka on this brisk Sunday evening, I knew I would never forget this year at the Alaska State Fair, or my coat.

26

"TIMMY"

DAWN

Dad had ended up letting Devan keep Missy, the Siamese cat she had found in the garage. I think it found her! Missy followed us everywhere. All of us kids packed her around, and soon she was one of the family.

It was late September, and soon the fall leaves were covered in snow as winter was coming early as usual. Mom was due to give birth any day and stayed home most of the time now.

Earlier this month, the two beautiful black fillies got beyond the electric wire and away from the other horses. Dad was at work and we were at school when they took off together and had been gone for a long time before we kids got home that day. Steve took Dungo out looking for them, not knowing which direction the fillies could have gone. The next day Dad rode Dungo out looking for them also with no success.

A few days later, the Montana station that was south on the tracks got word to Dad that there had been a sighting of one of the fillies. She was lying in the bank, ripped apart by a fast-moving train.

The very next day, we kids were hiking out to the bus on our usual trail when Steve thought he heard something. We all stopped and listened, and it sounded like grunting, only not like a bear. Then we followed the sound that was strange but familiar coming from a ditch alongside the train tracks close to the trail. I'll never forget what we saw that day down in the ditch and what happened next. The other black filly was lying there emaciated with a missing leg after several days. She was still struggling to breathe, unable to lift her head. Steve didn't hesitate when he saw her suffering so bad for so long. That's when he lifted up the twelve-gauge shotgun he was packing as if he knew what had to be done. We girls stepped back, holding in the tears as he pulled the trigger, putting her out of her misery.

The school district had changed its policy to starting the first grade at six instead of five. They had built a new grade school on the outskirts of town that held third through eighth grade. First and second graders still attended the little red school on Main Street in Talkeetna, where both Kristi and Joy would go next year. The high school was even farther out of town and was being rebuilt also for ninth through twelfth graders.

One very early morning the fourth of October 1971, Mom woke up with frequent labor pains severe enough to make her cry. The rare sound of Mom weeping made me crawl carefully around Devan, who was sleeping next to me in our small trailer bed. The hall was dark, and Lori's door was shut.

I could barely see as I made my way to Mom and Dad's bed at the other end of the trailer. The thick wool blankets were thrown back in a hasty fashion, and the room was empty.

Poking my head through the narrow doorway into the kitchen, I could see Dad putting his boots on. Mom was sitting at the table, stretching her short arms over her enormous belly, sobbing and struggling to put her own boots on.

It was getting so cold in the trailer at night now I could see my breath. Devan and I slept with our clothes on to keep warm, and so I was fully dressed in my jeans and long-sleeve cotton shirt.

I slipped into the kitchen quietly and got down on my knees to help Mom as she patted the top of my blond head. Dad and Steve went outside to hitch the sled to the snow machine as there was already four feet of snow on the ground.

While I helped Mom with her coat and in between labor pains, she used our one-way phone to call Grandpa Vern. She asked him to meet them out at the community center with their rig as a new storm had moved in with high winds and more snow.

While Mom was on the phone, I ran back into the trailer and woke Devan and Lori up, "Mom's going to have the baby!" All three of us ran down the dark hall toward the kitchen to see them off as we knew we had to stay home alone for a few days.

Dad helped Mom get into the sled onto a bed of blankets he had made that were already covered in snow. Mom wrapped herself up with another wool blanket and pulled her knitted hat over her ears as she hung on to the metal rails with her gloved hands. She smiled at us through her tears and said, "We're going to have a baby real soon!"

As Dad mounted the Polaris and started the loud engine, he yelled to all five of us kids standing there, wishing we could go, "Keep the fires going and take care of the animals and each other! Stay close to home until we get back in a few days!"

That empty feeling came back into my stomach as I watched Mom and Dad until they were no longer visible through the blizzard that was getting worse.

Shivering and covered in snow, we all ran back into the warm house, shaking the cold powder off us. Lori immediately started shouting orders as she enjoyed being in charge. "Devan, go out with Steve and Kristi to feed the animals. Dawn, help me make hotcakes."

We still had Aunt Wendy's horses and two of our own to feed and dogs and cows. Dad had given the sheep back to the Lankfords as they turned out to be hard to raise in the winter.

Last year during the fair, Uncle Norman stayed at our house while the whole family was away for almost a week. Little Lamb was only three months old and still nursed from her mother ewe. Dad gave his brother specific instructions on how to lay the ewe down so Little Lamb could nurse. He decided to give her canned milk instead, and by the time we got home from the fair, she was deathly ill. Dad did something I never thought would happen. He rushed Little Lamb all the way to Talkeetna to a local animal doctor to try to save her life. Little Lamb could not be saved, and poor Kristi was devastated.

After breakfast, Lori and Steve chased us around the house with rubber bands. Devan, Kristi, and I tried to find places to hide in our small house. Devan and I ran into the trailer and jumped up into the narrow closet across from our bed and shut the door. Lori and Steve were right on our heels and opened fire on us with stinging rubber bands as we were trapped in the closet.

Later that day, Lori gave us all jobs to do to get the house clean while she read her book on the couch and Steve kept the fires going.

I didn't sleep much that night as the wind howled and the trailer shook. I was worried about Mom having her baby so far away from us and no way for Dad to call if anything went wrong. Devan and I stayed up late talking until Lori came out of her room and shushed us.

Two days and two nights had gone by slowly before we heard the snow machine coming from a distance. Devan, Kristi, and I were outside with Steve building a fort in the snow behind the house.

Dad pulled the snow machine up by the garage with Mom in the sled. I ran over to them with Devan, Kristi, and Steve not far behind. It didn't look like Mom was holding a baby, and she was wrapped up tight with a blanket. It was still snowing, but the wind had stopped.

Dad got off the snow machine as Lori ran out of the house. Mom pulled her head out of the blanket and smiled at all of us standing there with a confused look on our dirty faces. She unwrapped herself from the heavy blanket, and inside she was holding a papoose-like bundle in her arms.

All of us circled in on the large sled, elbowing each other for a spot. Dad spoke up proudly as Mom unwrapped the top of the blue bundle, "It's a boy!"

Grinning at each other, we couldn't wait to see him as suddenly two feet poked out of the top of the bundle! Mom looked pale and embarrassed at the same time. She had been holding him upside down the whole ride home on the sled! Quickly turning him the right way up and unwrapping the blue blanket, there was a little baby boy with red curly hair, big ears, and blue eyes.

Mom looked tired as she smiled and said to us kids wanting to touch him, "His name is Timothy Vernon!" I wanted so bad to hold him, but Mom handed him to Lori as Dad helped her get out of the sled. Lori carried Timothy into the house as he stretched and yawned inside his blanket. Mom fed him from her breasts and then went to their bedroom to get some sleep. All of us kids got to hold Timothy while we sat on the long couch and passed him around.

Dad came in from feeding and stoked the fires. In between turns of holding our baby brother, I walked over to Dad, and brushing my long bangs out of my eyes, I asked him, "Dad, can we call him Timmy?"

The weeks went by, and Timmy got bigger where he could hold his head up and smile at us as we all made faces at him. Along with holding him, Devan and I got to change his cloth diapers and rinse them out in a bucket.

Winter was closing in, and the snowstorms were getting more frequent as we stayed in the house together, missing days of school. Dad made it into Talkeetna after a blizzard let up one day and rented the small cabin at the end of town. Mr. Kozlowski built it many years ago, and it sat empty by the welcome sign.

We packed up enough stuff for a few months and moved into the tiny log cabin at the end of Main Street right before Christmas. There was only a small room that was about half the size of our living room when you walked in and a loft above it where we kids would sleep. Mom and Dad and Timmy would sleep in the room below the loft, taking up most of it. A closet-size room was in the back with a sink, stove, and a toilet. The loft upstairs was barely big enough for the five of us kids to sleep in on our makeshift bed of blankets and pillows. Dad and Mom wanted to be close to town since Tim was born so close to winter, and we may get snowed in at the homestead. We kids didn't mind as we could play with our friends from school around town.

Christmas was challenging in the tiny log house, so Dad got us a small tree that sat on a table. Timmy was over two months old his first Christmas and could sit up without help. He was so cute with his round face and thick curly red hair. Since our cabin was so cramped, we got to spend the night Christmas Eve at the white A-frame with Grandma and Grandpa. Us kids slept up in the spacious loft with Aunt Wendy and our cousins. That was the night Devan, Kristi, Joy, Dougie, and I were told by Aunt Wendy, Lori, and Steve that there was no Santa Claus. We were anxiously awaiting his arrival, wondering if Santa knew where we were.

We also got to go to church every Sunday and play with the Valentine girls. Grandma and Grandpa went to the Talkeetna Bible Church with Aunt Wendy and Joy and Dougie now, and we had supper at the A-frame often. Grandpa bought a new Ski-Doo snow machine and tied an inner tube to pull behind it. All of us kids, even Joy and Dougie, took turns riding it as we bounced up off the snow all the way down their driveway as Grandpa and Aunt Wendy drove the snow machine. So much fun and no chores!

Our great-uncle on Dad's side had a daughter named Devon, who was Dad's cousin, making her our second cousin. She was having problems at home and had to leave, so Dad let her stay with us in the cabin for a few weeks. Devon was big and husky with strawberry-blond hair and obviously had a mental problem. They left her in charge of us kids whenever they were gone, and they had no idea how mean she was to us. None of us kids liked her and tried to stay away from the cabin when Mom and Dad were gone. Even Lori and Steve didn't want to mind her as she hit us and locked us out of the cabin several times while she sat and ate chocolate quick out of the can that she made Kristi run to Nagley's to get her.

My twin sister Devan's and my eighth birthday toward the end of January, Mom and Dad left for a few days to a Christian retreat in Anchorage and left us with our mean cousin Devon. We were still living in the small cabin in Talkeetna, and Mom had left a cake and presents for us to have with the few friends we had invited for a small birthday party. None of us kids wanted to stay in the cabin until it was time for the party, so we hung out in town with our friends. We ran out of things to do, so we went to the railroad tracks, which ran right through Talkeetna, and played and put pennies on the tracks to see them get flat. Next thing you know, cousin Devon came walking up to the tracks looking for us and caught all of us playing on the tracks. She marched us home and canceled our birthday party. When Dad and Mom got home a few days later, cousin Devon told on us, and we got a bad lickin' for playing on the tracks. Lori told Dad how mean cousin Devon was to us, and he sent her back home after that.

We had to make frequent trips to the community center to get into the homestead to feed the animals while we stayed in Talkeetna. Dad went back to work on the North Slope so Mom would drive us all there and then Steve would take the snow machine in the mile and a half to the house. One of us always went with him, and the first time it was my turn, Dungo was antsy again from missing his feedings and tried to take a big bite out of my head, mistaking my hair for hay.

We finally got out of the crowded cabin and back to our homestead the beginning of March. I had a new appreciation for our house in the bush, which seemed like a mansion compared to the little log cabin by the welcome sign in Talkeetna.

27

BROKEN SPIRIT

KRISTI

Almost six and losing my place as the youngest kid didn't bother me, as I adored my little brother Timmy. We were amazed at his enormous strength and his big hands. Timmy would climb up on the couch and then pull himself up and look over the ledge that divided the two rooms at just five months old.

I couldn't wait until my little brother was big enough to play with me so I could show him the ropes around our homestead.

Dad allowed us to ride our bike that all of us kids shared, down our dirt road. Determined, I had learned to ride it by myself last fall, standing up, because I couldn't reach the pedals from the seat yet.

The orange two-speed made a perfect taxi with one of us as the driver picking up our passengers. Always watching for grizzlies, we waited nervously for the driver to come back for us, standing alone on the long heavily wooded road.

After living here for five years now, we kids could almost sense if there were bears or other wild animals nearby. We also knew their most popular hangouts, like the spring and the creek. We avoided the beaten-down grass trails and dens that were dug out of the bank, wide and deep like an Indian cave.

Steve would take the large rifle when we went to our windrow fort in the field that also made an ideal place for bears to bed down.

Dad's warnings rang in my ears for us to never be too confident as a grizzly was keen and swift. They could easily drag a small child off, leaving no trace, never to be found again.

Climbing trees was a necessity in the bush, and I eagerly learned when I was only three. Pulling yourself up into a tall spruce or cottonwood, sitting on a strong branch overlooking everything, was part of survival and the million things to do out here.

Running fast across our endless fields was my favorite thing to do either on my pretend homemade stick pony or on big Jude. One of the requirements for Dad letting us ride the horses was we had to get on by ourselves and ride bareback with just a lead rope. Only Lori and Steve were old enough to bridle and saddle them up. With a fierce desire to ride horses, I learned real quick how to get on when Steve wasn't around to help me. Usually by getting on something like the lean-to by the big barn sliding down the slanted roof onto Jude's back. When I get a little taller, Steve said he would teach me how to shimmy up onto the horse's back from the ground.

The way I figured with the energy that was inside of me waiting to bust out all the time, I was an outside spirit. Not wanting anything to do with the chores in the house like cooking, cleaning, and laundry, I stayed outside with Dad and Steve most of the time. Fortunate to have three older sisters that helped Mom with the house, I was able to fill the shoes of another boy.

The morning after we got home from Talkeetna, our black angus milk cow Shorty was about to have her calf. Dad was on the North Slope, and Mom was at Bible study in Talkeetna. Steve, Lori, and I hiked out to the windrow where she was lying in the snow under the trees.

Another hard winter with five feet of snow on the ground still and more on the way with below-zero temperature. The snow machine couldn't make it in deep snow, making it time to get out the snowshoes, which we had only one pair. Most of the time we kids just hiked and made deep trails through the snow in hopes it would still be there the next day.

By the time we got halfway out into the field to the big wooded windrow, Shorty was trying desperately to push her calf out while bellowing loudly. While she lay there on her side, struggling, she brought her head up to look at us with her big brown eyes. She was the nicest of all the cows, and we all loved her.

Steve said, "The calf isn't coming out. We should help her!"

My big sister tied her straight red hair back and said reluctantly, "Okay, Steve."

I watched as my brother and sister started to pull on the tiny hooves sticking out of Shorty as she heaved around, trying to push the calf out.

After several rest breaks, Shorty finally pushed her calf out with Steve and Lori's help except it wasn't moving. I forgot to breathe as we stood there looking at the pale little female calf while Shorty licked it. "It's dead!" Steve said, because it came out backward, it might have caused it to die. Poor Shorty lay her head down on the ground, moaning, while Steve and Lori and I dragged it off into the field for the wolves.

When we got back to the windrow to check on Shorty, we couldn't believe our eyes! Shorty wasn't moving either anymore and had also died right there in the windrow.

Dad finally got back from the slope and sold our last two cows back to the Lankfords after pulling them into the barn from the deep snow where they were almost frozen.

Every month in the winter, Mom and Dad took the snow machine and sled out to the highway to the car and went into Anchorage for groceries and supplies.

Since we kids didn't get to leave the homestead very often, usually just school and church, only one of us got chosen to go with them since there was limited room on the sled.

It was almost my birthday, so Dad chose me for the first time to go with them, now that I was old enough to hang on in the sled for myself. I felt honored and didn't even look back at my siblings who were waving as we sped off on the trail out to the community center.

Mom stood on the metal platform on the back of the sled with Timmy in a Gerry pack on her back. He was bundled up and had mittens on with a stocking cap Lori had knitted for him on his round head. Timmy's big ears were tucked under the cap, but his cheeks were already red before we had left.

My long thick red hair, which was always in my way, was tucked into my hood that was tied around my face. I had my hand-me-down jeans on and my snow boots with my mittens sewed to the yarn inside my coat.

Dad steered the Polaris with ease, cutting a new trail and sliding down the steep banks of deep snow as if we were on a roller coaster at the fair. I squealed with joy!

When we got to the community center, we loaded up into the Bel Air while I sat close to Timmy in the back seat. Mom and Dad seemed like they were mad at each other, which happened often, and were talking loudly about some woman.

After we got the groceries and sacks of grain at the big warehouse store, Mom and Dad took us to Mr. and Mrs. Lok's Chinese restaurant.

Timmy sat in a high chair by a small table with me, and Mom and Dad sat at the bar talking to Mr. and Mrs. Lok. I fed Timmy his baby food that Mom had bought, while I ate some soft long noodles. Mom and Dad had raw salmon made all different ways, which now they call sushi.

After lunch Dad told me to put Timmy and myself in the car as we were going to go home.

Since Timmy didn't talk much, I had never felt so alone as I endured the long hundred miles to the community center, plugging my ears to the sound of more arguing. I didn't know why they were mad at each other, but I knew Dad was done with whatever it was and slammed the car into park as we pulled up to the snow machine.

Wanting nothing more than to get home to my sisters and brother Steve, who had no idea how bad this trip was, I quickly jumped out of the back seat and started unloading paper grocery bags out of the car.

Dad was quiet and his face was red as he stacked the four fifty-pound grain sacks into the back of the big sled and two full five-gallon gas cans up against the rails on either side. Then I helped him put all the grocery sacks into the sled in front of the grain and gas.

Mom got Timmy in his Gerry pack while I lifted him up so she could strap him to her back. Then I sat myself down in the middle of the sled with the grocery sacks around me in front of the grain and gas.

Dad pulled the long cord, starting the loud snow machine, and then walked back to the sled to see if we were ready to go. He looked down at me sitting in the middle of the brown paper sacks as the cold snow was starting to fall again and said sternly, "Don't let any of these groceries fall out of the sled!"

As Dad drove the snow machine past the large white community center and on down our trail, I hung on to the several paper sacks of groceries, of which one had Dad's favorite ice cream. Remembering Dad's warning and lickins from the past, I put both of my small arms over the top of the paper sacks, hanging on to them for dear life.

Looking back at Mom standing on the platform, hanging on to the big bar above me, she smiled down at me as we sped through the woods faster than usual toward the train tracks.

The icy snow stung my face, so I put my hooded head down and closed my eyes, still hanging on tight to the now wet sacks, wishing we were home already.

Suddenly my whole life changed. The several hundred-pound sled went airborne for a few seconds as Dad drove the Polaris up and over a large snow-covered hill just before the tracks.

As the loaded-down sled made its way back down to the ground, the force of impact was so hard I felt myself bouncing up off the surface of the sled into the air above the sacks! I barely saw the large metal V-hitch as my small right boot got caught somehow, sucking my whole body down into the large black triangle!

Darkness surrounded me as I opened my eyes, trying to make sense of this coffinlike place where I was suddenly thrust! All I knew was I was unable to move and I was pinned flat on my back with my right leg bent up. The cold, rough deep snow was under me with a flat board right above my nose as my body was being dragged backward.

What's happening? flashed through my now terrified mind, feeling helpless as the earth kept moving with me on it!

I knew where I was when I could hear above me Mom repeatedly screaming for Dad to stop the loud snow machine as he sped through the deep powder.

It seemed like a long time before the endless sliding stopped and I could no longer hear the loud whining sound of the Polaris. I just lay there in the dark with snow packed in around me and the sled above me, hoping Dad wouldn't give me a lickin'.

Mom was crying out hysterically, "Kristi's under the sled!" I heard Dad yelling something and unhitching the snow machine from the sled.

My parents might have thought I was dead until a pain I had never felt before broke my silence with uncontrollable sobbing. Dad's voice was muffled as I heard him say, "Hang on, honey. We'll get you out!"

The severe pain was forgotten for a second when the last light of the dusk came in on me. I lay there on the ground, looking up at Mom and Dad straining to hold the heavy sled up. Mom was crying loudly as Dad looked down at me and said sharply, "Crawl out of there quick!" Then the severe pain coming from my right leg came back to me as I tried to roll to my stomach to crawl out from under the big sled.

Feeling like a wounded animal and not wanting to get crushed, I dug my mittens into the deep snow under me and pulled myself onto my stomach. Screaming, I began dragging my broken body out from under the sled with my twisted, bent leg, making a trail in the snow behind me! Using my left leg to push and pulling with both of my arms, I dragged myself past Mom and Dad's boots and clear of the sled as it came slamming down. My hood was off by now and my long hair was matted into my tears as I rolled carefully onto my back, cradling my right leg with both of my hands.

The next few minutes seemed like a blur as my small body started to tremble uncontrollably. I could see the tall trees covered in snow above me as I heard Dad's voice echo to Mom loudly, "Her leg is broken! Evelyn, go into the woods and get a splint!" Mom was too hysterical to follow through, and I saw her wander around aimlessly, crying with Timmy still on her back. Dad was strapping his rifle over his shoulder while grabbing a blanket out of the box on the back of the snow machine.

Next thing I knew, Dad picked me up off the snowbank carefully into his arms and held me like a baby wrapped in the small wool blanket. Leaving everything behind, he started hiking through the snow up to his waist as he told Mom, "Let's get her to the house!"

With my boots dangling over Dad's arms, he held me as still as he could, moving quickly past the empty cabin, as I saw his rapid breath in the freezing air. Somehow I felt safe and the pain had even subsided some as I looked up at Dad's determined face through my wet swollen eyes.

The last half mile to the house, I could barely see ahead of us through the blowing snow but saw the light in the window as Dad hurried into the front door. I saw Steve running toward us from the kitchen, hearing me crying loudly, yelling at dad, "What happened to Kristi?" By now the rest of my siblings were around me as Dad laid me on the couch. I was crying and shaking so hard it was unbearable. I looked down at the upper part of my leg through my wet face and saw my bone sticking straight up against my jeans! The twins were crying also while Dawn was wiping my face with a washcloth and Devan covered me up with a blanket. Lori, who hardly ever cried, was holding Timmy, sobbing loudly.

Mom was still upset but managed to use our one-way phone to call Grandpa Verne. She could barely talk to him through her hysteria and asked if he could contact the town nurse Francis Wolfe and have her meet us out at the highway. After that she called Uncle Dave to tell him what had happened. Neither one could offer any suggestions how to get me out to the highway without causing too much pain but would head over to help. Just then Dad came in the living room carrying one of our snowshoes.

Dad laid the three-foot snow shoe on the picnic table in the kitchen and then came into the living room to get me. When he picked me up off the couch, I screamed in pain and continued to cry as he laid me on top of the snowshoe lengthwise. He took our large scissors and cut my pant leg open all the way up to my hip, exposing the broken bone pushing up against my skin.

Then after Mom got a sheet and cut several strips, the real pain happened. I think my siblings really felt my pain when they were all screaming and crying along with me. Dad pushed my right leg down to the snowshoe trying to bring the completely broken femur bone back together! I didn't know much about dying, but at this moment, I was sure this must be what it feels like. Mom was hysterical while she handed Dad strips of sheet that he used to splint my legs to the snowshoe with so he could carry me out to the highway. Through all the crying and screaming in the house, Dad managed to work quickly as he knew I needed to get to the hospital. As we were getting ready to leave, he turned to Mom and said, "Evelyn, pull it together! You need to be strong for the kids." Grabbing his flashlight, he continued, "I'll be home in a few days!"

Lori, Devan, and Dawn kissed me goodbye through their tears as Mom wrapped me up with the small wool blanket.

Steve put his winter gear on with Dad's big rifle around his back. Dad picked up the snowshoe with me on it, and with Steve hanging on to one end, they began carrying me out the living room door into the dark night. I didn't want to go wherever I was going, but I knew I wanted this excruciating pain to stop.

My nine-year-old brother had a hard time hiking in the snow carrying one end of the heavy snowshoe. Dad picked me up and put the whole big snowshoe on his shoulder and kept on hiking with Steve holding the flashlight.

Lying there bound to the snowshoe flat on my back, unable to move, all I could think about was, "Am I having a bad dream? Why did this have to happen?" Grandpa Verne and Uncle Dave met us halfway in to help Dad carry me all the way out to the community center. That's when Dad sent Steve home alone with his rifle after he said goodbye to me.

Through the blowing snow and darkness, shifting from one shoulder to the other, moving quickly through the deep snow, my grandpa, uncle, and dad got me to the highway. Then Dad laid me and the snowshoe in the back of a strange small car.

Suddenly a lady came to the back of the car carrying a black bag and stood over me, but I couldn't see her face in the dark. Dad was standing next to her and said to me, "She's here to help you." The pretty lady took a syringe with a needle out of her bag and stuck it into my already numb body. I usually dreaded the shots us kids had to get at the community center, but this time I didn't care.

Instantly, to my relief, the sharp pain turned dull and I could breathe normal and try to go to sleep. Surely this strange lady who came out of nowhere had to be an angel sent from God!

I'm not sure how long I had been asleep or how I got in this shiny white room with long bright lights on the ceiling. I was flat on my back in a bed with white sheets with long metal bars on either side. My right leg was straight up in the air strapped to some kind of metal contraption.

Only able to move from the waist up, I pushed myself up onto my elbows to look around the strange empty room. The big electronic equipment lined the walls, and there was a big window that had a view of a big green lawn as the day lit up.

A pretty lady with a white hat came in carrying a big tray with silver lids and put it on the small table over the bed. When I realized I was in the hospital and she was a nurse, my bottom lip started to quiver as a lonely feeling came over me, already missing my family who were nowhere in sight.

I really was hungry, but not able to get myself to even look under the silver lids as the tears were beginning to well up in my eyes. The tall, thin nurse looked down at me and said, "Go ahead and eat, you must be starving." I was about to ask her where my family was when Dad and a man in a long white coat came into the room. Wiping my tears away quickly, I perched back up on my elbows and said, "Hi, Dad!"

The nice doctor who was shorter and heavier than Dad introduced himself to me and said, "You're a lucky little lady!" I don't know how I could have been lucky as my world was changed instantly, but I listened on. "You have a twisted compound femur fracture and will need to be in this Buck's traction for six weeks." I stared at the kind doctor silently, not knowing how I could bear being away from my family for what seemed like forever.

Dad took a hold of my hands, looked me square in the eyes, and said, "This is something you have to do to let your leg heal so you can run again." My heart was beating fast, anticipating being left with strangers so far from home as Dad continued talking to me, "We'll come see you as often as we can, and before you know it, you'll be home!"

Dad stayed for a long time watching a Western show on the small TV that was in the corner of the room up by the ceiling. I gladly shared my hot roast beef, mashed potatoes, carrots, and chocolate cake with him, feeling a certain comfort, knowing he was still there.

After Dad left that night and the nurse turned the lights out, I cried myself to sleep thinking about my mom, my siblings, and how I just wanted to go home.

Dad did come back and sat with me often, watching Westerns on the TV for hours on end. I watched them with him and got to know a cowboy named John Wayne, who instantly became one of my heroes.

I squealed with delight when he brought the whole family on my sixth birthday and my brothers and sisters got to come in the room for a short time. There was some rule about kids being in the hospital at that time, so they made faces at me through the big window while playing on the lawn. I was so happy to see Lori, Steve, Timmy, and the twins running around having fun looking just the same as I remembered.

That was the last and only time I got to see my mom and siblings until Dad came to take me home a month later. I got to know the nurses and my doctor really well and became quite the card. They would often bring me candy of all kinds and coins for the piggybank one of them got me.

Two days before I went home, the doctor took me out of traction and put a heavy white body cast on me. It went from the waist down, covering my right leg completely and half of my left. He said I would have to be laid up in the cast for six more weeks!

As Dad drove me into the homestead and I lay flat on the back seat of the truck immobilized and unable to sit up, something happened to me. Even though I was happy to be going home finally, I knew it would be different.

Every day was a new adventure for me on our beautiful wild homestead, and it was torture thinking about being left out. I would miss riding the horses, running through the fields, riding our bike, and fishing on the slough with a long stick and fishing line I found in the beaver dams. I tried to forget about what I was missing and hoped that time would quickly pass.

28

TRAPPED INSIDE

DEVAN

I was so happy our little sister was finally home, even though she had gotten a little spoiled at the hospital in Palmer.

Kristi seemed sad, like she didn't care anymore. It was probably because she had to lie on the twin bed in the living room in a body cast most of the time. I knew it had to be hard for her being the active tomboy she always was. Dawn and I tried to spend time with her coloring and playing board games that were stacked on our big wood bookshelf.

Kristi liked books also, so Mom got her the Trixie Belden mystery series that she seemed to enjoy reading by the kerosene lantern.

We all wrote messages and our names on her big white cast that was dirty by now, and helped scratch her many itches. Dad cut a long skinny willow and made it smooth for her to scratch under the long hard cast.

She couldn't sit all the way up or bend her legs, so we girls had to put a flat pink bed pan under her and then dump it after she went to the bathroom. I could tell it was humiliating for her with no privacy and everyone waiting on her hand and foot as she couldn't get up.

When it was mealtime, one of us kids would take her a plate of food that Mom had dished up. She would prop herself up on pillows and set the plate on top of her cast so she could eat. After eating at the hospital, Kristi had become quite picky. Mostly she liked potatoes any way they were cooked.

One day we started to smell something rotten coming from that side of the living room where Kristi lay and decided to investigate. Mom looked around the small bed and just about threw up. She found a moldy pile of old food on the floor behind the headboard! Mom looked really mad as we kids all gathered around, laughing hysterically. She said to Kristi, "Why did you throw your food behind the bed?" Kristi looked up innocently at Mom and said with a half smile, knowing she couldn't get a lickin', "I didn't like it!" Even Mom burst out laughing at Kristi having the guts to throw her food behind the bed instead of just eating it like she usually did.

It was May and Lori had just turned eleven when all the snow had finally melted with the spring rain. I had just finished the breakfast dishes on this rare sunny day as I stared out the small framed window above the sink. I opened the kitchen door to dump the soapy water from the large plastic basin. Tipping the basin off the rail of the small porch, I looked down and saw something shiny. There in the grass was a bunch of our silverware that must have been in the dishwater we dumped all winter and was covered in snow. Just as I was running down the steps to pick the several forks and some knives out of the grass, a big strange pickup with plywood around the bed came roaring into our driveway. Dad and Steve were out at the big barn letting the horses out onto the field. Aunt Wendy had taken her horses last fall to their place where she and Grandpa had built a new barn.

Two men and a young boy about twelve jumped out of the faded red pickup as Dad walked up to them and shook their hands.

Missy, our Siamese, followed at my heels back into the house where Mom was stoking the fire in the kitchen as it was still cold and Kristi had to stay in bed. Mom said to me, Lori, and Dawn, who were standing in the kitchen wondering who our company was, "We're going to plant potatoes today!" My sisters and I looked at Mom, who seemed to know what was going on as she said, "Dennis went in on some seeded potatoes with that man outside to plant here in our field." It sounded like fun to me and Dawn looked excited too, but Mom told her she had to stay inside with Timmy and Kristi.

Lori and I ran outside and helped unload the fifty heavy burlap bags of seeded potatoes and carried them out to the field. Steve had already plowed up a couple of acres next to the road that led to the slough.

Lori and I had to make long rows in the dark silty soil while Mom, Dad, and Steve cut each potato into quarters, leaving one eye on each piece.

Then we all planted the quarters six inches apart, placing them with the eye down into the holes we had dug with our hands. After that we buried them in the rich soil, pulling the loose dirt around the planted potatoes, making a hill on top as the plants will get big. Lori and I used the hoes and pulled all the loose dirt back into the wide rows and then packed it down. The potatoes that took several days to plant would get plenty of rain, requiring some weeding, and would harvest in the fall.

Soon the big puddles and slush on the road from the long winter and short spring evaporated into soft muddy ground. The occasional June sun warmed everything, bringing new hope and a new love for our homestead. Kristi finally got to go to Palmer with Mom and Dad to get her big awful cast off. Before that, on warm days, we would all help carry her outside in the sun and lay her in a chair, which seemed to make her happy. Along with the good news Mom told us while we were outside working. "I'm pregnant again!" Timmy was barely seven months old and still in cloth diapers, and Mom was three months pregnant and due to give birth next January. That didn't matter to us as another sibling made us chatter with excitement.

Mom said when the doctor cut Kristi's dirty cast off and had her right leg x-rayed, he said Dad did a good job setting the bone on the snowshoe. After the traction and long-time trapped in the clunky cast, the bone had healed properly but was a half inch shorter than the other leg.

When she came home on crutches and slowly put weight on her right leg, it made me feel warm inside watching her up on her feet having a good time outside. One day Mom caught her up on the long metal slide someone had given us that was propped up on the cowshed as it had no ladder. Kristi, only one week out of her cast, was at the top without her crutches and getting ready to slide down. Mom and we girls ran outside while yelling for her to "Stop!" She looked disappointed but got down and agreed to wait a few weeks to try the slide.

Dawn and I liked to sleep in the blue wood camper in the summer that was across from the front door against the woods. It was fun to sleep up in the cabover, looking out of the rectangular window into the front of the house. We would stay up late at night after being outside working for hours and read our paperback books. Summer solstice had set, providing us with constant light perfect for reading. Our favorites were the Harlequin Romances Lori passed on to us.

After fishing at the slough, Dad put salmon eggs on a piece of chicken wire that lay on top of a piece of plywood to dry out for bait. It was right in between the camper and the house on top of a small trailer.

One night in mid-July, Dawn and I were lying under the covers on the thin mattress in the cabover. We had our small paperbacks open to the midnight sun while the rest of the family slept in the house.

Thinking about the drama in Tennessee where I had gone in the story, I looked up to gaze out the small window. My eyes froze on a huge grizzly bear walking right past the camper. I immediately got Dawn's attention by putting my hand over her book that was open as she lay on her stomach next to me. She looked up startled with her mouth open and couldn't help but see the big brown hairy hump as it passed under the window.

Grabbing on to each other, both of us stopped our breathing as we heard stomping around while the wood camper swayed back and forth. I figured the huge grizzly bear was after the drying salmon roe that was in between us and the house.

Just then the door to our homemade camper that was closed with a hanger and a nail started shaking as the bear walked around the camper. Dawn's voice squeaked into my ear, "Is the bear going to eat us?" I have to admit that I was as terrified as Dawn as I intensely watched the door. I tried to navigate a plan to get us back into the house where everyone was sleeping. We didn't have any weapons, and I could still hear the grunting sounds the big grizzly was making as he looked for food around the camper. We were trapped inside the camper with a grizzly circling it and could easily get in if it wanted to. Dawn and I hung on to each other under the covers as we heard the crunching sound of the twigs as it seemed the bear was going toward the outhouse.

We stayed awake the whole night, frozen with fear that the bear would come back and break into the camper. We didn't move or read our books and didn't dare go outside even though Dawn had to use the outhouse real bad.

The next morning we waited until Dad pounded on the camper door to wake us up, and then we told Dad about the bear. He saw the large grizzly tracks around the camper and the outhouse. Later that day, he saw a new animal carcass buried in sand next to the spring trail. Dawn and I decided to sleep in the house from then on in our bed in the trailer where we were safe with the rest of the family.

With such a big family, laundry was always a huge chore, and one day in early July, to Mom's surprise, Dad brought home a new washing machine.

It was white and round with a big drum and had four big legs that held it up. The open drum spun around with a rotating center. It had a big roller on top with a cranking handle to squeeze the clothes dry. It was electric and had to be plugged into the power plant to wash our many loads of clothes.

At first we kids were fascinated watching the drum wash the clothes swishing back and forth. Then we found out we girls had to hang the clothes on our two clotheslines behind the house where we kept the washing machine.

Even on crutches, I saw Kristi get back to her old self, staying close to Dad and Steve with the horses and outside chores. The rest of us kids saw a new toughness in her even though she never wanted to go on the shopping trip again.

29

THE BUCKET BRIGADE

STEVE

The light breeze cooled my face as I spent my tenth birthday on our new John Deere tractor, making a second cut in our many acres of high green grass. We still had our little tractor, but this one was more efficient at a good used price. It had bigger tires, making it ride smoother, and had plenty of room for passengers.

It was going on eleven o'clock at night, I noticed, as I looked down at the black plastic watch Lori had got me for my birthday. Dad got me my own fishing pole, and I got new jeans from Mom.

Lori was sitting on the big fender well beside me, swatting at the pesky mosquitos. Mom, Dad, and the twins were weeding the growing potato patch on the west side of the field. Kristi was in the house with Timmy sleeping. One more hour and we too would all go in the house, shut the dark curtains, and go to sleep.

Summer meant a lot of work, fishing, and not much rest. It also meant the fair was coming in August. When Dad was at work, he had Mom and me ride Dungo around the field for hours, keeping him in top condition. Cecil Premis sold Dad a tall palomino mare who was well broke and fun to ride. Her name was CJ, and she was yellow with a white mane and tail. She ran fast and could almost keep up with Dungo.

The next morning I rolled off the couch as usual, half asleep, and reached for my crumpled-up jeans on the floor beside me. Just as I was tying my tennis shoes, I heard a vehicle drive up, and I ran to the kitchen to look out the window. It was Uncle Doug and Aunt Kathy, as they were married now and lived in Talkeetna. He was busy gold panning and didn't spend much time on his part of the property and his cabin at the end of our field. Kathy was my new aunt and a schoolteacher at the new Talkeetna Elementary School. She was tall and pretty with brown hair, brown eyes, and a slim figure.

Pete and Dum Dum started barking, waking up the rest of the family, except Dad, who I could see was getting dressed in the trailer. Grabbing my jacket, I ran out the kitchen door with the dogs to greet them.

Uncle Doug shook my hand and Aunt Kathy gave me a hug, and then I ran out to the barn to let the horses out onto the field.

After Mom and the girls made biscuits and gravy with moose sausage for everyone, we kids went outside to start our daily chores.

Dad and Uncle Doug were getting ready to hike to the slough to go fishing for silvers. Mom, Aunt Kathy, and the girls were going to go blueberry picking and were standing by the house with empty silver cans and mosquito dope.

When I opened the wooden gate to the big barn to let our three horses out, Dungo practically ran me over as he barged his way out to the field. His strong, thick neck was bowed, and his head was high as he ran his powerful machinelike body into the cut grass.

As soon as I walked back over to Dad and Uncle Doug, Dad said to me, "Dungo's all hopped up from running and the hot feed. Jump on him and take him down to the spring for water." Then he turned to go into the garage to get the fishing gear together.

Not saying a word, I ran to the cowshed and got the halter and lead rope. I was used to riding Dungo now and wanted to show off my skills, and right now he was in perfect shape. When I got out to the field, he was eating the healthy grass and stood still while I put his halter on, and then I shimmied up on his bare back, taking the lead rope in one hand.

Just as I was bringing Dungo's head up, he bolted forward and took off at a dead run across the field toward the house. Pulling back hard on the lead rope and wishing I had the bit, I yelled, "Whoa!" It didn't even faze Dungo as we streaked past my family standing in the yard. As I gripped my knees hard against our powerful stallion's lean rippling muscles, I heard Uncle Doug yell out to me as we flew by him heading toward the spring, "Hang on, Steve!"

I leaned forward with my head down, hanging on to Dungo's thick neck and mane as he sped down our narrow trail as tree branches barely missed my head. I could feel myself slide forward as we went flying down the steep gravel hill the last fifty yards to the spring. Suddenly Dungo came to a screeching halt when we reached the springhouse. As he slammed on the brakes, I flew over his head into the air like a trapeze artist reaching for his swing. I then flipped over and came slamming down hard on my back on top of a fifty-five-gallon drum that was in the grass. Everything happened so fast as I slid forward off the sandpaper-like rusty drum, making my final landing on my face in the mud and water next to the springhouse. I felt a sudden pressure on my back and pulled my face up out of the mud to see what was on my bare back as my shirt was in shreds. Dungo was towering over me with his right hoof on my middle back as if to hold me down. As Dungo showed me who was in charge, he calmly drank from the overflowing water next to the springhouse.

"Steve, are you all right?" I heard uncle Doug yelling to me as he was running down the gravel hill toward us. Humiliated and hurting, I looked up with my mud-soaked face lying there on my stomach with the hide scraped off my back. With all the air knocked out of me, I managed to squeeze the words out, "I think so!"

When Uncle Doug got down to us, he grabbed the lead rope and backed Dungo up off me. Then without saying another word, using the strong lead rope, he put a half hitch on Dungo's nose and jumped on his bare back. I could tell my uncle was mad at Dungo for taking off with me as he jerked Dungo's head up and took off with him up the hill.

After peeling myself up off the grass and mud, I got up onto my feet and hiked all the way back to the house to get cleaned up. The rest of the day I spent in the field on the tractor cutting more grass. After that Kristi, Lori and I made a swing under the big cottonwood in front of the house. Dad let us use a long thick rope he had in the garage to hang from one of the strong white limbs. We found a big old tire behind the house and made a great tire swing that all of us kids could have fun on.

One warm August day right before the fair, Dad drove the blue Ford pickup to the Millers' house several miles away to buy a car. It was a tan Ford Galaxy that I had seen Denny drive and would replace our Bel Air that was no longer running and was parked in the woods behind the camper. Our Ford pickup that we brought up from Oregon was almost out of commission also, barely starting most days.

Before Dad had left this morning, he told me to cut the pile of birch wood that was in the yard with our big ax while the girls stacked it up against the house. He told Mom to take Dungo out for a run, and so she saddled him up and took off toward the river while we kids kept stacking wood.

Kristi was hobbling around the yard on her crutches, trying to keep up with Timmy, who had learned to walk at ten months old.

Not long after Mom had left, Lori and I pushed Kristi, Timmy, and the twins on the tire swing as they sat inside the black hollow ring two at a time. Lori and I liked to stand on top of the tire, holding on to the thick rope while using our bodies to get the swing to fly back and forth under the big cottonwood. Laughter ringing out from my sisters broke through the mundane of our chores as we took an extra-long break.

The familiar sound of Dungo's hooves pounding on the hard-packed trail came from the distance. I turned my head to see Mom running him at full speed straight for the house alongside the field. I had a lot of respect for my Mom, who had turned out to be quite the Alaska woman, and she sure could ride!

I knew something was wrong because we never let the horses run right up to the house.

Mom looked distraught as she dismounted Dungo and handed me his reins as he nervously danced around the yard. Catching her breath and pointing south toward the spring, Mom said to us kids, "I saw smoke billowing above the trees in this direction all the way from the slough! It might be coming from the community center."

Holding Dungo tight, I looked up at the black smoke that was too close to home and said to Mom, "Want me to go find out?"

Mom said to me as she walked into the house in a hurry, "Go ahead and come right back. I'm going to call Dennis at the Millers."

After Mom ran into the house, I jumped up into the secure leather saddle and then pulled Lori up behind me.

Dungo was full of juice, snorting along the trail with his head high, pulling against the steel bit. He was leery of the strong odor of smoke coming from a blazing fire in the tall trees ahead of us. As soon as the empty cabin came in sight, I could see the fire was coming from the train tracks far below by Goose Creek.

Lori hung on to the back of the saddle as I reined Dungo toward the tracks, loping as we got closer to the fire. Panic set in as I pulled Dungo to a sudden stop. Lori and I gasped as we saw the Trestle Creek Bridge engulfed in red and yellow flames in front of us. I immediately whipped Dungo around and ran him back up the trail to the house to tell Mom as Lori hung on for dear life.

As I loped Dungo up into the yard, I yelled out to Mom, who was standing there with the twins, "The trestle's on fire!"

She looked alarmed and said to all of us kids, "Dennis is on his way. Gather some buckets and saddle CJ and Jude!" Lori and I ran to the cowshed to get the tack for the other horses, while Mom and the twins gathered five-gallon buckets. As soon as we had the mares saddled up, Dad and Denny drove up in the driveway with both the pickup and the tan Galaxy.

Kristi stayed at the house with Timmy, while everyone else climbed up into the saddles, doubling up. There wasn't enough room for me, so I ran behind the horses, carrying the eight empty five-gallon buckets all the way back to the creek. The fire on the bridge had gotten even higher and was burning out of control, destroying the wooden bridge and the tracks beyond it. No trains would be able to get through, and I was hoping none were coming at this time.

There was a man with overalls and a baseball cap from the railroad company climbing off his railroad car west on the tracks. He had a big canvas water bag strapped around his shoulder with a long spicket to put the fire out. We all knew that was for putting small fires out that sparks from the train wheels would sometimes cause along the tracks.

As everyone got off the horses, Dad yelled across the hot wall of flames to the railroad man waving at all of us standing there, "We can help!" Then Dad told Mom and us kids to wade into the creek and line up while he and Denny climbed the gravel bank close to the fire.

Mom was at the beginning of our bucket brigade with the eight empty five-gallon buckets with Lori in between the twins. Wasting no time, my pregnant Mom started dipping the buckets into the clear creek, quickly passing them down the line until all eight full buckets were moving. I stayed at the end up by the bridge and heaved the five-gallon buckets up to Denny, who passed them on to Dad. As quickly as Dad reached for a handle, he threw the water onto the fire and reached for another one. The empty buckets were retrieved by Dawn and taken back down to Mom until we had a family rhythm going. There were few words being said as us kids knew how serious the situation was and kept working diligently to help put this horrible fire out.

At first it didn't look like we were making any progress on putting the fire out that was destroying the bridge we kids loved so much and the only way for trains to cross the creek. My arms were tired and sweat was dripping down my face as it seemed like a long time before the raging fire began to go out. Wet and dirty, we all stood around as the last ember faded to smoldering smoke.

As we kids cupped our hands to wash our faces and quench our thirst out of the clear cold creek, the railroad man thanked Dad and all of us for helping to put the fire out on the bridge. Then everyone mounted up again while the twins agreed to hike behind the horses. Tired, we took our time riding home, bathing our sore muscles in the warm rays of the bright sun.

A few days later, an official-looking man from the Alaska Railroad company came out to the homestead and talked to Dad.

In appreciation for us putting the Trestle Creek Bridge fire out, he said they would put a regular crossing over the tracks for easier crossing east of the bridge.

With all of us kids and Mom standing there proudly, the railroad man also presented us with a gold-plated wood plaque that had words engraved on it.

The plaque read, "In appreciation from the Alaska Railroad, to 'The Clark Family Bucket Brigade.'"

30

REMEMBERING MEARDHA

DENNIS

With one more mouth to feed on the way, I knew another job wouldn't hurt. So with Evelyn getting bigger and Timmy still a baby, I took a job driving the school bus in her place. It was mid-September, and I got to take the kids to school on the bus the first day.

I took Kristi, who was still on crutches, and Joy, whom we picked up at the A-frame along the way, to the little red elementary school in town.

When I walked them into the front door of the one-room school, I felt bad for my daughter after I introduced them to the teacher and the class. She was tough but still had to reluctantly use crutches for a few more months as her leg was still healing. I still felt bad about the sled accident and knew it was traumatic for her and hard to talk about.

They were both acting shy as the desks were already almost full of kids. Little Joy walked into the room first and took a seat quickly at a desk in the front row. Kristi flipped her long thick red hair back, and looking up at me with her already watering blue eyes, she said, "Bye, Dad."

As I was getting ready to leave the schoolhouse, I heard one of the students say, "What's wrong with her?" I saw Kristi take a seat silently as her cousin Joy spoke up loudly, "She broke her leg on a snow machine sled!"

It was potato harvesting time, and the cold weather setting in was already starting to freeze the ground. I was looking forward to having plenty of potatoes stored in our root cellar by the spring that Steve and I had dug out of the dirt bank. We secured it with extra lumber to keep the potatoes from freezing this winter.

For several days the whole family had been picking potatoes out of the rich dirt underneath their green leafy bushes. We had been working as fast as we could filling many gunny sacks, but the freezing weather was coming already. I noticed some of the kids were eating potatoes right out of the ground raw with the skin on like an apple.

The man I invested in growing potatoes with showed up with a special machine that dug the potatoes up from the soil and then dumped them down a ramp into a gunny sack. The next day he loaded his half of the one hundred and fifty bags of potatoes on a flatbed truck and covered it with a canvas. He had to drive all the way back to Anchorage and it was late, so he put a lantern under the canvas while he slept in his truck that night in our yard. We put our share in the big root cellar by the spring and a few bags in the trailer where the twins slept.

After a late September freeze, the next morning the man checked his potatoes and they were all frozen and it was snowing. Steve and I hiked down to the cellar by the spring and noticed a lot of our bags had frozen also. We packed up the bags that were good and put them in the trailer also to try to save what we could.

A couple of weeks later, the unused potatoes in the trailer all rotted, stinking up the house, and that was the end of potato farming in Alaska for us.

It was cold and snowing in October after Timmy's first birthday when I was driving the school bus one morning. Joy and our oldest five kids were loaded into the long yellow bus, along with eighteen other school kids on my route.

I was just getting into Talkeetna, passing the welcome sign and entering the main street, when I saw a dog with long red hair running down the gravel street going in the opposite direction. As the slender dog got closer its graceful gait of the Irish setter reminded me of Meardha. Our dog I had brought from Oregon had been gone now for three years, and we never knew what had happened to her. We all still missed our gentle and playful Irish setter.

I was staring at the beautiful dog as it ran by my slow-moving bus, and not able to take my eyes off it, I wondered, "Could it be Meardha?" I immediately stopped the bus right in the middle of Main Street and put it in park. Steve, who was right behind me in a seat with Lori, tapped my shoulder and said, "What's going on, Dad?" I turned to him and said, "Sit still for a minute. I have to get out."

I opened the door to the bus, quickly climbing down the steps to the street, looking in the direction the Irish setter had gone. I could see her small frame running toward the service station, and so I called out once, "Meardha!" The red dog stopped in its tracks several yards away and turned toward me and then just sat down and looked straight at me. I looked back at the bus and noticed the windows were steamed up from all the kids watching. Then I yelled a command like I knew she would remember, "Come!" Then something wonderful happened as Meardha ran as fast as she could to me, remembering who I was as she jumped up on me, licking my face. I was as happy to see her again as she was to see me, and I was sure it was Meardha, our dog.

I think we all forgot where we were for a moment in time when Meardha ran to our kids standing on the steps to the bus, smothering them with affection. Steve, Lori, Devan, Dawn, and Kristi were all talking at once and wondering if we were going to take her home. I had the kids get back in their seats and started the bus while Meardha sat on the street right below the steps looking in at me through the open door. I said to Meardha, "Come!" The next thing I knew, Meardha was bounding up the steps straight to me, jumping up on my lap this time as I sat behind the steering wheel. All the kids on the bus, including ours, were cheering as I had Meardha lie on the floor of the bus right next to my seat.

Pulling the long silver handle and closing the doors to the bus, I finished my route dropping all the kids off at their schools. As Lori got off the bus, she hugged Meardha and asked, "Are we taking her home with us?" All my kids' ears were perked as I looked at my oldest daughter and said, "You bet we are!" When we got to our road that late afternoon in the dark, Meardha knew the Ford pickup and jumped right up into the bed of it with the kids for the two-mile ride home.

When we got to the house, Evelyn was happy to see Meardha and told me that a couple of days ago, she was at the service station in town. She said a dog that looked like Meardha jumped up on the pickup window and she forgot to tell me.

The next day was Saturday and I had the day off, so Evelyn and I left our six kids at home and took Meardha into Talkeetna to the service station. Gary Johnson was the owner, and I had known him for some time. When Evelyn and I pulled up in the blue Ford pickup with Meardha sitting on the long seat in between us, he came out of the wooden station and walked over to us. Opening my squeaky door, I got out, leaving Evelyn and Meardha in the pickup and shook Gary's hand. He leaned around me and looked into the pickup at Meardha and said coolly, "Why do you have my dog?" Before I could answer, he reached through the open window and called her Moira. Meardha just sat there looking at him as she perked up her long floppy ears. I said to Gary, "We lost our Irish setter three years ago, and I'm sure this is Meardha. She came right up to me yesterday."

Gary turned towards me and replied, "I found her three months ago running along Parks Highway from the south. She had tags that say she came from Anchorage and her name is Moira." I was thinking hard about how to prove to Gary, who was a friend of my brother Doug's, that she was our dog as he continued getting more frustrated, "My kids are already attached, and we want to keep her. She can't be yours, Dennis!" Then I remembered she had gotten a broken pelvis in Anchorage when we were living there our first winter in Alaska. A car had hit her, and I was sure we had records at the animal hospital that treated her. I looked at Gary and said, "I'm sorry, but I had her for five years then she disappeared three years ago, and she remembered me right away when I saw her." He wasn't having it and tried opening my driver's side door, calling Meardha out of the pickup.

I just stood there as Evelyn was staring at me out the back window with a confused look on her face. Meardha didn't budge from the seat next to Evelyn. In fact, she lay down as if she was ignoring him.

Gary turned to me and said, "I don't want any problems with you, Dennis, but you will have to prove to me that Moira is your dog."

Tilting my cowboy hat back, I looked him straight in his brown eyes and said, "I'm taking Meardha home with us! I can get a veterinarian in Anchorage to prove to you she is our dog!"

Gary slumped off, waving back at me to leave, and said, "You can take her for now, but bring me the proof." I felt bad because I liked the guy and knew he had to explain to his family, but the miracle of finding Meardha overwhelmed anything else as I was glad to have her back.

That Monday morning, I took Meardha all the way to Anchorage to the same animal hospital that healed her pelvis five years ago. It cost me one hundred dollars to have her x-rayed again to prove what we already knew that she was our dog. I took the report to Gary and then drove home in the snow with Meardha sitting right next to me on the seat. She was looking out the front window, panting and smiling as if she knew she had finally made her journey home to her family.

As usual the snow continued to fall with plenty of blizzards and freezing weather. I continued to work on the North Slope and was gone from the homestead, leaving Evelyn with the kids for weeks at a time.

In November we decided to rent the small cabin again in Talkeetna for the winter as Evelyn was due in January and we could get snowed in on the homestead. All eight of us and our three dogs buckled down in the miniature cabin, awaiting the arrival of our seventh kid, making nine of us!

With the family in town now, we still had to keep our horses at the homestead and go in on the snow machine a couple of times a week to stock their feed. Evelyn's parents were close by and helped get Steve and Lori to the community center so they could ride in and feed when Evelyn needed rest. I felt a certain comfort knowing her family were there when I was away at work.

Evelyn's little sister Wendy was quite the firecracker and wasn't very fond of taking direction from anyone, especially me. Wendy had a love for horses, and even though she didn't agree with all my training methods, she respected my skill.

One day back in October, Evelyn, Wendy, and I took Dungo to Wasilla to a home for stud service where I could make some extra money. By the time we got close to Wasilla, it was getting dark and I couldn't find the people's home. We got lost and ended up on a lonely road in the woods that led to a small cabin that was overgrown with brush. I saw a dim light in one window and told Wendy to go knock on their door to get directions. Her straight red hair was clipped up on the sides, and her glasses were steaming up as she gave me a look and then climbed out of the pickup.

I didn't see the door to the cabin open after she had knocked a few times, and then Wendy ran back to the pickup, closing the heavy door behind her as she said, "Somebody yelled at me to go away, and a dog was barking!" I looked at her and said, "Go back and knock again!" Evelyn kept quiet, sitting between Wendy and me in the pickup as her teenage sister told me, "You go knock!"

I had to unhook the horse trailer just to turn around and had Evelyn direct me back to the hitch. I ended up getting frustrated and yelling at her when she couldn't get me straight on with it. Wendy was mad at me and took over. We successfully got the pickup hitched to the horse trailer again in the dark and then finally got to our destination. I have to admit, Wendy was a pretty tough girl and a handy person to have around. We ended up getting back late, so she stayed the night with us in the small cabin, sharing the loft with our other six kids and then later moved to the couch below.

It was almost Christmas now, and a few weeks ago I asked Wendy if she would help me get Dungo back into the homestead. I knew she was a good rider and thought we could get closer if we spent time together.

To my surprise, she agreed, and so the next day we went and picked Dungo up in Wasilla and headed back to the main road to the homestead.

There was no way the truck with the horse trailer was going to make it through the completely snowed-in road as we arrived to four to five feet on the ground. I decided I would have to ride Dungo in to the homestead. I turned to Wendy as I was getting out of the truck and said, "I'm going to have to ride him in on the packed train tracks and then hike back out. Do you want to go?" Wendy agreed reluctantly, and then while she bundled up, I unloaded and saddled my big red stallion up for the long ride.

It was snowing hard when Wendy put her boot in the stirrup. I reached down and grabbed her hand, swinging her up behind me on the large leather saddle. Dungo trudged a half mile through the deep wet snow until we reached the train tracks. The snowbanks between the thick woods and the tracks were at least six feet high from the railroad company blowing the snow. As I reined Dungo up onto the tracks, I thought to myself, if I could make it to the trestle bridge on the bare tracks without a train coming, then we only had a half mile to the house.

I turned to look at Wendy behind me holding on tight to the back of the saddle, her breath visible in the air. She must have thought this was going to be the scariest ride she ever went on when I told her, "Watch for a train coming behind us and I'll watch in front." Wendy looked startled as she said while I trotted south on the tracks, "I hadn't thought of trains coming!"

As we rode Dungo along the narrow snow-packed railroad ties, I noticed Wendy craning her head to look back for oncoming trains. I untied the red cloth always tied to my saddle and handed it to Wendy, "So if a train comes, you jump off," I said to her as she looked at the steep bank towering up with little room between it and the tracks. "I'll take off running as fast as Dungo can go, and you climb the bank and flag the train down." These days you could flag a train down with a red or white cloth anywhere along the route and stop a train to catch a ride.

Wendy's face was pale through her cold rosy cheeks, and I could tell she was scared as she said, "Let's pray I'm able to climb the bank quick enough!" I kept Dungo at a fast trot for the next mile on the tracks, and thankfully, no trains came until we finally got to the snow machine trail where the snow was still packed down. We both could breathe again, and we're grateful we made it to the homestead and back out again.

31

"MIKEY MAKES NINE"

LORI

Every winter the northern lights lit up the sky more magnificent than any fireworks show I had ever seen. I stood outside the small log cabin in Talkeetna with my brothers and sisters, mesmerized by the beautiful array of colors. The moon was half full, hanging in the background like it was part of the elaborate scene.

It was January, and Mom had gone into heavy labor a few days ago. Dad took her to the hospital in Palmer, leaving us kids alone with me and Steve in charge of our younger siblings. We went to school and did our chores as we anxiously waited for news. It was just like Christmas, only we were anticipating a special package. Dad was hoping for another boy, and Mom was sure it was by the way her stomach was shaped. She said he was strong and kicked hard like he was made of iron.

Our homestead that lay below the McKinley mountains had the best view of the northern lights. Our large field covered in the white snow acted as a large empty canvas. The fluorescent greens, blues, and pink reflected God's artistry for a moment in time for few to see. I would try and mimic the colors as I painted at night in my room on any kind of canvas I could find.

My dad was a great artist, and I loved watching him create paintings as he sat in front of his large wood easel in the living room.

Hoping I could paint like him someday, I would go into a trance watching his strong hands lightly stroke the canvas into something for my eyes to enjoy. The first painting Dad did in Alaska had hues of blue with a bucking bronc rider and cowboys leaning against the corral watching in the fog. It was one of my favorites, but he gave it to our friends the Seales in Anchorage. We kept a few framed and on our wall that were just as beautiful and made the living room come alive. There was one of a wolf howling at the moon perched on a cliff overlooking a canyon with a blue and white winter setting. The many large bald eagles we saw inspired Dad to paint them as they came to life. The big birds spread their wings over a large canyon above a carcass below using brilliant shades of red. I was thinking of asking for a set of acrylic paints and a canvas for my twelfth birthday this May.

It seemed like there was never a dull moment at our homestead, like last Halloween when Mom took us kids to the community center for a party. We all dressed up in homemade costumes with some store-bought accessories and hiked the snow machine trail there and back. Kristi and I went as witches, and the twins and Steve covered themselves in white sheets as ghosts. Mom cut holes in them for their eyes and mouth. There were lots of kids in costumes at the spooky decorated center with candy and apples to bob. All of us kids had a great time that Friday night, and to put us more in the spirit, on the hike home later, the wind from the oncoming blizzard blew Kristi's witches hat and more pieces of our costumes in the wind far above the trees. We kids ran around unsuccessfully trying to save the costumes we had worked hard on while falling into the deep snow laughing. The smoke from the chimneys and dim light in the living room door window came into sight, and Halloween ended for another year.

Right after that, Steve and Grandpa Vern went caribou hunting with Dad on his annual trip. They were gone for several days to Lake Louise in the Copper River Basin for the Valdez herd. Steve shot his first caribou at ten years old with the thirty-thirty rifle and then brought it home with the antlers as a trophy. Grandpa Verne shot his own caribou as well as Dad, and they proudly laid the large animals in the snow while Mom took Polaroid pictures.

The northern lights continued to shower their mystery over us as I sat on the wood deck in front of the small cabin with Steve. Meardha lay beside us, bathing herself in the affection of her reunited family while I stroked her soft red hair. The twins played red light, green light with Kristi and Timmy. Timmy was fifteen months old now and had a full head of curly red hair. He was shy most of the time unless he was singing to us, which he often did.

It was almost morning when we kids went to bed, and it seemed like I had just fell asleep when bright headlights shone into the cabin windows. As I shook Steve and pulled my long hair into a rubber band, the twins and Kristi sat up in their blankets, staring into the bright headlights like deer. I said to all of them, "I think Mom and Dad are home!" Kristi, who was off her crutches now and only had a slight limp, ran down out of the loft to greet Mom and Dad first. Mom came through the heavy wood door with the cold wind seeping in, giving me a chill in my long cotton nightgown. She had a certain glow in her face and held a bundle in her arms as the rest of us kids climbed down the ladder. Dad came in smiling after he had parked the pickup and said to all of us standing around Mom as she unwrapped the blue blanket, "Your new brother makes nine of us!"

All of us edged in, elbowing each other to win the chance of holding him first. There inside the warm blanket in Mom's arms was a beautiful baby boy stretching his little arms and yawning with his perfect mouth. He had blond hair with red highlights and big baby-blue eyes that looked gentle and wise as he gazed around at his big family. Mom and Dad took their coats off as we kids held our baby brother on the couch, taking turns.

Michael Dennis Clark was born on January 27, 1973, weighing eight pounds and ten ounces.

A couple of months later, right before we moved back out to our homestead, we all went over to Grandma and Grandpa Stanton's house for an early supper after church. My great-aunt Pat, who was Grandma Gloria's sister, was visiting from California with her husband, Charles Chase. He was the chief editor for the *Los Angeles Times* newspaper and was quite well-known. They had five daughters who were our second cousins and all in their late teens. Their names were Nancy, Teresa, Mary Jean, Patsy, and Caroline.

Mikey, which is what we siblings called our new brother, was lying in my arms as I sat in the front seat of the pickup as Dad drove up in front of the A-frame. Mom was next to me in the middle with Timmy on her lap. Devan and Dawn, who had just turned nine, were riding in the bed of the pickup with Steve and Kristi and our dogs. Lad came bounding across the snowy ground up to the pickup to greet us as we all climbed out.

Dad told us girls to see if Grandma needed help in the house with supper, while he and Steve walked out to the barn where Grandpa was standing. Mom took Mikey from me as we walked into the A-frame through the big orange door. Kristi and the twins took Timmy with them up the wood stairs to the loft to play with Joy and Dougie.

The house was full of company, but I didn't see my aunt Wendy or my second cousins. I asked Grandma, "Where is everyone?" Grandma Gloria was short and plump with graying brown hair that was set with curlers. Always smiling, her deep dimples lit up the room as she tried to keep a positive attitude with her strong faith in God. She turned from the pot roast cooking in the oven and told Mom and me, "Pepper's pneumonia has gotten worse, and he's going to die."

Mom looked sad as she said to me, "Go on out to the barn if you want."

As I raced out to the steel A-frame barn that sat up against the tall birch trees, I thought about old Pepper, who was born even before my aunt was. Dad let me spend the night with Wendy often, and I got to help her feed her two horses day and night. We would go for long trail rides, and I rode Pepper, who pranced and danced around when experienced riders were on him. When the younger kids were on him, he plodded along like he knew they were learning.

When I got to the barn and went inside, Aunt Wendy was crying and kneeling beside Pepper, who was lying in the hay. He was coughing, and there was mucus running out of his nose and mouth. Poor skinny Pepper had been sick for a while, and I could tell he was tired as I joined Wendy on the ground. Our second cousins were standing around Pepper, feeling bad for him and Wendy. Grandpa Vern was talking softly to Dad behind us, and I heard him say, "I can't do it, Dennis." Steve came in the barn with Dad's rifle as Wendy and I looked at each other as if knowing what had to happen. Grandpa Verne helped Wendy up off the hay and said to us, "Go to the camper and shut the door."

Steve, Wendy, Teresa, Mary Jean, Patsy, Caroline, and I all walked out of the barn toward Grandpa's new camper that was sitting on pallets in the yard. Wendy and I watched as Dad led Pepper away into the woods with tears in his eyes. One final wave goodbye, and they disappeared into the forest as we shut the door to the camper. We all knew Aunt Wendy was falling apart and wouldn't be able to stand hearing the gunshot, so all her cousins broke the silence, loudly talking and making jokes.

A little while later, Steve, who was looking out the camper window, said, "Dad's back!" All of us slowly got up and stepped out of the camper watching Dad walk back into the yard with his head down and his face hidden under the brim of his cowboy hat, as if it was something he hated to do. I knew it had to be one of the saddest days for Wendy ever because I had never seen her cry so much as Pepper left our lives forever.

Even though being in town was fun for all of us kids, the homestead never looked so good. Staying in the small cabin was cramped with all nine of us, and there was absolutely no privacy, making me appreciate my own room at the end of the trailer.

It was spring, and the warming temperatures melted the snow into large puddles and new ruts on the road and in the yard.

Mikey was adorable, and Devan, Dawn, and I fought over who got to carry him around. Until it was time to change his cloth diaper and rinse it out, then it was usually Dawn who volunteered. Mom breastfed him still while she sat in the living room in Dad and Meardha's easy chair often as he grew chubbier every day. We had fun looking through the family photo album, amazed at how much

Mikey looked like Dad. He had straight blond hair and sky-blue eyes like Dad did when he was young.

Timmy never left his new little brother's side, wanting to touch him and help us take care of him. He looked a lot like Dad too as they had the same nose and their hair parted the same way. Quiet Timmy had big round blue eyes that were innocent and kind. Someday Tim and Mike would be great pals, two different spirits balancing each other through life.

It was the end of April as a full moon, covered in shreds of black clouds traveling with a north wind, lit up the morning hours. We older five kids waved goodbye to Mom as we stepped out the front door to hike out to the bus. I had my long thick felt coat on that tied around the waist and my snow boots that went up to my knees. Kristi had just gotten a new Eskimo-style fox skin parka that was royal blue and had brown fur around the hood. Mom and Dad got it for her for her seventh birthday and then Grandma got Joy one just like it that was brown.

Steve walked ahead of the twins and Kristi, with me in the back, along our trail as we each carried our paper sack lunches in our mittened hands. Every school morning the twins and I made sandwiches for us kids to pack for school. It was usually tuna fish or peanut butter and jam. Dad was already at work for BLM, and Mom stayed home with Timmy and Mikey.

There was still a lot of soft snow on the sides of the trail that was lit up by the bright moon above us as we quietly trudged by the spring. The heavily wooded area before the empty cabin gave me an eerie feeling like there were eyes upon us. I almost ran into Kristi, who was in front of me, when Steve suddenly stopped to let a flock of ptarmigan scatter over the snowbanks.

We were just getting ready to continue on our way when we all froze right there in our tracks, staring straight at a huge scraggly gray timber wolf. His long black-and-gray hair stood up, and his skinny back was bowed. The large wolf's sharp teeth shone under the moonlight as he faced us off in the middle of our trail only fifty yards away. Steve didn't have a gun, and with our younger sisters with us, it would be hard to get away, I thought, as I grabbed on to them, pulling them against me. Steve slowly backed up to us and said quietly, "We may not have time to climb a tree!" The twins and Kristi held on to me tight, shaking with fear, trying not to make noise.

As Steve and I started to back us all up slowly, watching the fierce-looking wolf in our trail, another big wolf came out of the trees to join him. By now I was shaking in my boots and frozen with fear knowing the starving wolves could rip us all to shreds. My warrior brother Steve stood in front of his sisters as if protecting his tribe and was willing to be eaten first. I whispered to them quietly, "Keep backing up. There is a large spruce we can all get into if we climb quick."

Just as the words left my mouth, another big wolf came out of the thick dark curtain of trees and then another and another and another! We knew wolves ran in packs following the caribou runs. They were like the gangs of the woods outnumbering their prey without discrimination. The twins and Kristi were whimpering, trying not to cry. I slowly pulled on their coats to keep them backing up with me to the big tree only a few feet behind us. Steve and I knew we only had a small chance of surviving this hungry snarling pack of wolves without a gun or flame to scare them off. All I could think about was that Mom and Dad would lose five kids in one morning and would never recover from the tragedy. In the seven years we had lived out here, I had never seen a pack of wolves this close to us, facing us off, ready to attack.

I quickly counted seven of the vicious animals standing on the trail, bowing their backs and gnashing their long sharp teeth at us in the moonlit morning. Steve's face was pale and his golden eyes were wide with fear as he looked back at me and said with a trembling voice, "Lori, get yourself and the girls up into that tree behind us. Don't look back!"

Tears started to freeze on my cold face as I stared at my brother as if it was for the last time. He turned back to face the wolves and whispered loudly back to us, "Now!" Even though Kristi had a bad leg, she could still climb a tree like a squirrel, so instantly I grabbed her around her parka, picking her up as the twins clung on to my long coat.

I did what Steve said and stepped back to the large spruce, heaving Kristi up onto the first branch. Then grabbing Dawn, Devan and I pushed her up behind Kristi, who was already pulling on Dawn's hand to help her up.

It was only seconds before all four of us were climbing up into the spruce as we kids knew the drill. I could hear the wolves snarling, and as I looked down to the trail at the wolf pack still lurking, I didn't see Steve!

Just as I was about to scream for him, his red head popped up into our tree as he was reaching for branches to get higher. Steve was out of breath and shaking uncontrollably as I reached for his hand to help his drained body to the larger branches where I had the girls.

Devan and Dawn were holding on to each other tightly on a sturdy branch, and Kristi was above us on another one hanging onto the tree trunk.

I gave Steve a quick squeeze, grateful he made it out alive as the pack of wolves slowly gave up on us being their breakfast. We watched from the tree as their scraggly gray bodies sauntered off into the dark woods.

Steve and I knew we couldn't get out of the tree until we felt safe, and besides that, we were too scared to get down. Devan said as we stayed on the branches, still in a state of shock, "Our guardian angel must have been with us!" I smiled and then started crying as my body trembled with gratefulness. Steve put his arm around me and said, "Don't cry, Lori. I'm gonna carry the rifle with me from now on!"

It seemed like hours before daylight broke through the long needles of the spruce branches where we kids still sat talking about the wolves. Steve's watch said nine o'clock, and we knew we had missed the bus for sure. So we climbed down out of the big spruce and headed home as fast as we could. Steve was leading the way carrying a dead branch to use as a club. Mom was surprised when we burst through the front door, all of us out of breath, talking at once about our close call with the large pack of timber wolves. It was a story never to be forgotten as we kids grew stronger and wiser to the wilds of Alaska.

32

"WHAT A RIDE!"

KRISTI

Freedom swept through my long thick red hair, raising it like an open flag as I gripped my bony knees against CJ's bare back. My small hands pulled on the thick lead rope attached to her halter to keep control as she raced across our field toward the mountains. It felt wonderful to ride against the wind cutting through the high grass without a care in the world. Our golden palomino was flying like a magic carpet with me as the Indian princess warrior. Throwing grass and mud out behind us with her large hooves, she rounded the windrow, unaware of her light load.

Riding bareback was the only way I knew how to ride a horse, and I did it well. Dad had taught us how to sit properly with our backs straight and shoulders rolled back. Then we would grip our knees against the ribs of the horse and relax our behind. I figured out real quick if you did those exact things, you would naturally flow with the movements of the unpredictable animal and not fall off!

CJ's big blond mane hit me in the face as I lay lower to cut the wind. When we got close to the other horses in the field, I stopped her and slid off to the ground, landing on my feet. Unbuckling the halter from her big head, I gave her a nudge and walked back to the house. Meardha, Pete, and Dum Dum scampered across the yard to meet me at the edge of the field.

I barely remembered Meardha the first time we had her before she was kept in Anchorage for three years. When she finally came home, she was pregnant by a black Lab the Johnson family had, and this spring she had puppies, which were whisked away down to the frozen slough. The harsh reality of feeding seven kids and several animals that were multiplying year after year was known to all of us. Lori was the only one that had the guts to argue with Dad in situations like this, defending her love for animals. It usually got her nowhere.

A couple of days later, Mom and Dad were gone to the McCulloughs to buy a pickup George had found for Dad. We kids were playing on the tire swing under my favorite cottonwood in the yard when we heard yelping noises. Meardha jumped up off the ground where she was lying and perked her floppy ears up as she stood on all fours. Pete and Dum Dum started a barking contest as they all were looking down the dirt road toward the slough. Steve, Lori, Devan, and I all stopped playing and walked closer to the kitchen porch to see what was coming. Dawn was in the house with our younger brothers as they were napping in the built-in bunks.

Straining our necks and holding the dogs back, we saw a tiny black dot running down the dirt road toward us. Meardha became frantic, straining against her collar to run to what looked like one of her puppies only a few days old. Lori let Meardha go as she ran to her baby running on its short toothpick legs, lucky to have survived. By now Dawn had come out of the kitchen door as we all ran to the road to pick the only surviving puppy up off the ground where it was easy prey for large animals. The little black puppy with Meardha's floppy ears was so cute and hungry as it latched on to her nipples, and as its belly filled, it fell asleep on her stomach.

Mom and Dad got home later that evening and saw the little black puppy in the living room next to Meardha by the barrel stove. Dad was surprised and said we could keep it, and so we kids decided to name him Lucky.

It was July now, and the homestead was green everywhere, from the emerald fields to the thick woods. I decided green was my favorite color, so I would always remember our life out here. There were lots of other brilliant colors from all the different kinds of wildflowers God created and planted on our homestead. I especially liked the dandelions when they turned to a ball of a feather substance to blow in the wind. I also thought the pussy willows were fascinating with their cottonlike blossoms. The bluebells were beautiful with their dainty bells hanging down in clusters.

Last summer in my sixth year of age, I discovered the art of whistling with a wide blade of grass. I desperately yearned to whistle like my siblings, but my lips failed me. My friend Holly had the same dilemma and told me that she could whistle using a blade of grass. After much practice, a loud trumpetlike sound echoed the woods as my older siblings and I hiked down the bus trail. I especially got a kick out of annoying my sisters as my lips pressed gently on the thin side of the big blade of grass hanging from my lips. With a deep breath, I could make a long, loud, deep whistle that changed its tone and went on forever.

When I got back into the yard with the dogs, I noticed Uncle Dave was at the house as his Lincoln was in the circular driveway. The twins were playing cars under the big Birch with Timmy in the dirt.

Steve came out of the big barn carrying a shovel on his way to the garage to put it away. I met him halfway and said, "Are you done with your chores, Steve?"

His freckles crinkled a smile as I followed him to the garage. "Yeah, do you want to go for a bike ride?"

I wanted to go anywhere my brother Steve went as I watched his every move and always felt safe in his presence.

Our three-speed bike with the white seat and handles was leaning against the big gray garage. I jumped up on the heart-shaped seat and rode it around the yard while Steve put the shovel away. As he was coming out of the garage, he told the twins to keep the dogs and Lucky with them in the yard. I got off the bike so Steve could pedal us and jumped up in one swoop on the straight handlebar.

My tan shorts still had CJ's hair on them from riding bareback, and my light-blue tank top was stained from chores. I pulled the rubber band off my wrist and tied my tangled curly red hair back into somewhat of a ponytail. My sisters were always trying to get a brush through my waist-length tangled mess, and Dad threatened to cut it off if I didn't take care of it. Even though my hair got in my way, it did keep me warm in the winter, but I didn't like the way the kids at school made fun of it. It was as if redheads weren't like other people and got treated as such. The names like Carrot Top, Ketchup Head, and Red just made me tougher as I and my siblings had to fight to earn the respect of our peers. I ended up with lots of friends, including Holly, Beth, Anne, Jason, and a native girl named Renee, who also had twin sisters, and they lived across the Parks Highway a few miles away.

Dad let me spend the night with Holly a couple of times when we were staying in Talkeetna, and we had a great time running all over town. I got to watch TV with their electricity, and they had water that ran out of faucets. I don't remember ever living in a house, even the small cabin, with electricity or something they use to bathe called a shower.

I hung on tight to the handlebars with my skinny white legs dangling on either side of the front wheel. Steve pedaled and steered the orange bike away from the yard. I bounced and hit my bony butt when he hit a rut by the big barn as we were going down our dirt road toward the tracks. We were having a wonderful time riding the bike slow and enjoying the light breeze on this hot day. It was fun when Steve hit the ruts and dips in the packed dirt road, and I was loving the ride as he pedaled harder. The fully bloomed trees and underbrush lined either side of the road, making it feel like a tunnel in a maze of forest.

We got to the ninety-degree bend in the road that was marked by the tall cottonwood with the big knotted branches. Steve suddenly put the brakes on and stopped the bike right before the corner that was heavily brushed. He was acting strange, like something was wrong as he told me to get off the bike. I didn't think he needed a break yet from pedaling, and so I asked him, "Why are we stopping?" Steve stood next to the bike with me on the left side of the road by the trees and said, "Stay here for a minute." Steve wiped his wrinkled forehead, looking concerned. He was sweating in his blue jeans, black tennis shoes, and short-sleeved striped shirt as he walked farther away up the dry dirt road. I stood there watching him walk around the corner by the big cottonwood, which was several yards from me and the bike.

A bald eagle soared above me close enough to see its long yellow beak. The fascinating bird distracted me as I looked up at it soaring over the tall birch trees.

Steve's loud command brought me out of my trance as I whipped my head around to see him running at me, "Get on the bike!" I thought maybe he was playing a joke on me, and so with my hands on my hips, I yelled, "Why?" Right as Steve yelled back, I saw what he was running from. "Get on! Get on!" I flipped the small bike around facing home and jumped up quickly on the handlebars after I saw a huge brown grizzly bear on all fours behind Steve. My brother was running so fast I thought he might trip and fall on the dry dirt as he slid in on the bike like it was first base. Steve was already pushing us down the road as he swung himself up onto the pedals, which were in motion before I could look back. "Hang on, Kristi! Hang on!" Steve yelled in my ear as I turned my head around to see the enormous grizzly up on his hind legs behind us only about fifty yards. The ferocious animal had his big mouth open and was walking behind us, growling loudly. I could almost feel Steve shudder as he pedaled so fast his thick red hair was all on top of his head. My hands hurt from gripping the handlebars so hard to keep my body on the fast-moving bike. I felt every rut all the way into my stomach as I bent my knees to grip my feet onto the bike frame. Neither one of us dared to look back again as we flew down the bumpy road, hoping we could outrun this huge bear that was known to outrun a horse. I think Steve and I both knew we might not make it home. We had lived in the bush long enough to know if the bear wanted to catch us, it would drop to all fours and make it to us in seconds.

"How did you know?" I asked Steve just to hear his voice.

His usually soft voice was quivering as he answered me, still pedaling for dear life, "I had a feeling something was around the corner!" He yelled louder as he stood up on the pedals to gain some speed as we finally made it to the field. "I almost ran into him, and he looked right at me!" It was the first time in seven years a grizzly had charged at any of us as we often rode the bike down the main road.

It seemed like a long time down the quarter mile but was only minutes before the house came into sight. Steve was out of breath and his legs were a blur as he pedaled through the yard and came to a screeching halt at the kitchen porch. I practically flew off the handlebars and landed on my feet at the steps. Steve and I both climbed the steps to the porch and then looked back to see nothing behind us. We gave each other a pale glance and then ran in the house to tell Dad.

Everyone was in the house getting ready for an early supper and stopped what they were doing when they saw the two of us standing there, shaking and out of breath. Steve told Dad and Uncle Dave about the large grizzly that had charged at us down the dirt road. Dad said, "There's no way you can outrun a grizzly." Dad acted like we were telling a tale as he got his thirty-thirty out of the gun cabinet, still longing to get his grizzly hide. He turned to Uncle Dave and said, "Let's go check it out!"

Dad never found the bear that day, but he and Uncle Dave did discover fresh bear tracks on our road that were from a large grizzly.

My double cousin Joy and I had become best friends like two peas in a pod. We were only three months apart and had a lot in common like riding horses. Joy and Dougie had lost their mother when they were really young, and now my grandparents were raising them. I always felt bad that I still had my mom around and Joy didn't. She was more like a sister to me, and I could tell by her big blue eyes that her heart was still broken.

Joy liked to come over frequently and spend the night, and sometimes Dougie would come with her as they were really close. I saw the way she looked at my mom with a certain kind of longing to be around her and be loved. Even though Joy was only two years old when Aunt Joyce had her tragic accident, I think Mom made her feel close to her memories. It made me feel happy inside when I saw Mom and her together, and I didn't mind sharing. Sometimes I wished Mom and Dad had taken Joy and Dougie to raise them with us kids. She didn't even mind the lickin' she and I got from Dad for slamming the living room door, as long as she could be at our place.

It was July 19 and Steve's eleventh birthday. Grandma, Grandpa, Aunt Wendy, and her new boyfriend Jim, along with Joy and Dougie, came out to the homestead for a picnic. Jim was older than my sixteen-year-old aunt, and she said they were just friends. He was short but stocky and Japanese. Jim was quiet and kind but strong as an ox, and I really liked him.

It was a warm midmorning, and Steve, Devan, and I had just gotten through bringing up fresh water from the spring. We each carried two full five-gallon buckets up the steep spring hill and then the rest of the way home. Steve had the long shotgun strapped to his back and carried the heavy buckets with ease. Devan and I struggled and had to take a few breaks.

The seven older siblings all took our turns packing water up from the spring, developing our arms and legs into solid muscle.

When we got to the house, our relatives were in the yard, looking at the pigs Dad had just brought home several weeks ago. He and Steve built a pigpen out of dry birch next to the cowshed. Dad bought the four pigs in Palmer, hoping to raise them and have them butchered for meat. The biggest one was soft, pink, and friendly, and soon we were pals. She let me ride on her around the pigpen, and we all decided to name her Jennifer. I asked Steve to make a wish when he blew out his candles not to have her butchered. She taught me how to grunt like a pig using only my throat.

After Steve helped us dump our buckets of fresh water into the reserve drum, I skipped over to see Joy. There was a certain art to skipping fast that I had mastered since my sled accident, and it just seemed a lot more fun than running. Right when I jumped up on the slanted gray boards of the pigpen next to Joy, she asked me, "Do you wanna go for a ride, Kristi?"

I said back to her, as I thought it was funny, "Ride what, the pigs, bike, or horses?"

My pretty cousin flipped her shoulder-length wavy brown hair back and giggled as she said, "The horses, silly!" So Joy and I crept away to the big barn to get the lead ropes while the rest of the family were walking back to the house. Dad, Steve, Aunt Wendy, Jim, and Grandpa Vern were going fishing at Goose Creek for silvers.

Mom, Grandma Gloria, Lori, and the twins, who were carrying Timmy and Mikey, were heading in the house to prepare the picnic.

The inside of the big barn was huge with a big round rafter that went all the way across. In the corner was a haystack so big it reached the open window at the top of the barn that faced the house and part of the field.

We kids liked to climb up to the top of the loose hay stack and look out the window at the millions of stars on a clear dark winter night. Devan and Dawn had good voices and would sing out loud, echoing from the top of the barn out the window like they were famous.

I pulled the lead rope off the large hook on the birch wall of the barn as Joy asked me, "Do you want to ride double?"

I knew Dad didn't care if we went riding double on CJ bareback as we had before, so I shrugged and said, smiling eager to ride, "Sure!" My cutoff jean shorts went to my knees and worked perfect for riding in the summer. Mom didn't like it so much that I dirtied my clothes often, and so did my little brothers even though she had a nice round washer out behind the house.

I threw the thick lead rope over my right shoulder and started to walk out to the field with Joy beside me. Joy had shorts on too as we stepped over the rows of freshly cut grass to get to CJ, who was grazing with Dungo and Jude. All three horses shied away as if they knew we wanted to take them off their endless pasture like it was a delicacy. I put the lead rope behind my back and slowly walked up to CJ, telling her, "Easy, easy." As she continued to mow down the grass, she snorted at me and shook her blond mane as if to tell me, "Not now!" I knew once we got on her, she would enjoy being ridden, and so I walked bravely up and put my arms around her big long neck.

Our golden mare brought her head up and stood still while I slipped the black lead rope around her, fastening the steel clip onto the halter. Then with one jump and a few shimmies, I pulled myself up onto CJ's bare back, swinging my legs around to sit.

I reached down for Joy, who put her tennis shoe on mine to use as a stirrup, and then she hoisted herself up behind me. Joy hung on around my waist as I led the big mare away from Dungo and Jude and began trotting across the field toward the house. When we got close, I could see Dad, Grandpa, Wendy, Jim, and Steve walking the dirt trail toward the slough alongside the field. I was glad Steve got to go fishing today since he was usually on the tractor in the field this time of year.

Mom, Lori, and Grandma were in the front of the house shucking corn. CJ pranced by the house with her head up, barely feeling Joy and me as we were both small and light, gripping our bony knees on her big back.

When we passed the house and kept going toward the spring, we waved at the corn-shucking party and giggled as CJ trotted faster than usual. She had a smooth gait, unlike Jude, who was choppy, making it hard not to bounce.

I didn't want to go all the way to the spring because it was bear season and they had cubs to protect. I pulled back on the single lead rope that I had in my left bare hand, bringing CJ's head back, slowing her on the grassy trail to a trot from a lope. Joy and I were having a blast holding our arms out like we were flying as we rode a little farther toward the spring. The smell of the dry trees and flowers was in the aroma that filled our noses as we sat high up on our imaginary wild horse.

Then I was caught totally off guard when CJ decided to turn on a dime and head back home. Both Joy and I were gripping our knees, and I had the lead rope in my hand when the big palomino jerked to the right in the middle of a trot and made a ninety-degree turn. "Hang on, Joy!" I yelled as I felt her squeeze my small waist with her arms. As CJ spread her legs to the wind and headed home at a dead run, I pulled back on the rope, burning my hand, yelling, "Whoa! Whoa!" I knew she wasn't going to stop until she got to the house, so I buried my fingers into her mane, gripped my knees, and hung on. The house was like a blur when we flew by on CJ kicking up dirt and gravel as I heard Lori yell, "Hang on, girls!" Everything happened so fast. Before we knew it, we were heading out onto the field to Dungo and Jude, who were a long ways out past the windrows.

I didn't want to get to our stallion, who sometimes got riled up when the mares were in heat and might try to mount them while you are still on.

As I was gritting my teeth and hanging on to every piece of CJ's long blond mane, I yelled to Joy, who was still squeezing me tight, "Jump off!" My brave cousin didn't hesitate as we were starting to slide off of her anyhow. CJ ran like she was in a race, and she knew I couldn't stop her.

Then Joy let go of my waist and the grip from her knees and for some reason went flying up into the air and got sucked up into the wind. I could see her doing somersaults in the sky out of the corner of my right eye. As I started to slide down CJ's right flank, thinking it might be a better way off this enormous animal, I heard Joy scream as she hit the ground with a thud. CJ never slowed down as I let go of the lead rope and let myself just fall to the ground after I slid halfway off and was hanging from her like an Indian in the Westerns. However, I didn't plan to fall underneath the big horse as I hit the ground and felt her hooves hit me all over like somebody was punching me hard.

It was only seconds before the big mare was off me and running the rest of the way across the field. I lay there in the grass without breath and holding my stomach as she had stepped right into it with her hoof. I didn't hear Joy and was worried about her as I heard Lori yelling, approaching me lying in the grass, "Are you girls all right?"

Devan and Dawn had seen CJ running away from us also and were right behind Lori, out of breath as we were quite a ways out into the large field. Then we heard Joy moaning from a distance in the grass toward the windrow. The twins ran over to her as Lori was looking me over. "CJ trampled on me!" I struggled to get the words out as I moved all my limbs, hoping I didn't have another broken bone as my big sister helped me to my feet.

Mom and Grandma were watching from the edge of the field as my sisters wrapped their arms around Joy and me, and we gimped back to the house, broken and humiliated. They laid us on the twin beds in the living room, and that's where we stayed the rest of the day except to join Steve's birthday picnic.

Joy's body was sore all over from hitting the ground rolling. My body ached all over too, and I had a large red hoof burn directly under my right rib cage. Another inch and she would have crushed my tiny ribs, possibly ending in my demise.

When Dad got back from fishing, he laughed and wasn't mad at us for letting CJ take off running, and he went right out and bridled her up.

Steve and Dad took turns riding her through the field, making her stop at a dead run. Dad was planning on racing her this year in Palmer, and I knew after that ride, she was going to win for sure!

33

THE HAUNTING OF GOOSE CREEK

DAWN

I t was time to harvest our garden on the edge of the field and that's what Devan, Kristi and I were doing on this unpredictable August day. There was a north wind blowing, and black clouds blocked the sun as we picked strawberries from Mom's patch and ate a few while we were at it.

This time of year, we got everything from our small garden and canned it to save for winter before the ground froze over. The greenhouse had been destroyed by high wind blizzards a few years ago, and the cows ate the Visqueen off the outside of it.

We were still picking raspberries, blueberries, and cranberries to make jams, ketchup, syrup, and desserts. Dad liked his desserts, and so did I. My sisters and I helped Mom in the kitchen often. We made bread pudding, whacky pudding, parfaits, and cobblers of all kinds, including rhubarb, which we grew wild on the homestead.

The swiss chard we planted were tall and dark green with wide leaves. We planted them along the edge of the field and were full of nutrients and good to eat. We kids would break off the long dark-green bumpy leaves from the long thick stalks. Then Mom boiled them until it was like spinach, and with a little homemade butter and vinegar, swiss chard was delicious.

Dad was in the garage getting fishing gear together for the coming weekend. Grandpa Vern and Aunt Wendy were coming over to go silver salmon fishing at the mouth of Sheep Creek.

Devan and Kristi just got a lickin' with a willow this morning for getting into the fishing poles the other day, tangling them all up. Dad asked us all who did it. Kristi and Devan confessed and had to go cut a willow with the pocketknife Dad gave them. We siblings knew better than to bring back too thick of a willow, because Dad would go cut a better one. As we plucked strawberries off the vines and put them into the tin cans, both Devan and Kristi were quiet.

Dust rose up off our dirt road as a root-beer-colored Rambler drove up into our driveway. I saw Uncle Norman get out slowly. He kept the door open, and out jumped a beautiful golden dog. All our dogs were barking except Dum Dum, who had disappeared a few weeks before the fair. Someone Dad knew saw him get hit by a truck on the Parks Highway where he lay several miles away. We were all so sad to lose our friendly big dog we had gotten from the McCulloughs.

Meardha, Lucky, and Pete ran ahead of us as we went to greet our uncle. Dad came out of the garage. Mom, Steve, and Lori came out of the house. I couldn't help but stare at the strikingly beautiful golden-haired dog as he ran around, getting to know everyone. He was a short-haired golden retriever with floppy ears and big brown eyes. Lori crouched down beside him, letting the friendly dog lick her face as she said to Uncle Norman, "What's his name?" Dad, Mom, and all of us kids including Timmy, who had walked out of the house rubbing his eyes, were standing around, admiring Uncle Norman's dog as he humorously said, "His name is Goldy. Do you want to keep him?"

We kids immediately looked at Dad and waited for a response. "Sure, if you don't want him!" Dad said with a half smile.

I felt like squealing with joy as I pet the rambunctious dog as Dad took his cowboy hat off. Then he ran his fingers through his thick brown hair and said, "He looks like a good bird dog."

Uncle Norman stayed for a few days and then left Alaska for a while, also leaving behind his 1969 Rambler.

Soon the weekend came, and so did our company. Grandma brought her homemade gooey sweet apple pie with real whip cream. Mom cooked up some pink salmon and fried potatoes. Devan and I made a big green salad with everything from our small garden and homemade thousand island dressing.

A few days ago, Lori, Devan, and I made several loaves of white bread for the afternoon feast and enough to last our family a week. The fresh hot bread smelled delicious and filled the house with an aroma that made me feel warm and cozy. The best time to have a slice was right out of the oven with our homemade butter melted into the soft thick center with the crusty outside. When we had our cows last year, Mom skimmed off the cream on the fresh milk and put it into mason jars. We often sat in the kitchen by the stove shaking the jar until the cream turned to butter. Then Mom stored it in wax paper in the little cellar under the kitchen floor to use for many months.

When Grandma and Mom said it was time for supper, she sent Devan and me outside to gather the family. We found Kristi showing Joy and Dougie how to ride our pig Jennifer in the pen next to the cowshed. Steve, Lori, and Aunt Wendy were just bringing the horses in from a long ride across the field. I knew how to ride Jude and sometimes would ride behind Devan, who wasn't afraid of horses like I was.

A couple of hours passed as we all gathered in the house for a prayer and a big meal that everyone enjoyed with lots of talking and laughter. After supper everyone packed up to go fishing, except Devan, Kristi, Joy, Dougie, and me, who were left to watch Timmy and Mikey.

Besides, there was a huge pile of dishes stacked up in the sink and on the counter from the family supper. Mom told us kids to have the dishes done by the time they got back from the creek.

Hide-and-seek seemed much more fun than doing dishes. Besides, it would be awhile before the adults returned. With the trailer attached to the house now, there were great hiding places for hours of fun. It was dark in the long trailer as we all ran to find our favorite hiding places.

As pale-yellow curtain on Mom's bedroom window reminded me of last winter when the most embarrassing thing happened to me at school. I was ten years old then and was tired of wearing the same old clothes and always looking identical to my twin sister. So one morning while Mom and Dad were gone for a couple of days, while no one was looking, I pulled the old faded yellow curtain down. With only a T-shirt and underwear underneath, I found a pair of Mom's nylons crumpled up on the floor in the corner of the room and decided to put them on. They had long runs in them and were too big. The hose bunched up everywhere and hung from my crotch. I figured that no one would see them anyhow under my elegant gown.

Devan was out at the outhouse with Kristi and Timmy, and Lori and Steve were getting dressed also, so quickly I wrapped the long curtain under my arms and around my barely developed breasts. It fell to my feet like a wrap-around dress as I pulled it snuggly three times around. The big safety pins Mom kept on her dresser worked perfectly to keep my pale-yellow gown together. Then I ran to the living room and zipped my coat up over the surprise dress I had made all by myself. I felt like a princess and just knew all the kids at school would think I looked grown-up.

I felt so pretty as I took my coat off in Aunt Kathy's class and walked as gracefully as I could in my white tennis shoes to my desk and neatly tucked my long gown under me as I sat down. Devan was sitting next to me in her desk and said, "Dawn, why did you wear a curtain to school?" Aunt Kathy called my name just as I turned and smiled at my twin sister. It was my turn to read the assigned essay I had worked for hours. The whole class had their eyes on me while I picked my essay up off the desk and stood up proudly, flipping my combed blond hair.

Suddenly a draft of cool air hit my body as my elegant pale-yellow dress hit the floor, leaving me in only my underwear and oversized nylons. I was devastated and humiliated as all I could hear was laughter as my face started heating up. My feet were embedded into the wooden classroom floor as I reached down and yanked the curtain back up around me and ran out of the room. I couldn't even look at Aunt Kathy as she was sitting at her desk as I flew by. Devan was right behind me as I swung the bathroom door open, feeling like I was going to faint. She quickly helped me pull the yellow curtain back up around me and repinned it with the safety pins still attached. Becky and Debbie came into the bathroom just then, laughing at me, and at that point, I just wanted to cry. I dreaded wearing my home-made gown the rest of the day and all the way home, even though everyone knew it was a curtain by now. Devan told Lori on the bus, and neither one of them laughed at me and never told anyone else.

HAUNTING

Before we knew it, we had been playing for an hour and a half and the house was beginning to get dark as well as the outside. We hadn't lit any of the propane lamps yet, and we knew if we didn't get the dishes done soon, we would get in big trouble.

Kristi, Joy, and Dougie started for the kitchen, with Devan and me close behind to light the lamps. As we were stepping up into the kitchen, Devan and I practically ran into Kristi, Joy, and Dougie as they stopped suddenly in their tracks. A dark shadow crossed in front of us, leaving a cold breeze. The dark figure looked like it had a brim hat on and no facial features. It was shaped like a real person and was literally floating above the floor, making its way to the front door.

Devan and I clutched onto each other in total fear, not able to speak an utter word. Kristi was frozen as Joy and Dougie backed up against us, shaking with fear.

Suddenly the shadow turned and floated back by us and then disappeared into the trailer entrance. None of us kids could move as it literally stopped for a second to look at us.

Our group attached to each other peered into the kitchen entry, straining our necks to look into the opening to the trailer where the figure had gone, and we could not see it.

Then, *slam!* We heard the door that was at the end of the trailer where Lori's bedroom was banged shut! Why would a ghost use the door? Then terror filled me as I remembered hiding in that very same room under the bed.

When Devan, Kristi, Joy, Dougie, and I looked at each other, our faces were as white as snow as we seemed to be saying, "Did you see what I saw?"

Then suddenly, on the ceiling, circular white lights appeared and were swirling around in no apparent pattern, as if someone was using a flashlight to scare us. This went on for a few minutes, which seemed like an hour. Completely terrified and in tears by now, we hung on to each other, slumped down by the gun cabinet in the living room, too afraid to move much less do the dishes.

A few minutes later, the front door opened, and in came Mom, who noticed the house was dark and the dishes were not touched. After explaining about seeing this figure and the lights, Mom laughed and went outside where Dad was filleting the fish they had caught and told him what we had seen. He was so amused we didn't get a lickin' that night, but we had to stay up till all the dishes were washed, dried, and put away.

That wasn't the last time we heard from or saw that figure again. We wondered if he was an old sourdough that at some time maybe lived and died at our homestead and never wanted to leave.

34

LINDSTRAND'S CABIN

DEVAN

September brought the colorful orange and red fall leaves down from all the gigantic trees that surrounded our bus trail. Dawn and I had our fur-lined hoods over our heads as we hiked up to the spring with our eleven-year-old brother Steve leading the way. He had his stocking cap on and his brown coat with Dad's thirty-thirty rifle tucked under his right arm pointed toward the ground. Lori was behind us with Kristi, who was crunching over the leaves with her tennis shoes, full of energy for the second grade, happily whistling on a blade of grass.

The still-dark morning had a cold bite to it as our noses turned an apple red and our breath lingered as we all talked to each other loudly. As we siblings approached the top of the hill down to the spring, we stopped to look briefly at a big new mound that was buried under dirt and gravel.

Lori said, "Wonder if the grizzly killed a moose or a horse?" None of us wanted to find out as we continued down the trail past the spring to the empty cabin on the knoll. Besides, the dirt was fresh, meaning the dangerous hunter was possibly still nearby. When the carcass ferments under the mound, it lets off a pungent smell overwhelming the pleasant forest aroma.

There was something different about the brown wood cabin that stood empty for the six years we had lived out here. Oftentimes we kids would stand on our tippy-toes to look into the already furnished one-room birch-sided structure. There were thin blue transparent curtains that hung loose over the three rectangular red-framed windows that wrapped around to a front door. An old tattered lime-green couch was placed directly under a huge window on the other side of the room, and there was a big bed on the right side against the wall. The roof had tin on it and one smokestack that for the first time had puffs of smoke swirling up into the still dark early morning. Steve held up his free hand, stopping his sisters right in front of the cabin, and said, "Hold up! There must be someone living here now."

Before we could say anything else, the light-brown tarnished door to the cabin opened suddenly. A tall thin man with a floppy fisherman's hat stepped off the two concrete steps onto the wet ground. He had short brown hair and glasses that were round on his friendly face looking slightly younger than Mom and Dad.

The young Clark tribe didn't know what to say except "Hello" in unison using our best manners. The strange man, who didn't seem like a threat, stood in front of us as the light was barely breaking through the morning.

Standing close together and looking up at him, we listened to his soft, kind voice, "My name is Doug Lindstrand. Who are all of you kids?"

Dad always taught us to shake hands and introduce ourselves to adults and be respectful, so that's what we did. Steve shook Mr. Lindstrand's large hand first and said, "My name is Steve, and we're the Clark kids."

Dawn and I introduced ourselves and shook his hand also as I noticed he had soft brown eyes. Then he knelt down on one knee on the twigs and grass, looking Kristi straight in the eye, and said, "What pretty braids! What is your name?" Our little sister, who was a little shy at first, put her bright-blue eyes down to the ground as she made a hole in the soft dirt with her shoe and said, "I'm Kristi, and I'm seven years old." Mr. Lindstrand showed his straight white teeth as he let out a friendly laugh and got up off the ground.

Lori, who was the oldest kid and the most outspoken, adjusted her knitted multicolored cap as her straight long red hair lay in front of her shoulders. She reached her thin hand out to our new neighbor and said without hesitation, "I'm Lori." He smiled at her as she continued, "Nice to meet you, Mr. Lindstrand. We have a homestead a half mile north of here toward the mountains. This is our bus trail." Now that he could get a word in edgewise, Mr. Lindstrand said to all of us, "I'm a photographer and an artist, and I travel all over Alaska to take shots of wild animals mostly. I've been renting this cabin since this area is infested with grizzlies and moose."

Then he turned to Steve and said, shaking his head, "That's an awful big rifle. Are you old enough to shoot that thing?"

My proud brother's golden eyes sparkled as his big freckles stretched across his dimples into a grin. "Yes, sir, I'm eleven now and been shooting my dad's guns since I was six! Even have a few of my own." The nice man seemed impressed and watched us hike down the knoll toward the tracks as we waved goodbye and headed for the bus. He yelled out into the faded distance between us, "Call me Doug!"

The big yellow school bus pulled into the new grade school where Dawn, Kristi, and I attended on the outskirts of Talkeetna. The three of us scooted off the smooth green seat where we were sitting together and got in line with the other kids to get off the bus.

My twin sister and I were wearing the same black, red, and white checkered skirts with black tights and black shiny dress shoes. Our short bob-style straight strawberry-blond hair flowed neatly around our white turtleneck sweaters. Last year Dad cut mine and Dawn's long hair after the rats that had developed were impossible to comb out. With only one bath a week, our hair became tangled and greasy, and we didn't smell very good either.

One time last year, I went with my class on a field trip to McKinley National Park where we stayed overnight in sleeping bags. McKinley Park was renamed Denali National Park years later. That was when I discovered the rat in my hair and the confirmation that I stunk. Never did I feel so humiliated when one of my classmates who was in the sleeping bag next to me said loud enough for everyone to hear, "Ooh, you stink!"

Mom often dressed Dawn and me the same when we were little, and people sometimes couldn't tell us apart. Now that we were both nine, dressing different wasn't unusual but still fun to confuse people with matching outfits.

Last night, Dawn and I lay in our bed in the trailer, giggling our way through our mischievous plan to trade places. It wasn't the first time or the last we successfully confused teachers and students, wondering if they were ever going to catch on. It became a fun game bound by a pact we had made to each other to not tell anyone in hopes Dad would never find out.

Dawn had Aunt Kathy for her fourth-grade teacher, who was strict but kind and patient. Even though she didn't want to play favorites with her nieces, Aunt Kathy always made us feel special.

My class was down the hall with Mrs. Brown, who was in her late fifties with silver hair and steel-blue eyes. I dreaded going to her class because she was not very nice and raised her voice a lot. I especially didn't want to go today since we had a hard math test.

Dawn didn't want to go to Aunt Kathy's class only because she had to stand up and read her English essay. So we figured since Dawn was good at math, she could go to my classroom, and since I wasn't afraid of speaking in front of the class, I would go to Aunt Kathy's room.

All three of us waved goodbye to Lori, Steve, and Aunt Wendy at the back of the bus where the teenagers sat as we stepped off onto the sidewalk. Dawn and I walked Kristi to her classroom at the other end of the hall, and then I turned to Dawn and said as we couldn't help but giggle, "See you at recess, Devan!"

I walked to Aunt Kathy's class with Dawn's English essay in my hand, ready to read it as passively as I could not to give away our secret switch. It was about our pug Boots that we brought from Oregon who was killed by a grizzly in our garden. As I walked by Aunt Kathy, who was at her big gray metal desk, she smiled, deepening her dimples and said, "Good morning, Dawn." I smiled and waved like Dawn would have, not exposing her teeth, and took a seat at her desk.

The day went as planned and I had no problem reading Dawn's well-written essay in front of the class, and even Aunt Kathy joined the applause afterward. Kristi met us in the cafeteria at lunchtime where we opened our paper sacks and ate the peanut butter jam sandwiches Lori had made us this morning. Right after we ate lunch, Kristi decided to show off her cartwheel skills and did a whole row of them perfectly all the way across the cafeteria. She was sent to the principal's office where he gave her five swats with his big wood paddle and she had to miss recess. Dawn and I pushed each other on the swings and hung out with Amy and Beth Valentine until the bell rang, signifying the switch was back on as we returned to each other's homeroom, having a great day being each other.

Huge butterflies of yellow, orange, and some black and white perched on the many wildflowers that were starting to fall to the ground as winter was right around the corner. The purple fireweed had blossomed to the top of its peak, and the frost was setting in.

My siblings and I knew not to touch the beautiful delicate wings of the many friendly butterflies that circled our heads as we hiked our dimly lit trail home. We learned very young to have respect for all of God's creation, only harming to defend each other, tiptoeing quietly through the forests of wild-animal domain, only using and occupying what is necessary for survival, leaving enough for our fellow creatures, respecting their need to defend their families the only way they know how.

Steve led the way across the train tracks with a firm grip on the big rifle while we girls hiked behind without words for once. We were all tired and hungry from the long day at school and noisy bus ride home.

The only sound was Goose Creek that roared beside us, lapping its high waves against the big rocks on one last run before the winter freeze.

We had almost forgotten about our new neighbor until the whirling of gray wood smoke became visible from the bottom of the steep knoll.

Not wanting to disturb Mr. Lindstrand, Lori told us to walk softly by the occupied brown cabin that was only inches from our trail. Hiking in a perfect line, the five of us stepped lightly on the soft grass and leaves that blanketed the narrow path. As we made it to the end of the long narrow cabin, a soft voice broke our determination to respect the privacy of others. "Hey, there you are! I was getting worried." I know the butterflies were not only in the air but also in my stomach as Mr. Lindstrand's gentle nature made me feel welcome as he continued to talk to us kids as if he had known us forever. "Hold on a minute. I made some cookies." Our tall new friend was sitting on a wide tree stump in between the cabin and his outhouse with a large sketchbook propped up on his crossed leg. A partial drawing of a bald eagle etched so perfectly was coming to life for the whole world to see. We held up on the trail, smiling at each other as if all of us felt his warmth and talent that ignited our curiosity and our taste buds as the aroma of warm cookies seeped through the cabin windows. Mr. Lindstrand pulled his floppy round white hat off his short thick brown hair and put his sketchbook on the stump after getting up off it. "Grab a stump and rest!" he said to us as he turned and went around the house to the front door.

Steve leaned Dad's big heavy rifle on one of the many tree stumps in the tall grassy yard. As soon as we all took a stump, Mr. Lindstrand was out of the cabin with a large metal plate of fresh chocolate chip cookies, offering each one of us hungry kids several of them. Eagerly, we thanked him and let the soft cookies melt in our mouths.

The nice man sat down with his sketchbook while his large hand made dancelike movements on the white page. The large bald eagle came to life right before us, holding his white feathered head up proudly as its black wings and huge talons engulfed the rest of the canvas.

Talking with strangers was my specialty, so I struck up a conversation. "Mr. Lindstrand, our dad is an artist too."

A big smile broke into his friendly face as he looked straight at me to the left of him and said, "You kids can call me Doug since we are neighbors and friends now."

We all nodded as he adjusted his round glasses and continued our conversation. "I would love to see your dad's art. What is his name?"

I perked up on the wide tree stump Dawn and I were sharing and raised my voice proudly while my siblings ate their cookies. "Dennis Clark, and our mom's name is Evelyn!" Not wanting to be left out, Lori joined in the chat while neatly wiping her porcelainlike face of cookie crumbs. "I like to draw too and have learned a lot from watching our dad, who paints mostly Western art and wild animals."

Doug curiously shifted around on his stump and seemed to be enjoying our company as all of us kids eventually joined in. He told us of his travels around Alaska and how he had never met kids like us in the bush and maybe we could possibly give him a few survival tips. Dawn told him we had two baby brothers at home making seven of us kids.

Kristi shared her story of her broken leg, which made him sit perfectly still, gazing at her with a compassion I had never seen.

The late afternoon turned into dusk that would soon blanket our path with darkness. Steve got up from his stump, picking the big steel rifle into his small arms again. The rest of us followed his signal, thanking Doug again for his cookies and conversation. He yelled out to us as we headed down the narrow dark trail engulfed with the thick woods and underbrush, "Be careful and stop by again for hot cocoa!"

Waving back, happy to have a close neighbor, we kids hiked on by the spring and the rest of the way to our warm lit-up house. Dad and Mom listened as we all talked at once about our new neighbor while sitting around the picnic table next to the black iron stove, devouring hot moose roast. They said it was okay to visit with Doug as long as we minded our manners and got home before the night would blind the trail. Kristi told Dad about the principal spanking her for doing cartwheels in the cafeteria as she knew he would eventually find out. Just for fessing up honestly, Kristi didn't get a lickin' from Dad.

The next day after we had got to school, Dad showed up there and paid a visit to our principal. He told the principal behind closed doors to never lay a hand on one of his kids again or he would spank him the same way.

35

HARD TIME

STEVE

Winter came upon us early as usual after Timmy's second birthday in October. Unlike Mikey, who was still crawling and pulling himself up on furniture at nine months old, Timmy was growing like a weed and following us kids everywhere. He especially liked it when I rode him on the handlebars as I pedaled our bike all over the homestead.

Timmy had thick curly red hair that bounced around on his head with big blue eyes and was extraordinarily smart for his age. He was shy and quiet except for when he was belting out the only song he knew, "I Saw the Light." Mom and Dad got him a miniature guitar for his birthday, and he already figured out how to play his favorite song on it.

Right before Halloween, on which we attended the community center party again, temperatures dropped below freezing and the snow was accumulating on our soft dirt road. Our bike had to be stored in the garage for now until spring breakup to keep it out of the mile-high snowbanks.

Summer work and play were done, and now it was time for winter games inside—Monopoly, checkers, scrabble, Yahtzee, cards, and a new game I had learned to play called chess. I won a new chess set in a drawing at school that was handmade. A lady from our church made it out of Sitka clay. Lori and I moved the knights, bishops, queens, and kings across their shiny black-and-white checkered platform every chance we got and couldn't wait to teach our siblings.

The house had cooled off during the night, and I woke up shivering under the two wool blankets that covered everything but my long white feet. It was impossible to keep the blankets tucked into our soft brown couch, exposing my red toes to the cold air. Dad always stoked the fire before he went to bed at night, and when he was gone, it was my job.

Mom, Timmy, and Mikey went with Dad to Anchorage yesterday, leaving us five kids home alone for a few days. I wasn't exactly sure when they were to return. Dungo and Jude were stuck along the Copper River somewhere after one of Dad's hunting trips with a dear friend that went bad. That's all I have to say about that as the memory is too sensitive to talk about. Dad had barely survived the trip, finding his way miles from home on foot with no food for several days.

Dad had me help him hitch up the horse trailer yesterday in the two feet of snow on the ground, hoping to make it out of the homestead. He had confidence in his newly bought strong red 1961 Ford flatbed. After a few more days of white cold rain from above blanketing every inch of the homestead, Dad knew the real challenge would be driving the horses back in our undriveable road. He always packed his saddles and riding gear for the horses. One never knew when our horses would be the only transportation down the long narrow treed road into the bush.

Mom said goodbye with last-minute instructions for my sisters and was loading the boys into the pickup when Dad gave me the usual speech. "Steve, you and Lori are in charge of making sure your little sisters are safe!" Dad's black Stetson was tilted to the right, dusted with snow, and the fringes danced in the wind on his favorite tan leather coat that was now missing a bottom button. His long, narrow nose was turning red and dripping from the cold. "Keep the fires going in the stoves and take the rifle with you on the trail." I made sure I kept my eyes locked in with his stern questioning navy-blue eyes. When Dad spoke to us, he was always making sure we were listening and retaining every word for our own good. A lot of times he repeated what he had said or quizzed us to make sure it stayed in our heads. As I took in every word my dad said to me, standing by our big barn in the rare light of the day, a slight fear of being responsible for all of us and the animals made me shiver as I said to him, "Yes, Dad, we'll be careful and stay close to home except to go to school."

That's exactly what we did this freezing Monday morning as I jumped off the couch to start the big barrel stove up again. Having a certain love for this place was a must to endure being cold most of the time, never enough layers to keep the whole body warm. My numb toes tingled like needles finding the hard linoleum beside the couch as I slipped on my dirty socks and three-day-old jeans and long-sleeve red shirt. The liners to my snow boots were beside the stove after drying last night beside six other pairs that were mixed up most of the time. I slipped the wool liners over my feet and then into the knee-high snow boots that had lasted for a few hard winters now. My thick brown suede coat felt good as I zipped it up to the top and put on Dad's leather gloves.

With plenty of dry birch wood outside the living room door, I kept it open to carry in several armloads to stack by the stove. The snow had stopped falling, and the sky was moonlit with clusters of stars glistening from the heavens. When the freezing wind hit my face upon opening our old wood door, it stopped my breath as a moose trampled around in the brush, scraping the bare trees for something to eat. The big dark shadows of their hairy bodies gave way their disguise as I watched them move clumsily in the woods close to the outhouse. Steam puffed out of their large nostrils as they took notice of me. I wasn't scared as a moose was almost a daily sight.

The birch wood faithfully lit up, slowly making a crackling noise that woke Kristi up, who was in the twin bed next to the wall as she sat up yawning.

I moved the gray logs around with the long metal rod, poking the fire, staring into the red and yellow flames, wishing we could stay home today. Lori liked school though and wouldn't have us staying home unnecessarily. She was in the kitchen, packing our sack lunches, dressed neatly in jeans and a white turtleneck sweater. The twins had matching green outfits that were pantsuits Mom had made and came through the trailer door as I slipped out to feed the rest of the animals. We didn't have our big pig Jenny anymore but still had two hogs to butcher next spring. Dad had Jenny butchered last summer, and we were still eating the pork that was stored in the kitchen cellar. Kristi refused to eat it as she loved Jenny, and Dad let her get away with it even though he told her not to get attached.

After we all gulped down a hot bowl of oatmeal with brown sugar and homemade butter, it was time to hit the trail. Kristi and I had our heavy coats on with our thick snow gloves covering our hands. Our black snow pants were hard to walk in, but we wanted to get on the bus dry. I tied Kristi's hood and put on my dark-red stocking cap that folded down into a ski mask. It wasn't cold enough yet to cover our faces at only twenty below, and the wind wasn't blowing very hard. Lori and the twins bundled up the same as I turned the barrel stoves damper down and left the dogs in the house. Meardha was already outside climbing on top the one big snowbank we had so far from Dad plowing our driveway. She liked to play king of the hill even this early in the morning, while Goldy and Pete barked at her as if paying respect.

Lori shut the faded brown door and checked the copper knob to make sure it latched, or snow would blow in all day. We had no locks on our doors as we were probably just lucky to have the knobs. The almost full moon lit up our trail as I kept my right hand on Dad's twelve-gauge shotgun that rested over my shoulder in the leather sling. Even though most of the bear population was already in hibernation, starving moose and timber wolves caused some slight delays in our hike out to the bus. Every time we kids hiked past Doug Lindstrand's cabin, we hoped to see his smiling face, feeling better knowing he lived a half mile away.

This moonlit morning was no different as I saw him dancing with his shadow behind a kerosene lantern as his right arm brushed the large canvas. He must have seen us as we topped the knoll looking down the steep snow-covered bank. I heard the familiar creak of his door opening as Doug stepped out into the cold air. "I know you have time for hot cocoa!" Lori and I grinned at each other as the twins and Kristi looked at us with puppy dog eyes, knowing we had left early enough like Dad always told us to in case of emergency.

I waved and nodded to Mr. Lindstrand as all five of us hurried into his warm cabin after shaking the snow off our boots. We all stood around his hot woodstove as he ladled five cups full of steaming dark rich cocoa. After that, our artist neighbor topped each one with two large marshmallows, not to miscount one cup, and then carefully handed them to us kids watching his every move. My mouth started to salivate as I sipped the sweet hot chocolate from the tin cups that made me warm all the way to my toes. Doug showed us his painting of a mother grizzly bear defending her cubs. He told us he was going to be gone for a few weeks to see his family for Thanksgiving. After we thanked him for the hot cocoa, I threw the big rifle over my right shoulder and said, "We have to head out."

Lori, Devan, Dawn, and Kristi put their cups in the sink and followed me out the door as Doug waved goodbye and said, "Be extra careful!" I felt like he was a friend, and so I turned around before the knoll and yelled back, "Thank you, Doug, likewise!"

My black snow boots pounded the snowed-over playground, making a running trail for Chad and me to play tag. He followed behind me, packing the trail even wider as we rounded the large metal swing set. All the boys liked to run and play tag or throw the football, while the girls made several igloos to play house in. By January their perfectly formed domes made of packed snow squares were weather resistant and fun to sit inside. They saved their milk cartons and little Styrofoam ice creams from lunches gone by and stored them in the igloos for recess.

Some of the boys in my fifth-grade class were bullies, and I tried to steer clear of them. One was named Tommy, who was black and aboriginal. He was really athletic and could outrun every kid in school. Chad shook me from behind, directing my attention to Tommy as he stood over by the igloos, glaring at us. Tyler Smith joined our group as we ran around our trail, tagging each other until we were out of breath. Watching Tommy roll huge snowballs out of the corner of my eye made our game not seem as much fun. Suddenly and without warning, Tommy and his band of bullies started to fire their arsenal straight at us. My friend Tyler was a maniac and began throwing snowballs back at them while yelling, "Let's get 'em!" Chad and I looked at each other while making our own bombs out of the hard snow. We then whipped our heads around to see Tommy go into some kind of a crazy frenzy screaming like he was going to kill us. Just as I looked him square in the eyes fifty yards away, he released a huge ice chunk from his glove coming at me, and with the speed of a bullet, it landed right between my eyes. Next thing I knew my feet went right out from under me as I landed on my back on the hard-packed trail we had made. Chad grabbed my gloved hand and helped me to my feet as Tommy took off running through our well-formed trail and messed it up with his boots as he laughed hysterically. My head pounded and my temper boiled as I felt my cold ears burn with heat. I sure didn't want him to get away with trying to knock me out, so I ran as fast as I could after him, holding back the tears that were welling up in my eyes from anger.

The bell rang, and all the kids ran for the lineup to go back to class from recess as Tommy ran too far ahead of me to catch, laughing hard with victory. As I skidded in line with my face streaked with tears, the teacher's aide, who was Mrs. Valentine, looked me up and down as I caught my breath, and she said, "What's wrong with you, Steve?"

I knew it was wrong right after the words left my mouth, and I never felt like I was prejudice but somehow it made me feel better. "That little nigger threw ice at my head!" I thought Chad's mom was going to have a heart attack right there on the playground as all the kids' heads turned to look at my red face. Chad snickered behind me as Mrs. Valentine yelled all the way from the front of the line, "How would you like it if he called you a redhead freckle face!" I decided not to say anything back about how he already did call me that and instead looked away and got back in line. Chad was never allowed to spend the night at our house again after that incident, but she never did tell my dad what I had called Tommy.

The bus ride home was long and silent as I gazed out the small fogged-up window at the train lights through the tall trees. Darkness was setting in already as the big yellow bus pulled into the community center. Lori grabbed her books and slid off the seat into the aisle behind the twins, who were sitting in front of us. Tired and hungry, we kids got off the bus and zipped our coats up for the long hike home. I reached down into the brush to grab Dad's twelve-gauge shotgun behind the community center and then looked ahead to assess the trail. "Let's go," I said to my four sisters, who were arguing over who had to make supper for us when we got to the house. That included packing snow into our large metal bucket to melt on the barrel stove for water. The spring froze every winter no matter what Dad did to prevent it. The twins were almost ten and could cook as good as Lori. Kristi never liked housework, including cooking, so Dad always let her help me feed the animals and get the woodstoves going.

Our path was lit up by the moonlight breaking through the late afternoon darkness, and the air was still but freezing. The faster we walked, the warmer we stayed, which was a familiar exercise in the bush. Our boots made deep prints in our packed trail as we crossed the railroad tracks after stopping to run across the bridge and back.

There were still pieces of the old red Ford that was smashed by a train last year lying under the snow with its rusty metal sticking out. The man and his son who harvested potatoes with us came back to get a second load, and their red Ford pickup broke down before they crossed the tracks. They had a brilliant idea to push it up onto our railroad crossing to fix it because the crossing was wooden and had a flat surface. The Alaska train ran often, as we kids knew very well. Sure enough, before they could fix the truck, a train came roaring around the sharp corner on schedule. Just as the man and his son jumped out of the way, the big locomotive hit their truck, ending any reason to fix it now.

Doug Lindstrand's cabin was dark when we hiked by it, and then we continued on past the spring. An eerie feeling came over me as I gripped the shotgun tighter, remembering Mom and Dad were gone too.

By the time we kids got to the cold, dark house, we were all worn out and my head was still sore from the ice chunk that almost broke my skull. We knew we had to get our chores done right away, and so that's what we did. First thing I did was start fires in our two woodstoves to chase the cold out. Lori and the twins made a nice hot dinner of homemade moose pot pie in our white cook stove. Then we had Jell-O they had made the day before. Most of the time when Mom and Dad were gone, we would get the little boxes of Jell-O Mom had hidden in her room and dip our fingers in and lick the sweet powder. After supper Kristi and Dawn used some of the hot water and did the dishes.

After a long game of Monopoly with Kristi and the twins, I looked at the glow in the dark wind-up clock on the kitchen ledge. It was getting late, and we had to get up early to hike out to the bus again in the morning. Besides, I had taken most of the property and money from my sisters. Devan put the Monopoly game away, and Kristi and Dawn got ready for bed. Lori was in her room at the end of the trailer, reading. Soon all would have to sleep in the living room except Mom and Dad because the trailer was impossible to heat.

Just as I was turning the dampers down on the black iron stove, huge bright lights piercing our kitchen windows startled me. Company was rare especially late at night, and my heart began to pound as I couldn't see who it was through the stream of light. Meardha, Lucky, and Goldy all woke up and started barking. Kristi and the twins ran into the kitchen in their pajamas to see if Mom and Dad were home.

Rushing my sisters back into the living room, I followed and grabbed the twelve-gauge shotgun that was propped against the wall by the barrel stove. Lori came running out of the trailer just as a loud knock on the living room door startled me again. She came running beside me, grabbing our loud dogs as I said deep and loud, "Who is it?"

An even deeper voice from a man said back through the door, "Trooper Bunker!"

Lori opened the living room door slowly as I kept my right finger close to the trigger on the ready rifle. Dad knew trooper Bunker, but I had never seen him before. He stood in the doorway with a blue uniform and a brim hat on with a badge on his thick brown coat.

Lori was tall and stood at eye level with the friendly sheriff who was of medium build and had brown hair.

"Come on in," I said to Trooper Bunker, who was there by himself. He stepped into the living room and spread out his large hands over the hot barrel stove. The trooper looked over at the twins and Kristi huddled together on the twin bed by the bunks with a wool blanket wrapped around all three of them. Then he turned to Lori and me to tell us something we didn't want to hear. "There's two escaped prisoners on the loose in these parts. They're dangerous and already have broken into that cabin close to here and stole a .22 rifle." Trooper Bunker focused in on me, locking eyes as I knew it was Lindstrand's cabin the prisoners had broken into. He then continued speaking as he stared at me. "Where's Dennis and Evelyn?"

Lori spoke up nervously, "Mom and Dad are in Anchorage for a few days." The trooper never took his eyes off me as I was still gripping Dad's rifle that was pointed toward the floor. He said to me, "You know how to shoot that twelve-gauge, boy?"

Not realizing I was biting my lower lip, I put my shoulders back and answered him, "Yes, sir, Mr. Bunker."

He put his gloves back on and headed toward the door as he turned to me and said, "Keep it loaded and stay awake." After Trooper Bunker closed the living room door, Lori and I looked at each other with horror.

We didn't want our sisters to be more scared than us, so Lori tucked them into the twin bed together and told them to get some sleep. I pulled Dad's big easy chair that Meardha was sleeping in across the living room and up against the door. Lori and I put a metal folding chair up under the knob of the kitchen door since we didn't have locks. The only other door was at the end of the trailer in Lori's room, which had a lock and was secure. She and I put blankets on the couch in the living room and sat there together wide awake. Our adrenaline was so high and we were so terrified there was no way we were sleeping. Never once in the six years we had been on our homestead had I thought of people to be a threat. Mostly we had to be weary of wild animals and winter storms.

Before we knew it, the early morning hours came upon Lori and me as the woodstoves crackled in the silence. We didn't dare talk too much, in fear we would miss a sound as we stayed up the whole night.

Even though it was morning, it was dark, and so Lori and I continued to stay on the couch awake. My eyes were drooping, longing for sleep, when we heard a rig coming up over the two feet of snow into our front yard. Headlights shone into our windows again. We both jumped up off the couch and the girls stirred in their bed as the dogs started to bark.

I recognized Glenn Valentine as he shone his flashlight in the kitchen door window. Lori was right behind me as I pulled the metal chair away from the doorknob and let him in the house. He smiled at us and said somewhat out of breath, "Are you kids all right?"

Still holding Dad's shotgun, I said, smiling back at him, "We stayed up all night, but sure glad to see you!"

Mr. Valentine sat at our kitchen table as the twins and Kristi joined us all around him. He said to us, "The escaped prisoners were headed up the tracks, and Trooper Bunker and his men found them lying by the tracks hiding a mile from here."

Knowing how close they were to us, my eyes got wider as I said to him, "When did they catch them?"

Mr. Valentine shifted around on the bench and looked at me. "Just an hour ago, son. I was there right after and saw them being hauled away. I knew your mom and dad were gone and word was all over Talkeetna about the escaped prisoners in this area." Lori shivered next to me as he continued, "I was worried about you kids out here in the bush alone with them on the loose." Devan got Mr. Valentine a cup of hot cocoa before he got up and left a little while later. We never made it to school that day, and Mom and Dad came home the next day to hear us all talk at once about how we barely made it through the night with escaped prisoners on the loose.

36

THE GREAT KASHWITNA

DENNIS

E very winter I flew eight hundred miles north to Prudhoe Bay to put my welding and mechanical skills to work on the pipeline. It was hard leaving Evelyn and the kids out at the homestead this time of year for weeks at a time with no power or running water. We were snowed in most winters with the only way out on snow machine, foot, or horseback.

Christmas was spent in our shack with only a few gifts for the kids and a moose roast browning in the oven. Vern and Gloria made it out with Joy and Dougie on their snow machine and sled but had to spend the night because of an unexpected blizzard. Wendy was with her fiancé, Jim, and his family this year. Wendy and I might not always get along, but she was Evelyn's little sister, and I still wasn't sure of Jim. He seemed like an honest man and wasn't afraid of hard work. Jim was taller than most Japanese and had a stocky build. He liked to hunt and fish and came out with Wendy to the homestead often. I guess I just thought she was too young to marry.

We found a nice spruce for our seven kids to decorate with the strings of popcorn they had made for evenings on end. Bulbs and ornaments the kids had crafted over the years hung from the thick green branches that Steve and I had trimmed just right. The snow kept falling, and the temperature was as far below zero as it had ever been, freezing all the creeks and blowing the icy wind into the Visqueen on the outside of our old shack. Turned out to be a wonderful Christmas as 1973 came to a close.

Light-green and purple fluorescent beams spread out over the top of me and glowed on my face as my long legs sunk into the new snow in front of the house. January was a perfect time to see the northern lights that showed off a magnificent array of beauty to all of Alaska only visible during the coldest months of the year.

Steve and Kristi were dumping our tin bathtub onto the snow after all nine of us had our baths since it was Saturday night. It was late and time to kick up the woodstoves. This summer Steve and I cut plenty of dry birch and some poplar while the rest of the family stacked the twenty cords under the big tarp and against the house by the front door.

In the morning Evelyn made a big hot breakfast, which we all sat at the table and ate together after the chores were done. The twins bundled Timmy and Mikey up in their snow suits, gloves, and mittens for the cold ride out, while Steve and I warmed up the Polaris and hooked up the sled.

I had left the Ford pickup out at the community center in hopes we could make it to church this morning. Even with Evelyn behind me on the snow machine, the kids barely fit in our big sled, but the extra weight would help make a packed trail for the ride back in. This last October, when the snow started to fall early, I taught Steve how to drive the snow machine so the kids could get out to school.

After the escaped prisoner incident, I also showed all my girls how to shoot the .22. We spent many hours target practicing on old soup cans that were propped up on a stump behind the house.

Talkeetna Bible Church was barely visible from the highway as I pulled the big Ford in with five of the kids in the back trying to stay warm and dry under a blanket. The big red-and-white Quonset hut was hidden behind tall snowbanks and a poorly plowed driveway. There was one more spot in the parking lot next to Denny Miller among the many vehicles that were already covered in snow. We didn't always make it to church every Sunday, but our friends there saved us a row anyhow just in case.

When we finally walked into the large warm room with red carpet and soft maroon benches, everyone was standing praising the Lord in song led by Dick Smith. Evelyn saw her mom wave at us to sit in the long row they had saved for us in front of them. They got rid of the old metal fold-up chairs and green carpet a few years ago when all the men in the church helped to remodel the old Quonset hut.

Gary Calhoun got up after the singing and gave a fire-and-brimstone service about how riches are not gold. Denny Miller, who was sitting across the aisle from me, cleared his throat and then looked at me and smiled. I knew why he was grinning at me and told the whole story after church during the big potluck with all the congregation listening, except for the kids who were playing Ping-Pong.

Last fall I had a vivid dream one night about finding the headwaters of the great Kashwitna River. The wide and strong body of water ran high above the timberline east of Goose and Sheep Creeks out of the Talkeetna range. Most locals in Talkeetna knew about the great Kashwitna and the deserted gold mining claims over the tundra. After my dream, Denny agreed to ride the horses miles from home with me. Dungo and CJ were packed up with food, guns, and sleeping gear. I had already been planning to go for a few years now and had made another attempt with my brother Norman. We went the wrong time a year and got stuck in a snowstorm. We couldn't find our way out until I let CJ go and she followed the old tracks out of the mountain. She was good for navigation, while Dungo cut across, taking the shortest route home regardless of the treacherous trail.

Goose Creek was starting to freeze, pushing huge chunks of ice downstream as it got ready for winter. Denny rode CJ and I was on Dungo as we crossed Sheep Creek's icy waters and on into the tundra below the mountain range. From my previous trips up here, I knew about the bog holes in the tundra making it unpassable. An unfrozen part of the ground creates a sinkhole that can go down as far as fifty feet filled with mud. Riding through the tundra was like playing in a minefield, never knowing where the bog holes were. So I headed Dungo straight up the timberline toward the top of the lowest peak with Denny behind me. Only yards away, the Kashwitna River was the only thing we could hear as the great river almost a mile wide roared in our ears. Its peaks were visible hundreds of yards away and then went back down again as the queen greeted us. Beside the river we headed straight into a canyon where the wind began to really blow, making it nearly twenty below. We were about halfway to the mining claims when I decided to stop and set up camp. The high wind and wet snow falling on us suddenly made it impossible to start a fire. I finally came upon a hole in the huge rocks with somewhat of a cover. Denny and I unloaded the horses and set up our tent in the cavelike shelter. Then we realized the pack with our food was not on CJ and nowhere to be found. Cold and hungry, we chopped dry wood and started a fire in the cave while the horses snorted and danced around outside in the storm.

As we sat there in the dark cave warming ourselves against the small fire with only a flashlight, we talked about how we forgot our food supply. Denny was sitting across the fire opposite of me on a big boulder, and I was facing the entrance of the cave. The wind continued to howl outside, blowing snow in as I got up to check on the horses. Something moved quickly and awkwardly into the cave as I was nearing the entrance, causing me to stumble back, almost falling. Denny heard the commotion and jumped up with his .41 magnum just as I was able to shine the long black flashlight on our intruder. Unafraid and determined to get out of the storm, a huge porcupine waddled closer to the fire as Denny and I backed up so we could chase it out. My stomach growled as if it knew there would be no food tonight, and so I turned to my best friend, who had to be hungry too, and asked, "Supper?"

Denny and I not only had the same name but could almost tell what the other was thinking as we were a lot alike. He pulled up his pistol and pulled the hammer back to take aim at the porcupine. It was black with long white needles as a coat and was staring at us only feet away. Knowing we had several hours of riding tomorrow to reach the mining claims, I said to Denny, "Why waste a bullet?" He looked at me and laughed as I shone the flashlight on his round friendly face. I reached down by my saddle pack to grab my thirty-thirty rifle and turned it over to use the stock. Denny used the handle of his long heavy black flashlight to chase the porcupine my way as I stood toward the entrance of the cave. I swung my rifle into the air, bringing it down onto the angry porcupine. Barely stunned, the fat rodent ran back toward the fire toward Denny, whose laughter echoed inside our makeshift shelter as he hit it back to me with the long flashlight.

I had never eaten porcupine before but was about to find out what it was like as it finally fell to its death after we chased it back and forth for quite some time. With my leather gloves on, I took my hunter\s knife and slit the belly open and then skinned the quill-covered hide back. Denny held the legs while I cut them and the hindquarters off at once. That's where most of the meat was and roasted up to a delicious sizzling brown over our small cottonwood fire. The meat was tough and stringy but hit the spot in our empty stomachs and actually tasted a little like chicken.

Dick Smith, Gary Calhoun, and several of our other friends in the church stopped eating for a while as I continued to tell the story.

Leery of bears or other wild animals making their way into our dry cave, Denny and I took turns staying awake with the gun. The morning hours came upon us even though it was still dark. The storm had stopped, leaving new snow on the ground. We dried the horses and then saddled them up to finish the journey we had started to the top of the first mountain peak where the mining claims were. Several hours and narrow trails through the thick timber later, we finally reached the destination that took us several attempts to get to safely. The snow was too deep to do any mining and would have to wait until summertime and another trip. Denny and I gave the horses a rest and then headed back down the mountain. We had a good time riding down through the timberline, recalling the poor porcupine who became our supper. Once again my faithful mare CJ led us through the completely white forest as I told Denny to just let her go while I followed behind on Dungo.

After my story, I challenged Denny to a Ping-Pong game, and then Evelyn and our seven kids loaded up into the pickup so we could make it home before dark.

37

THE DUET

LORI

The wooden mouthpiece felt just right as I moistened the reed and then inserted it into the end of my black clarinet. The gym at the high school was almost full for the annual talent show. I was almost thirteen now and was feeling confident but a slight bit nervous. The whole family was in the audience sitting in the metal bleachers, including Grandma and Grandpa. I stood behind the blue velvet curtain, waiting for my best friend Robin, who was in my band class and played the clarinet also.

My arms were chilled under the short-sleeve red blouse I had tucked into my bell bottom blue jeans. Every time the double doors opened, more people came in, bringing a gush of forty-below wind into the auditorium. It was causing the curls on the ends of my long straight red hair to come out as they lay in front of my shoulders neatly. I had borrowed Mom's big pink sponge-like curlers and bobby pins and left them in my hair while I slept last night. This morning I had perfect curls and hoped they stayed in.

Dad got back from the North Slope the end of January, just in time for Mikey's first birthday. We were snowed in and running out of firewood, and the extreme cold and heavy blizzards caused us kids to miss a lot of school. Some people Dad knew up on the Parks Highway offered their house to us for a month while they were out of town. The talent show came just in time before moving back out to the homestead in March as we wouldn't have been able to make it out otherwise. That made me remember a funny story, which thinking about it calmed my nerves.

One day we kids were getting ready for school at the rental house on a clear but cold day. Mom was already gone to work driving one of the school buses while Timmy and Mikey rode with her. As always, the twins were taking forever to get their hair combed and teeth brushed. Kristi was waiting for the bathroom to get her tights and skirt suit on. Even though she was a tomboy, Mom made her wear skirts and dresses to church and school.

We were right by the highway where the bus pulled right up, allowing us more time in the mornings. Somehow we kids managed to be running late. Anyhow, I didn't like being late ever and watched nervously out the front window for the big yellow bus. It appeared suddenly as Steve and the twins were putting their coats on and Kristi was still in the bathroom. I yelled to her as Devan opened the front door, "Kristi, the bus is here!"

Just as Steve, Devan, Dawn, and I were hurrying out the front door, Kristi came running out of the bathroom, grabbing her coat. We all ran for the bus that was waiting for us with a new man driver. Kristi was behind us, zipping up her blue parka. The tall narrow bus doors swung open as an older man with dark hair and a white smile greeted us as we all raced up the steps into the long bus. Devan and Dawn took a seat in the front, and Kristi sat with Joy. Steve, Aunt Wendy, and I walked to the back of the bus. Some of the high school kids were smoking marijuana. The bus pulled out onto the highway as Steve and I found a seat amidst the cloud of funny-smelling smoke.

Then the funniest news made its way to the back of the bus via the twins. They were trying to get my advice on a disastrous situation. After I heard it, I made the mistake of telling Wendy in her ear to possibly figure out what to do. When she stood up and yelled out to the whole bus, finding the situation humorous, I felt bad for my little sister, who was crying in her seat at the front of the bus. "Kristi forgot her skirt!" With the rush of getting out to the bus, Kristi forgot to put her skirt on over her tights and didn't realize it after she put her parka on. When we got to the high school, I had Kristi get off the bus with me to wait to transfer to Mom's bus. Then after Mom got a good English laugh about the missing skirt, she took Kristi home for the day.

Robin was late as usual as we were next to go on stage for our duet. She came running in the backstage door with her short brown hair sticking out and her wrinkled white blouse out of her bell bottom jeans. I helped straighten her hair out as she tucked everything in just as our principal announced our act. My stomach did a flip and my heart began to race when Robin and I took the stage overlooking hundreds of familiar faces. We sat with good posture in the two metal folding chairs that were positioned in the front center of the stage. Our families were sitting directly in front of us. I saw Dad sitting next to Mom behind my siblings and felt like I needed to do my best to express the artist in me so he would realize I was a lot like him.

The big colorful stage lights suddenly dimmed, and then small bright round ones appeared with a bang on our black music stands to light up our notes. Robin and I looked at each other with confident eyes and knew it was time to start playing the song we had practiced for months.

We picked up our long black wooden clarinets in unison and held them up to our mouths with our lips firmly around the mouthpiece. My hands were slightly trembling as my long white fingers took their place on the little round metal keys. The whole building was silent in anticipation to hear the two girls who were first-time entrees into the talent show.

I was to the left of Robin, and as I tapped my right foot four times, we began to play "The Entertainer." The audience remained silent except for several oohs and aahs that lifted my confidence, and then I really began to play like never before. My long white fingers danced across the round metal keys as I used my tongue to execute perfect beautiful notes. Robin sounded good and in time with me as we both knew the song by heart and really didn't need the white pages in front of us with the musical notes.

"The Entertainer" unfolded and filled the gym with a graceful and upbeat story that everyone seemed to be enjoying. No fancy words were needed to explain the well-constructed and famous song that Robin and I played with ease. It was hard to see my family in the dark audience, but I thought I saw Dad take his cowboy hat off and wipe his eyes. He as well as Mom loved music and hoped all of us kids would play an instrument.

Steve and Devan had started playing the clarinet last year and joined the school band with me. Dawn played the flute quite well and finally got up the nerve to join the band this year.

There seemed to be a disappointment in the audience when our beautiful melody came to an end as the last few notes lingered on, echoing the perfect duet. As we finished playing, my good friend Robin and I stood up and hugged each other, shedding a few tears of happiness and relief. When we turned to face the audience hand in hand, I saw that they were all up off the bleachers, giving us a standing ovation.

My whole family yelled and cheered for us, and it made me feel so proud. I then realized practice does make perfect and we should always use the gifts God gave us.

Robin and I won the talent show this year at the high school, and we each got a blue ribbon to show for it. Both of us suddenly gained some popularity at school after that talent show, and I have to say, it didn't bother me.

Dad moved us back to the homestead the beginning of March even though it was still snowing and we had to take the snow machine and sled in making a few trips. When we got into the house and set-tled in, Dad told the twins to go out to the garage and feed our dogs. As they were doing what they were told, several meows got the twins' attention. Devan's big Siamese cat had given birth up in the attic to two kittens that were male and female. Dawn boosted Devan up into the rafters where she crawled into a small dark space to pull the two cute little newborn kittens out and her cat Missy.

They then brought them into the warm house where Dad looked at them and shook his head as if we couldn't keep them. I was the only one of us kids that ever challenged Dad, and this was one of those rare occasions. "There's only two kittens, Dad. Can't we keep them?" By then the whole family was standing in the living room, admiring the kittens. Dad looked at me, squinting his eyes and cocking his head as a big smile broke through, showing his straight white teeth. Then the words he said to me next made me know Dad was proud of me and made me feel good inside. "Lori, if you play that song for me again on your clarinet tonight as good as you did at the talent show, I'll let you kids keep the kittens." And that's what I did as the snow continued to blow by our lantern-lit windows and the stoves crackled into the close of another night.

38

THE POWER PLANT

KRISTI

It was 1974 and unusually hot for an early July day. At noon the thermometer nailed to the wall outside the kitchen door read ninety degrees. It was a good day for Timmy and me to be outside, and we were.

The huge white birch tree that stood in the front of the house had large branches that provided an abundance of shade. The bed of it was built up with pretty pansies Mom had planted the first year that came up every spring. Perfect place to play matchbox cars pretending the flowers were our trees. With our denim-covered knees in the dirt, we made lots of miniature roads beneath the shady tree that led to our make-believe town. We had hours of fun imagining this was where we really lived and these were our own cars, trucks, vans, and buses.

Mom had told us during breakfast that she was going to wash our many loads of dirty clothes. She would be plugging the big white round washing machine into the power plant that sat on a small trailer in the front yard.

Dad had pulled it from the garage before breakfast and put it outside of the kitchen and made sure it had plenty of fuel.

The power plant was a large blue square machine that was also a welder Dad used often. At the other end of the power plant, facing the tongue of the trailer, was a flywheel with four large blades that spun very fast when running. A screen formed a cage over the wide blades, leaving narrow gaps. Dad had warned us many times to stay away from the power plant running or not! When Dad said to stay away from something, we knew we had better listen.

The silvers were running at the mouth of Goose Creek near the end of the slough in large schools. Their large shiny bodies jumped in and out of the water, waiting for a colorful lure to bite on.

Dad, Steve, and Lori hiked up the half-mile trail ending at the mouth of Goose Creek to try to catch the challenging salmon. Steve was just days away from twelve years old and an expert fisherman. He helped Lori tie her lure before casting out into the rapid creek, with Dad's .41 magnum strapped around his thin waist.

Grizzlies were abundant this time of year, and even though their diet mostly consists of vegetation, they may become aggressive. We had great respect for all bears in the wild, being careful not to be a threat to their habitat.

Sharing the same forest, land, and riverbeds, they seemed to know us as the years went by and knew we were not of harm to them and their cubs. Before Dad had left, he instructed Devan and Dawn to watch us younger kids while he was gone.

I had turned eight in March and did not need a lot of supervision, but Timmy was almost three and Mikey was only eighteen months old.

I looked up and saw Mom come out of the house in her cropped light-green pants and a white sleeveless blouse with her long wavy red hair tied up in a blue handkerchief. She walked over to the power plant, turned the key, and started it. Then she plugged in the one-hundred-foot extension cord to plug into the washing machine Dad got Mom a few years ago.

The power plant was loud but didn't bother us as we kept driving our cars down the dirt roads under the huge tree.

This went on for about twenty minutes when suddenly I heard a loud scream that came from behind us where the power plant was! I jerked around and stood up to see Mikey standing at the end of the power plant with his arm into the cage that enclosed the flywheel!

He was looking at me, struggling to cry with his little mouth open.

I sprang up off the ground, running as fast as I could to Mikey while screaming toward the house, "Mom! Mom! Help!"

Timmy was right behind me, screaming, "Mommy!"

Mikey's right hand was stuck in the flywheel that was spinning and chopping at his fingers.

I knew I had to pull his hand out of the flywheel as there was no one else around except Timmy, who was behind me sobbing loudly.

So quickly getting behind his tiny body, I reached out and grabbed his right arm. With both of my hands, I pulled back as fast as I could, and his hand was released from the chopping blades. I couldn't help but see blood and bone hanging from his hand as his little blond head fell back against my chest.

Mom came running out of the house faster than I'd ever seen her run, almost stumbling. She swooped Mikey up from my stiff arms as I held his weak body. He was crying and screaming at the same time.

I just stood there in the yard with my little one-year-old brother's blood on my green T-shirt in shock. I didn't know what to do. It was like a real bad nightmare.

Devan and Dawn trailed behind Mom, sobbing uncontrollably in disbelief that Mikey was hurt so badly. Mom held Mikey's limp body close to her as she ran up the two steps to the deck. Devan opened the new screen Dad had put on the kitchen door to keep the mosquitos out.

By now Timmy was clinging on to me with his arms around my waist, and I knew I had to pull it together for him. So I grabbed his hand, and we ran into the house.

Screaming "Oh my god! My baby, my baby!" Mom frantically grabbed a towel from the kitchen counter and wrapped poor Mikey's injured hand tightly to stop the bleeding.

"Dawn, go get your dad!" Mom commanded her through her flood of tears.

Devan stood by Mom, trying to keep her calm and comfort Mikey at the same time. I just stood there, nervously trying not to bawl and wanting to help.

So I kept an eye on Timmy, careful not to let him out of my sight as he was upset but didn't know what was going on.

"Dennis! Dennis!" Mom cried as she rocked in her big wood chair by the stove, holding Mikey close to her chest.

I hardly ever saw our mom cry. It was only when one of us was hurt or in danger that she would lose control, unable to function. That was how I knew how much she loved us.

I couldn't believe what was happening. Was Mikey going to die? The blood was soaking through the towel around his tiny hand onto Mom's white blouse. Mikey just laid his head on Mom's shoulder, sobbing loudly. Devan told me to get another towel to wrap around Mikey's hand while she wrapped a blanket around Mom and Mikey's shaking bodies.

LORI

I was standing with my dad on the bank of Goose Creek, admiring the sixteen fish we all had caught and cleaned.

Dad heard something from a distance and shushed me quickly.

Steve was a hundred yards down the bank, trying to catch just one more fish before we had to leave.

"It sounds like one of the twins!" Dad said.

"Dad! Dad!" Dawn screamed as she ran as fast as her legs would go to our well-known fishing spot.

We looked up to see my sister Dawn running toward us, her face streaked with tears and yelling, "Mikey's hurt real bad!"

"What happened?" Dad said to her sternly as he grabbed his big rifle and instructed me to grab the fishing poles.

"He got his hand in the power plant and is bleeding badly!" Dawn said through her tears.

"Let's go!" Dad was worried as he ran up the trail, packing our catch on a stringer toward the house with me running not far behind.

STEVE

As I looked up from the long silver I had just caught, I saw that Dad and Lori were gone. They weren't on the bank anymore, and I only saw the friend of Dad's that had just showed up to fish.

He was standing where Dad and Lori were, so I yelled down the bank to him. "What happened? Where did everyone go?"

The guy, whose name was John, yelled back to me, "Something about your little brother getting hurt real bad!"

My heart began to beat rapidly as I grabbed my fish and ran up the bank to the trail. I was thinking that Dad must have been really upset to have left me behind and not told me about my little brother.

KRISTI

It seemed like a long time since Dawn had left to get Dad, and Mom was getting more hysterical, crying and screaming, "Help us, God! My baby!"

Just then Dad came bursting through the kitchen door with Lori and Dawn right behind him, slamming the screen.

He ran over to Mom and Mikey and could see instantly that Mom was hysterical and said to her sternly, "Evelyn, pull it together. We've got to take care of Mikey!"

Dad knelt down and rubbed Mikey's sweat-soaked head. Then he carefully unwrapped the towels that were soaked in blood from Mikey's tiny hand.

Dad's face turned white as we all saw the permanent damage the flywheel had done to Mikey's fingers.

His pinky finger was chopped off right above the knuckle, and the finger next to the pinky was hanging by fragments of bone and skin.

Mom looked down at Mikey's right hand and started screaming, "Oh my god! Oh my god! His fingers!"

Dad then reached up and slapped Mom firmly on the side of her left cheek, which startled her instantly back into reality.

"We have to tend to these wounds right away!" Dad said, knowing Mikey was at risk for bleeding and infection.

Dad yelled toward us kids standing around them, not knowing what to do but cry, "Get some gauze and Vaseline!"

Mikey started to sit up, trying to extend his arms to Dad while sobbing and shaking. Dad wrapped the towels around his hand again and picked him up and held him tightly in his arms.

We all knew Mikey had a special place in Dad's heart 'cause we could see a twinkle in his eyes when he watched Mikey do anything.

Lori and I ran as fast as we could out to the tack room that was in the barn to find supplies Dad used for the horses when they were injured.

Grabbing two rolls of gauze and a tub of Vaseline, we ran back to the house, handing the supplies to Dad.

Mom was still crying but was able to hold Mikey as Dad sat him on her lap as he doctored his hand. He pulled a big glob of Vaseline out of the jar and packed it onto Mikey's mangled fingers then took the roll of gauze and wrapped his hand several times, securing it tightly with electrical tape.

Just then Steve came running into the kitchen, out of breath, to find all of us standing around Mikey while Dad was wrapping his tiny hand.

Dad instructed Steve to get the Ford Galaxy ready to go and gave Mikey to Devan to hold.

"Evelyn, get your purse and jacket. We need to get to the hospital," Dad said to Mom and then continued, "We'll stop at the Lankfords' and use their phone to call Francis Wolfe so she can give Mikey something for pain."

Mom had told Lori through her tears to crush a baby aspirin with sugar and water on a spoon to give to Mikey for pain. Lori was trying to give it to him as Dad was carrying him out the kitchen door to the car where Steve had parked it in the driveway.

Mom ran behind him while telling us to clean up and stay away from the power plant. Dad said as he was loading Mikey onto Mom's lap in the seat of the car, "We may not get back for a few days and won't be able to get a hold of you kids. Steve and Lori are in charge.

Do what they say!" He continued while shutting the door on his side of the car, "You have enough water for a few days, so stay close to home until we get back!"

Leaving a trail of dust, the tan Galaxy sped out of sight down our dirt road as our hearts sank watching our little brother go away with Mom and Dad.

I was praying in my mind that Mikey would come back soon and his fingers would be all better.

After stopping across the tracks at the Lankfords', Dad drove the rest of the way to the highway to meet nurse Francis Wolfe, who gave Mikey a shot to ease the pain. Just like she did when I broke my leg when I was five.

After Mom and Dad had left, Steve and Lori picked up the two buckets of salmon they had caught and started filleting them on the wooden table behind the house. They threw the heads and bones in a bucket to be buried in our small garden.

Devan and I helped by taking the rich red meat into the kitchen and wrapping each one with Saran wrap tightly. Then we placed the fillets into the root cellar under the house.

The fillets would need to be brined and smoked within the next few days or put in the Lankfords' freezer as they let us do in the summer.

Dawn got Timmy to take a nap and then pulled the clothes from the line and started folding them on the couch.

After all thirty-four fillets were put away into the root cellar, Lori and Devan made us all tuna fish sandwiches.

We sat at the table, silently eating our sandwiches, staring at the blue power plant that we could see through the screen door in the kitchen.

I'm sure we were all thinking different thoughts, but I was wishing I would never have to see the power plant again.

After we ate, Steve and Lori dragged the trailer with the power plant into the garage and closed the two large doors.

Later that evening, Steve and I headed out to the field with three halters and lead ropes to bring the horses in for the night. Even though I was only eight, Jude followed me with ease. She had foaled this spring from being bred by Dungo, and her little brown filly colt followed behind.

The big powerful bodies of Dungo and CJ hid Steve as he was in between them, trying to hold them back.

After the horses were all put away in their stalls, we threw them each a flake of hay and a half can of sweet feed.

On the way back to the house, we fed our two hogs.

Meardha, Goldy, and Lucky followed us around as we fed all the animals. We didn't have Pete anymore as Dad gave him away after he lost his mind and ran in circles all the time.

Palmer Community Hospital sent Mom and Dad to Providence Hospital in Anchorage, which was another forty miles, for Mikey to see an orthopedic specialist.

The surgeon at Providence saw how distraught Mom was and advised Mom and Dad to go have some dinner and let them take care of Mikey.

He said that Mikey's two fingers on his right hand, the pinky and ring finger, would be lost down to the first knuckle.

The surgeon told them he was fortunate not to have lost his whole hand. Mom and Dad went to the Seales' house in Anchorage for the night where Joe and Jeanette prayed with them and fed them dinner. Mom said she could hear Jeanette crying all night long.

The next morning I awoke to the sound of Lori opening the dark curtains in the living room to let the never-ending light in.

Steve was already dressed and putting his boots on. "Get up, Kristi, and come help me feed!"

I jumped out of bed, eager to go outside and help with the all the animals. Besides, it got me out of helping in the kitchen. I put on some clothes—blue jeans and a little red T-shirt—and my blue tennis shoe with no socks.

After pulling my long tangled red hair back into a rubber band and putting on my sneakers, Steve and I headed out the front door with the dogs.

Later that day, all of us kids were outside doing chores when we could hear someone coming down the dirt road with a cloud of dust behind them.

As soon as we could see the vehicle, we knew it was Mom and Dad.

We all wondered if Mikey would be with them.

They pulled up into the yard, and we could see that Mom was holding Mikey with his brown and white plaid shirt on in her lap. Dad got out and went around the car to take Mikey so Mom could get out.

We all ran over to the car, eager to see our baby brother, who was perched up in Dad's arms with a large bandage around his right hand. He was smiling at all of us, and I could tell he was glad to be home.

I remember a sense of pure happiness and peace at that moment in the yard when we were all together again and thankful.

39

DOWN UNDER

STEVE

All summer long Dad had us skin spruce logs up by the slough for our new house. All four of my sisters and me straddled the long trees Dad had cut down with his chainsaw. We worked all day unless the often rain poured down on us too hard.

He gave us tools that were long thin blades with a handle on each end that were meant for skinning the bark off the fallen trees.

Our house was crowded with all nine of us now, even with the long trailer attached that we couldn't keep warm in the winter.

A couple of weeks ago, Dad and I built tall narrow wooden footings for filling with cement for a basement and foundation for the new house. Dad said he always dreamed of having a daylight basement.

Something new about my mom that I didn't know but admired her for was that she is a well witcher. Mom took two thin long copper rods to hold in her hands while she pointed them toward the ground. She was looking for the best place where we could dig for a well.

Mom explained that some people have a certain energy in their bodies that blend with copper to detect water minerals deep below the ground.

As she walked the property close to the new house, the long copper rods vibrated right in her hands in certain spots. One area close to the foundation made the copper rods vibrate really strong as we kids and Dad watched her. As she did her magic, Mom said by the way the rods were bouncing she could tell the well would be deep with plenty of water.

They marked the spot on the ground with a big post so the well drillers would know exactly where to drill.

I couldn't believe we might have running water and plumbing in our house like most of my friends did in Talkeetna. No more hauling five-gallon buckets of water a half mile from the spring mostly uphill or packing and melting snow on the barrel stove in the winters for baths, dishes, and drinking.

When gathering snow, we kids watched for the yellow snow that was commonly around the house in the winter as none of us wanted to visit the dark outhouse during the night.

This year in July, right after Dad turned thirty-four years old, we took advantage of the warm weather and hayed our field as fast as we could. There was a lot of rain this summer, making it hard for me to pull our new hay baler with the pickup through all thirty acres.

Dad took the Rambler Uncle Norman had left with us and cut the back off to make it shorter. Then he poured concrete in the back of it after removing the back seat to make traction in the wet muddy ground.

Dad welded a hitch on the back of the Rambler to hook to the hay baler. Then I drove it up and down the field, while my sisters kept the bales from hanging up on the baler. Driving the Rambler was a lot of fun and made haying season bearable for me.

August brought us cooler days, just in time for the Palmer fair and the races. I had been jockeying for several years now, developing a passion for the win. Horses were a way of life for me, and Dad had taught me everything I needed to know to stay in the saddle. On our homestead we had many uses for horses—hunting, fishing, transportation, and sometimes the only way out of the property.

The biggest challenge was keeping the horses warm during the winter and safe from the many bears wandering throughout the bush during warmer seasons.

Grandma and Grandpa Stanton wouldn't be at the fair this year as they were moving to Trapper Lake, which was about twenty miles northwest. Grandpa Verne wanted to live on a lake, and they found the perfect spot with a cute log cabin that he had remodeled himself. The only way into Trapper Lake was by airplane as many other places in Alaska.

Aunt Wendy didn't move with them as she was getting married to Jim Sakaguchi in October. She took home studies to Jim's parents' house close to McKinley Park and stayed with them. Joy and Dougie were going to homeschool with Grandma Gloria as their teacher on Trapper Lake.

August brought some darkness at night, putting an end to summer solstice. The days were cooling down to the forties above and the nights below the freezing mark, leaving a glisten on the leaves and crispy ground.

Dad was up at sunrise, which was 5:00 a.m. and had all of us kids up at once scrambling to get ready to go to the fair. The chores were done and the old wood camper was loaded and so were we within the hour.

The fair was my favorite time of year, and I was especially looking forward to this one. Dad usually had me jockey Dungo, who made all our other horses a breeze to ride. This year I got to jockey our palomino mare CJ, whom I'd been training for the big day for months. She was quick out of the gate and fast at running, but not as fast as Dungo, who beat most horses every year. CJ was in prime shape this year, and her rippling muscles and shiny golden coat showed it.

Last year Dad let Lori, for the first time after months of her prodding, jockey CJ. My older sister was lightweight and a good rider. CJ took third place, and Lori had the time of her life. Dad promised to let her jockey sometime again soon. She was still a big help in the stalls and walking Dungo and CJ before the races.

Dad also thought about eventually putting Kristi in as a jockey since she rode bareback just like an Indian with her long braids flying in the wind.

"Steve!" I practically tripped in my oversize cowboy boots that Mom and Dad got me for my twelfth birthday on July 19. They were brown leather with one-inch heels and pointed toes, and I wore them almost everywhere in the summer. Mom always believed in buying our new shoes at least one size too big so they would last longer.

Dad was yelling for me from the pickup and horse trailer to help him hitch up and load Dungo and CJ. Within split seconds, I was at the back of the red Ford one-ton guiding the hitch directly over the ball of the horse trailer.

I raised my right arm with a fist indicating to Dad to stop. He jumped out of the pickup and began winding the jack handle to lower the hitch onto the ball. I knew better than to wait for further instructions from my dad, and so I headed with a sprint in my step to the barn to halter up Dungo and CJ.

Jude, our big chestnut mare, had to stay home with Meardha, Goldy, and Lucky for five days. She foaled this last spring and had a pretty little brown stud from Dungo. We named him Star because he had a big star-shaped white marking on his forehead. We watched him grow as he awkwardly followed Jude out to pasture to graze.

Both big horses full of piss and vinegar were pulling on the halter ropes as I had to run in between them using my huge muscles to hold them back.

Dad was loading two bales of hay into the tack compartment, then he walked over to me and took Dungo's lead rope. Then we both led our powerful prize-winning racehorses over to our blue-and-white horse trailer.

Mom, Lori, Devan, Dawn, Kristi, Timmy, and Mikey were already loaded into the camper and pickup with food and supplies for camping out at the fairgrounds.

The horses loaded into the trailer right in step with just a quick gesture from Dad's hand as he and I dropped the lead ropes at the same time.

I sure looked up to my dad as he continued to teach and amaze me with his knowledge and many talents. Spending a lot of time with him reassured me that my skills in the bush and riding horses came natural to me like Dad. While my dad and I shared this, I felt like my personality was more like Mom's of an English nature, finding softer ways of resolving problems.

The camper rocked around as Dad pulled the pickup and trailer into the Palmer fairgrounds. My stomach leaped when the hammer came into sight as I knew it was a gut-wrenching ride I looked forward to every year.

Last year I met a little cowgirl my age who was a jockey for her dad on a brilliant black thoroughbred stallion. I was caught off guard by her nice-looking, perfect white smile and long sandy-brown hair. Her name was Sissy, and every time I spoke to her, I stared at her dark-brown eyes as if in a trance. I was already kind of spoken for in Talkeetna by Farah Smith, who was my best friend Tyler's older sister.

I sure was hoping Sissy would be here this year so we could hang out again and become great friends.

After unloading the horses into their assigned stalls, Dad said we kids could have some free time and handed us each five dollars. Mom made us bologna sandwiches before we ran off to ride the carnival rides with our free passes. Lori dared me to ride the octopus with her, Devan, and Kristi. Dawn took Timmy and Mikey on the teacups, cars, elephants, and other kids' rides where she had the most fun. Dawn seemed to have a nurturing heart when it came to babies and little kids more than horses or anything else. She always stayed close to Mom as if she were her own personal nanny.

After a few hours and tons of fun riding the big carnival rides and filling our bellies with cotton candy, all seven of us headed toward the camper to check in with Mom and Dad. When we got back to the camper across the fairgrounds, Dad had CJ saddled and was warming her up in the arena. There standing by the corral was Sissy with her dad and black stallion.

As I walked up to the arena, I forgot all about my brothers and sisters behind me as a huge smile cracked my face without trying. "Hi, Steve!" Sissy's assertive but soft voice called out to me just as I had imagined in my mind. I felt my face heat up the closer I got as I threw her an eager wave. Dad saw me coming and dismounted CJ and led her out of the arena. He handed me the reins and said sternly, "Take her out to the track and run a few laps."

Even though I was already tired from the carnival rides, I knew Dad was serious and wanted CJ to stay in top shape. So I tightened up the cinch and put my cowboy boot into the stirrup, swinging myself into the saddle. Besides, I didn't want to miss a chance to show Sissy how my riding skills had improved.

CJ made winning time around the track with Sissy and her stallion running close behind me as we made several laps practicing for the cowboy race. Every year before the big cup race on Sunday, we had an old Western tradition of lap and tap racing, where all the horses line up on a chalk line in front of the gates. An old-fashioned air horn was blown loudly for the takeoff.

The next few days, Sissy and I hung out with my sisters at the carnival rides where got to know each other better. In the evenings, she and I worked our horses in the arena and then slept in the stalls to keep watch over the horses at night. I slept with my sleeping bag in the loose straw next to the plywood wall with CJ. Sissy was with her horse in the stall next to mine, and we ended up talking late into the night. I found out she was a Palmer basketball cheerleader.

Sunday morning came too soon, bringing the nervous jitters about racing against Sissy in just a few hours. Dad had warned me about distractions, and I knew it was time to get serious and competitive. Yesterday, I raced Dungo and took second place, winning a red ribbon and two hundred dollars. Sissy's brother raced her big stallion, and the saddle came loose during the race. Her brother went over with the saddle, and it hit the track with him in it right under all the racing horses. He turned out fine.

CJ pranced around, proudly tossing her silky white mane that Lori had brushed and braided. I sat up in the Western pony saddle Dad had got for me because it was small and light and still within the rules of the race. The race announcer said my name and CJ's while I rode proudly erect in the little saddle. I could hear my whole family cheer from the bleachers as they all stood up and waved at me. Dad was standing on the side of the track, waiting for the race to start cheering for us as well. I heard Sissy's name called as she gracefully rode her shiny big black stallion up to the grandstands. When it was time to ride up on the big chalk line with the other seven horses, I made sure I was next to Sissy and her stallion. She turned and looked at me just as the loud air horn sounded, and I looked at her and then yelled, "Yah!" CJ bolted into the air, landing at a dead run as I kept yelling like Dad taught me, "Yah! Yah! Yah!"

One by one CJ passed every horse like a streak as I gripped my knees on the small pony saddle. As we took the inside of the track, we passed Sissy and the others for an easy win. How I loved the cheers from the crowd and the dust flying behind me for the victory on our faithful mare.

Just as CJ was making the last two laps, my light leather saddle suddenly became loose, shifting sideways to the left, taking me with it and throwing her off stride. Now my mind was racing, imagining the saddle taking me all the way down to the track under sixteen hooves behind me that were quickly gaining. "I have to stay on!" That voice inside my head screamed at me as I reached forward and grabbed CJ's mane with the reins between my fingers. Then somehow I lifted my legs off the saddle, and with my left hand, I pushed the saddle off her back so I could finish the race bareback. The crowd screamed and the cameras flashed as CJ ran faster than ever with the little saddle under her belly. It was as if the other horses were standing still as we pounded dirt on the inside, coming in second place the best way I know how to ride—bareback!

40

FATAL CRASH

EVELYN

U pon our return to the homestead after the state fair in Palmer, in less than a week, our long dirt road was covered in dry leaves already. A north wind was blowing hard, stripping the wild animals of their shelter and food supply. The big colorful cottonwood, birch, and spruce leaves were turning brown from the frost that had crept in early this year.

The moose were more visible through the thick trees as they stretched their long necks up into the branches, scraping for vegetation. The bears were filling up on plants, berries, salmon, and carcasses of all kinds before hibernating for the winter with their cubs.

When we passed by our big barn that day as we made it home from the fair, where Steve made an amazing finish to his race on CJ, Jude and her colt were standing by the road with our dogs.

Dennis had left the barn open while we were in Palmer so Jude and Star could graze on the field and still have shelter.

Our seasonal electric wire was up around the back of the homestead to keep the horses out of the woods.

Thinking it odd that Jude and Star were standing by the road instead of grazing on the field, Dennis stopped the pickup with the camper and the horse trailer right in the middle of the road only a hundred yards from the house. As soon as he got out of the pickup,

Meardha, Goldy, and Lucky began to bark, and then as Star came around from behind Jude's huge body, we knew what was going on.

Dennis yelled, "Evelyn!" I gasped at the blood spurting out of the little stud colt's wounded neck. I struggled to get out of the pickup over Timmy and Mikey, who were sleeping in the cab.

Even though Mikey's hand was still tender, I don't think he realized part of his two fingers were missing because he ran around with the rest of the kids playing in the dirt. Then he would accidently hit his right hand on something and cry out in pain from the damaged nerves.

The camper door flew open, and Steve ran over to Dennis with a towel from the fair supplies. Lori, Kristi, and the twins were right behind him.

Star walked right over to Dennis, and that's when we all saw a large gaping flesh wound deep and wide on the left side of his little brown fuzzy neck.

Steve haltered Jude, while Dennis applied pressure to the big hole in the little stud's neck and turned to us and said with great disappointment in his voice, "Looks like a grizzly took a swat at this little guy." He stroked the colt to calm him and then said quietly, "Steve, let's get Jude and Star to the barn where I can doctor him. Lori, find me an upholstery needle and fishing line." Kristi followed Dennis to the barn with the bag of lime he told her to fetch from the outhouse as I pulled the pickup into the front of our house.

After Devan and Dawn helped me to unload Timmy and Mikey from the pickup and into the house to finish their naps, we ran out to the barn to see Dennis try to save the recently mauled colt.

Steve held Jude close to Star as Lori held the little colt's halter lightly while Dennis washed the wound with peroxide. The four-month-old stud colt gave them a challenge as he danced around from the cleansing sting. "Is he going to live?" Kristi asked Dennis as we all watched him pack the grapefruit-size gash with pure clean lime powder.

"Maybe if I can keep infection out," Dennis said as he threaded the thin fishing line through the upholstery needle. "Hold him still,

Lori!" he said sternly as Star started backing up as if he knew what was coming.

Then I stepped in and helped Dennis by holding the borders of the huge wound together as he started stitching into Star's tough hide.

Jude whinnied and fought the halter rope in Steve's hands as Dennis made the final stitch. The large needle and fishing line closed most of the big wound and was probably better than a veterinarian could have done.

September went by fast as we prepared for my sister Wendy's wedding that was to be held the same day as Timmy's third birthday, October 4, 1974. She and Jim were to be married at Kent and Martha's lodge one hundred miles north of here on the edge of the impressive Mount McKinley National Park. Dennis couldn't go as he was heading out on a hunting trip into the mountains with the horses. He wasn't thrilled about going to the wedding as he still wasn't sure about Jim Sakaguchi.

On his way to the mountains, he took Tim, the boy he had brought out to our homestead for a week, back to the boys' ranch. Dennis got a part-time job working for a boys' ranch in Willow as a counselor. He thought about starting his own ranch for troubled boys at our homestead eventually.

Tim was of native descent and had dark skin. He was tall with an afro that was colored red or more of a burgundy. Dennis was good with Tim and taught him how to work on a ranch and ride a horse. Then he caught Tim smoking marijuana behind the barn and told him he didn't want that stuff around our kids. We never saw him again, but many other young boys came and went.

The wedding day was finally here, and it was snowing buckets on the homestead, leaving a heavy wet foot of it to drive through with our tan Galaxy. It was running good for the ninety miles the kids and I had to go to get to McKinley Park, if we could just make it through the snow on the way home.

Last night we all enjoyed the birthday cake the twins baked for Timmy, and he opened his presents a day early.

I wanted to arrive at Wendy's wedding early so we could all help with the preparations. I pulled the tan Galaxy into the snowed-over parking lot. It was wet, heavy snowfall and even more of it up north at the lodge.

Jim was standing outside, looking handsome in his dark three-piece suit with my mom and dad and his parents.

Steve, Devan, Dawn, Kristi, Timmy, and Mikey stayed outside in the snow with their coats and hoods on while Lori and I ran into the Smiths' cabin where my sister and her two best friends Ruth and Robin were waiting.

Wendy looked beautiful in her white wedding gown, and her cheeks were glowing bright red. She was not even eighteen yet and getting married to an older man at twenty-four. As I took a good look at her standing there with her long red hair curled at the ends under the veil, I said, "I'm happy for you, sis, wish Ginger and Joyce could be here."

Fifteen minutes before the ceremony was to begin, Lori and I were still in the cabin with Wendy when we all heard the drone of a plane outside above us. Lori and I headed for the door to see who would fly a plane in this wet, heavy snowfall.

Wendy whisked by us to step out of the cabin to look. She stepped off the deck into the wet snow, straining to get a look.

"Get back in here. Your hair will get wet!" her friends yelled to her as she looked up into the sky. "I hope it's no one we know flying in this weather!" Wendy yelled back as we caught a glimpse of the hardworking loud small plane coming through the white clouds just above the trees.

The white plane had mouth and teeth on the nose and continued to circle right above us like it was trying to land in the bad storm.

Wendy went back into the cabin in a frenzy while Lori and I joined everyone else outside in the falling snow.

The plane started to circle back toward the highway, and as we looked up, it was losing its engine and starting to come down toward us fast.

The crowd of family and guests standing outside with us ran quickly toward the lodge not knowing where the plane would land.

Then as we watched in horror, the little white plane with the mouth and teeth came rapidly crashing nose down into the earth close to where we were all standing.

There was a brief explosion in the back of the plane, shaking the ground. Then everything went silent except for the disbelief of the wedding crowd.

Delores McCullough ran to the cabin with Lori and the twins to let Wendy know what had happened without spoiling her wedding day. My dad and Jim ran into the lodge to get preacher Kent and the other men. Then they ran out to the plane that was nose down and tail up in a snowbank while I ran behind with Steve.

When we got to the crashed plane and saw the two men in the cockpit slumped over, I knew they couldn't have survived the hard impact.

Dad and Jim opened the cockpit door with a crowbar Pastor Kent had retrieved, and after a struggle, they pulled the men out of their sudden grave. Steve and I went back over to the lodge with the rest of the family, not able to see any more of the fatality.

Dad, Jim, and Pastor Kent moved the bodies to a nearby dump truck and then notified the local park ranger.

Lori and I went back over to the cabin where Delores had Wendy and the other girls singing "I Saw the Light."

The wedding went on as planned an hour late and was beautiful even though only a few hundred yards away was the tail of the small plane sticking straight up out of the snow.

Jim and Wendy said their vows to each other, trying to forget about the fatal crash but still remember the lives lost of the two unfortunate men on their wedding day.

All the way home from the McKinley Park that night before dark, the snow continued to fall like a lace curtain in front of me, sticking and freezing to the windshield of the Galaxy. I was barely able to see the unplowed highway staying in the tracks of the car in front of me through a foot or more of snow. It was twenty below zero and almost nine o'clock, and the kids were restless, poking at each other, anxious to get home.

When we finally made it to the homestead, Dennis was there from his hunting trip early. After we all unloaded from the car, I asked him why he was home so early from his trip with George McCullough.

He said they killed a large moose but couldn't get it out through the tundra and had to leave it. There was another man with them that was having heart attack signs and needed to go to the hospital.

Dennis said the moose rack was the biggest he'd ever seen and wanted to go back and get it.

So the next day Dennis and I headed up the mountain range toward Copper River on horseback. We tied Dungo and CJ off at the timberline just before the tundra. Then we hiked up in the snow to where the moose carcass was, avoiding the bog holes.

Dennis had a good idea where the big moose was shot, and sure enough, we came upon it in a thicket of spruce trees, as the snow fell harder.

Only the huge eight-point antlers were oddly propped up against a huge mound of dirt made by a grizzly. The moose carcass was claimed quickly and buried under the soft brown dirt of the mountainside.

Dennis and I knew the grizzly was nearby as the high grass around us was beaten down and the mound had fresh bear scat on it.

I said to Dennis as he loaded his twelve-gauge shotgun and held it under one arm, "We had better get out of here!"

There was a cold north wind blowing, and the mound of dirt was being engulfed by the heavy snowfall. I got a chill down my spine as it felt like we were being watched.

Dennis walked over to the grizzly's mound and picked the heavy antlers up off the dirt and swung it up onto the back of his tan leather coat. "Let's go, he might follow us," Dennis said as he turned to look at me with apprehensive eyes.

The .41 magnum was heavy on my right hip as I hiked behind Dennis down the mountain through the tundra as fast as we could go. I kept looking behind me as I stumbled through the wirelike tundra, watching for soft ground.

When we got back down to the horses, we were both out of breath and Dennis was completely worn out from carrying the heavy moose antlers. There was no time to rest as we had to get the antlers off the mountain. Dennis tied them securely to the back of Dungo's saddle where the rack hung completely over his butt, which made him hop around until he got used to it.

We finally made it back home, and a few days later, Dennis hung the huge trophy moose antlers on the front of our big wood garage.

41

THE BALANCING ACT

DEVAN

C hristmas was my favorite holiday at our homestead, where my
senses were filled with the spirit of the Father himself.

There was really no need for fancy store-bought decorations or
too many gifts. The forest he created with his own two hands was
covered in a white blanket of pure snow from above.

Our wood fence of worn spruce that bordered part of the field
from the road had large mounds of snow on its railings. It was partly
buried into the deep snow that covered the field and entire property.
Mount McKinley was covered with snow, as well as all the other
peaks of the Alaska Range behind the field.

The rare sun glistened over the shiny white winter snow,
blinding our eyes like a bright star. Then the gold rays seeped in, and
it was like heaven on earth.

The smell of the wet forest was like having a million Christmas
trees as all the branches hung low with the weight of the heavy snow.

Squirrels still ran amuck gathering new fallen gifts from the
trees as their large furry bodies scampered up to their winter homes.

All the cars and tractors were put away for the winter under
several feet of snow where you could barely recognize their outlines.

Every new year the northern lights gave us a splendid light show
that danced its Christmas like colors off the glistening snow, overtak-

ing the moon. When Dad could get the ice clear on the slough, we kids got to skate for hours under the natural light that lit up our rink.

Huge mounds of snow from Dad's attempt to plow made a playground for the dogs as they ran up and down the large hills with us kids chasing close behind. We played king of the hill, pushing each other off the bank while the dogs barked and our three Siamese cats ran for cover. We didn't have cows or pigs anymore as the hard winters were nearly impossible.

Early on Christmas Day, we kids each eagerly opened our presents and got into our stockings. Dawn and I each got new books to read, and so did Lori. Steve got his very own basketball as he had joined the team at the high school so he could see his girlfriend Sissy when they competed with Palmer. Timmy got a new guitar so he could sing to us loudly but oddly in tune almost every night. Mikey got a brand-new shiny red tricycle that he could only ride around inside the house for now, and he did. Kristi got a whole big book of cut-out paper dolls that were stiff and punched out of the paper of the book with paper clothes. She liked to take Mom's JCPenney magazines and cut people and furniture out of them and play house. Kristi had a good imagination and no problem entertaining herself inside or outside.

Grandma and Grandpa Stanton came to town from Trapper Lake for Christmas to see friends and family. Right after breakfast on Christmas Day, they came roaring up on Grandpa Vern's nice yellow Ski-Doo with its matching sled. Joy and Dougie were in the partially enclosed sled, and Grandma was behind Grandpa on the snow machine.

After the chores were all done, Grandpa pulled us kids around on an innertube that he tied to his snow machine. We took turns as he sped the Ski-Doo across the field, weaving back and forth to get the innertube with several of us at a time to spin out of control. We all went in soaking wet from being thrown into the deep wet snow.

The whole family sat in the kitchen together to feast on scrumptious fatty moose roast with its rich drippings, in which Mom made her amazing gravy to pour over her seasoned dressing. Our family picked plenty of cranberries this fall to make a sweet tart sauce that tasted delicious with Mom's candied yams. Lori and Dawn loved to bake and spent all of Christmas Eve making us all homemade soft rolls and blueberry pies. Even though I had to help bake bread once a week, it wasn't my favorite chore to do. Really, it was an all-day project with other little ones in between while the twelve loaves with towels draped over them tripled in size. Since we had a fairly small oven, the trick was to make the loaves of white bread in a sequence so that they wouldn't all rise at once. In the winter we put the loaves in the pans by the hot woodstove to help the yeast work better.

Along with the other berries we picked every year, I especially liked the big juicy raspberries that grew on the thorny bushes along Goose Creek. The trail to Goose Creek was so pretty in the summer with the cottonwoods and poplars so thick and green hanging over the dirt trail. Tall blades of grass and raspberry bushes intertwined with colorful wildflowers that filled my nose with the fragrance of the woods.

While the whole family was skinning spruce logs this last summer for the new house, Dad had me ride Dungo bareback down to the creek to keep him in shape. Before that, some man borrowed Dungo and took him down into a canyon where he slid off a bank and broke his back.

Even with a broken back, Dungo was hard to hold back and cantankerous when I got off him to let him drink from the cold, clear creek. Sometimes he would nip at my ankles while I was standing next to him, holding his lead rope.

With only a few warm months a year, the wide creek that was like a river never warmed up. That didn't stop us kids from swimming in it as often as we could. Sometimes after skinning logs Dad would let us run down the narrow trail and cool off in the creek, while he threw a line in.

After Christmas, Grandma, Grandpa, Joy, and Dougie left to go back to Trapper Lake, where they would stay most of the winter.

The year 1975 came in with sixty-below temperatures and heavy blizzards. Dad was already back on the North Slope working and had to leave right after Dawn's and my eleventh birthday. Us kids missed a lot of school this winter as even the snow machines couldn't make the deep snow and often wouldn't start. When the chores were done and the fires were lit, we would play board games or read by the lanterns.

On Mikey's second birthday at the end of January, all of us kids gulped down the gooey German chocolate cake Mom had made and headed out to the big barn. The big piles of loose hay were fun to jump in, and the stacked bales made an easy way to get up onto the long thick rafter poles that went from one side to the other. The one in the center was a huge round spruce log, and when we climbed up on the bales of hay, we could sit on it and dangle our feet.

After all seven of us climbed to the tall stack of hay bales, Steve dared me to walk across the huge beam like a trapeze artist. We had all attempted to keep our balance and walk a few feet out on the rafter from the stack of bales but never had the guts to keep going all the way across.

I had always thought I had good balance and was up for a challenge on this cold winter day where the big long beam seemed perfect for practicing.

As my brothers and sisters watched, I carefully put one foot in front of the other and my arms straight out for balance. The rafter was wide enough for my small feet, and the first several steps seemed easy.

Everyone kept still as I had made it to the halfway mark before making the mistake of looking down at the ground. "Devan!" As the barn started to spin and my body was teetering out of balance, I heard Dawn yell my name as if I was going to fall to my death. Dancing my feet around on the wide round beam was my last effort to keep from plummeting several feet to the hard dirt floor of the barn.

Everything happened so fast as the next thing I knew, I was lying flat on my back, looking up at six faces that belonged to my siblings. I thought maybe I was dead as all my breath had left when the hard ground made impact with my body. I could see what they were doing but couldn't hear them, just like a silent movie. Lori was shaking me, and Dawn was crying. Kristi ran off to get Mom, and Steve looked worried.

A few minutes later, Mom came running into the barn as I was finally able to breathe but couldn't move as my back had an ache. Mom made me move my arms and legs to make sure nothing was broken, and then had Steve help me into the house where I stayed in bed and recovered.

I lay there and wondered how trapeze artists make it all the way across the wire without falling off. They must have guardian angels like we do that gently guide their landing even better than a safety net.

42

THE BEES

KRISTI

M y short red hair was sticking straight out after Dad had cut it all off into a Dorothy Hamill style. To the disappointment of my teachers and myself, my thick curly hair wouldn't bob like the famous ice skater. I got comments all the time on how they missed my long hair. For me it was easier to take care of since I could never find a brush with three sisters around.

My long skinny legs hung over the side of the twin bed as I heard Steve stoking the fire in the barrel stove. Trying not to wake my two little brothers, who were sleeping in the bunks that were close to the end of my bed, I slipped on my jeans that were crumpled up next to the bed on the floor.

It was an early Saturday morning in the middle of May, and we had company coming to our homestead today. I was hoping for sunshine.

Denny and Jean Miller were coming to visit with their two sons, Jason and Jeremy.

Last week Dad and Steve cut down several trees and had plenty of firewood to share as winter was still hanging around with patches of dirty snow and big, deep mud puddles. While they were in the woods cutting the fallen trees into firewood, Mom and my sisters sat in the house and visited with Aunt Ginger and her husband, Dan Work.

I rode our bike down the dirt road, splashing through every puddle to where Dad and Steve were falling trees. Then they threw the cut pieces of birch and spruce into the bed of Dad's red Ford pickup.

They were both busy, and the booming echo of chainsaws running and trees hitting the ground rang throughout the woods. "Timber!" Steve yelled as a tall, heavy spruce towered over and then shook the whole ground as it hit hard a long ways. Dad looked over at me standing by the pickup and yelled, "Kristi, get in the back of the pickup while these trees are falling!"

I heard Dad and jumped up onto the tailgate and then into the bed of the pickup, sitting in the middle of the woods with big tree stumps all around it. After I got tired of bouncing up and down in the bed of the pickup around the many pieces of wood, I decided to test my balance. So stepping up on the railing of the bed, I put one foot in front of the other like we did on the barn rafter. My hand-me-down white tennis shoes had good traction as I carefully walked around the whole bed several times without falling.

Devan and Dawn showed up just as I got so good at walking around the bed of the pickup almost at a run. Devan yelled up to me as I was concentrating on keeping my balance, "Kristi, you're gonna fall!"

She and Dawn started throwing loose pieces of firewood into the bed of the truck, and I kept my balance on the five-inch railing.

Then as I picked up some speed around the bed of the truck again, dodging the pieces of wood, my right foot slipped off the rail.

Next thing I knew, in an instant, my body was sailing forward off the side of the pickup headfirst. My arms were flailing in attempt to catch my fall, but my face beat it to the punch. I came down hard on a wide tree stump right on my chin, causing my neck to jerk back and my body to stop.

Then the woods became silent as I couldn't hear my sisters who were trying to help me get up off the hard tree stump.

My hearing came back a few minutes later as I started to cry, and then I heard Dawn yell to Dad, "She's bleeding!"

My chin stung real bad and was dripping blood onto my brown T-shirt and onto my hands. Even though my chin and my pride were hurt, I got up from the stump, leaning on the twins.

Dad told the twins to get me to the house after he put his handkerchief on my gaping chin and had me hold it there firmly.

When we got to the house, Mom and Aunt Ginger put a butterfly bandage on the huge wound right on the bottom of my chin, pulling the sides together without having to have stitches.

She said I would have a scar on the bottom of my chin for a long time, and Mom said I would never forget it.

I could hardly wait for the Millers to get here and just knew Jason and I would have a great time no matter what the circumstances.

Jason was short and stout with brown hair and was an unusually rough boy. Denny was even stricter on his boys than our dad was with his kids, which really said a lot. I liked Jason and he liked me because we accepted each other just the way we were made, and he wasn't afraid to do anything on the homestead.

Since Jason moved here from Iowa several years ago, we'd become great friends even though he was only six and I just turned nine years old.

Every day after school, Jason stood outside my classroom to walk me to the bus, and as if we were a couple, he carried my books.

My friends giggled when they saw Jason waiting outside my aunt Kathy's classroom door for me, but I paid no attention to them.

The Millers lived eight miles north of us on the main highway toward Fairbanks. We went to their house often, where Jason and I rode his bike and played target practice with his BB guns. Jason and I sometimes played real cowboys, aiming our BB guns right at each other as we ducked behind the trees. The small round metal BBs stung our flesh as we both had good aim. Dad had taught all of us older kids how to shoot a .22 rifle a couple of years ago. We got to shoot at empty soup cans on top of the wood fence on the edge of the field.

As Steve and I were heading out the front door with the dogs to feed the horses, we could hear Mom and Dad getting up out of bed. It was still dark outside, but the full moon gave us enough light to feed along with Dad's big flashlight.

Then we joined the rest of the family around the table for hotcakes and homemade syrup. Salmon warmed up with syrup on it went good with the hotcakes. Fluffy fresh scrambled eggs were the finishing touch as we passed them around our big picnic table in the kitchen with all nine of us.

Mikey still sat in his metal high chair only tucked in under the table without a tray. He was getting big but not very tall, and his hair was the same color as the butter we made ourselves from cream. Mikey had a lot of guts and would try just about anything even at two. You could say he was made of steel, and the accident with his hand made him even tougher.

Timmy was big enough at nearly four years old to sit on the benches with Mom and us kids. He was thin and tall for his age and had thick curly red hair and lots of freckles. Timmy was shy and really smart. He tried hard to keep up with his little brother as he felt it his duty to protect him.

We said our prayer like we always did before a meal and then started passing the food around the table. Taking only what we planned to eat was the rule as we had to finish everything on our plates. Then we asked to be excused from the table, which I did, eager to get back out to the horses.

Dad said, "You may be excused, but you have to help with the dishes." He must have seen the sour look on my face but didn't react as I quickly removed it.

Dad was still talking as I looked straight at him. "Steve and I'll put the horses out to pasture. If we all pitch in, maybe we can go fishing later and enjoy our company."

A couple of hours later, after the rain had stopped, the Millers came driving up in their own pickup right about noon. The sun was peeking around the dark clouds, making me feel warm a little at a time.

My sisters ran outside to help carry in the Tupperware bowls Jean had brought with food she had prepared for our picnic. Mom opened the screen door to the kitchen to let everyone in the house.

I was outside by the cowshed playing with my new dog that Mom and Dad gave me for my birthday. They got her from the Seales in Anchorage, and she was a six-month-old white malamute husky with blue eyes. I don't know why I named her LuLu, but it seemed to fit her as I got her to chase me around our big birch tree in the front yard.

Joe and Jeanette Seale were staying close by this summer in their own cabin north up the tracks. Their son Alan was only a few years younger than me, and we were friends. His younger sister Becca was only three and really cute with her long curly brown hair and rosy cheeks.

I rode our bike to the cabin a lot to visit with the Seales. Jeanette made something delicious called granola, and she gave me all I wanted and seemed to enjoy my company. I liked her happy personality and took her horseback riding when she asked me to teach her how to ride. I let her ride Jude since she was gentle, and I rode CJ, our palomino. We both rode bareback, and she taught me a new song called "You Are My Sunshine."

Jason brought his bow and arrow to show off to me as he carried them over to where LuLu started to bark at him, only it was more of a yip.

After Jason and I shot several arrows off into the woods behind the house, we ran off together to play in the old cars that were parked behind the house.

"Let's get fishing," I heard Dad say to Denny as we passed by them in the garage. Dad and Denny grabbed the poles and guns while Steve picked up the tackle box and followed. Dad had his .41 magnum strapped to his hip in a leather holster. His big shotgun had a sling that fit snugly around his shoulder to rest on his back.

Mom, Jean, and the girls stayed in the house, talking and giggling, preparing the picnic for later that day.

Jason and I could smell the caribou roast in the oven basted with its own juices and smothered in onions. Homemade bread in the oven was delicious with melted butter. Mom's apple pie for dessert with homemade ice cream was a real treat. Jean brought candied yams and a green salad with fresh tomatoes.

Even though the smells of our later supper were overtaking us, we couldn't resist playing in our Bel Air that had broken down a few years ago. Jason got behind the wheel and pretended to be my husband and drove us out to dinner.

To get into the passenger side of the car, I had to remove some weeds that had collected in the front floor board and through the open window.

"I want to drive now, Jason," I told him while he put the long silver shifter on the steering wheel.

"But husbands are supposed to drive!" Jason said as he got out of the car reluctantly.

My faded jeans got a new hole as something sharp caught on them as I hopped out of the passenger side of the Bel Air. Making my way through the willows and high grass, I noticed Jason was opening the large heavy trunk. "What are you doing, Jason?" I said to him as I rounded the sharp corner on the back of the Bel Air.

Before I could stop him, Jason opened the trunk of the car, and a mass of bees swarmed at us and then above us like a tornado.

I stood perfectly still like a statue, but Jason started to scream and turned to run. Without one single sting, the huge cloud of bees swarmed off and followed Jason, stinging him as he screamed and cried in terror! I ran after him as fast as I could, yelling at him to stand still, but he just kept running. I ran as fast as my legs would go to the house to get help.

Mom and Jean heard me yelling before I even got to our front door. "Help! The bees are attacking Jason!" I screamed as Jean grabbed our broom and ran toward Jason in the woods.

Mom took the blanket off the couch and told Lori to get a pail of cold water. By the time Jason's mother got to him, he was on the ground, rolling like a log, trying to get the bees off himself.

I had never heard Jason cry so much as Mom and Jean killed the bees with the broom. Then they doused him with cold water and brushed the remaining bees off with a towel. I felt really bad for him and saw the huge red welts from all the stings he got.

Jean picked up her little boy, wrapping him up with the blanket Lori had in her hands. Then she carried him into the house and laid him on the couch.

Mom knew what to do by making a paste made out of baking soda and water to rub on all the bites. Jason's face was swelling, and he was unable to see out of one eye. He was still sobbing, rocking back and forth as if to comfort himself.

After a while, Jason started to calm down as the baking soda drew the sting out of the numerous bites he had all over his body.

By the time Dad, Steve, and Denny got back from fishing, Jason was asleep on the couch and dinner was on the table. Everyone squeezed into the picnic table to eat, hardly saying a word to each other.

Dad spoke up, laughing, "One thing I don't understand, Kristi, is how did you not get stung by the bees even once?"

I answered proudly, "I pretended like I was a statue."

Dad laughed even louder as we all relaxed at the table. That was what he had taught us to do as a lot of bees shared our homestead too.

43

VICTORY BIBLE CAMP

DAWN

The warm and rainy days of summer went by fast as the frost of fall set in everywhere and the hours of darkness increased on the homestead.

The fireweed, bluebells, white daisies, wild roses, and all the other striking wildflowers lost their petals, bowing down into the strong cold wind. Pussy willows shed their cotton blossoms onto the wet ground. The variety of tall trees spoke to me in a strong voice of wind, showering spruce needles, covering my head and the ground. My eyes squinted into the bright sun, peeking around the clouds as it glared off the white birch trees in the woods.

The grizzlies and black bears started to head for their dens with cubs trailing close behind. Giant moose ate frantically from the tall trees in the woods as if it were their last meal. The bald eagles circled in and out of the dark clouds. A rare closeup at the brilliant hunter perched on our fences and barns looking sharply around for prey was fascinating. The enormous size of a bald eagle up close took my breath away as I stood in awe of its majesty.

There was a certain peaceful silence as the frost blanketed the ground in warning to all that winter was coming.

The salmon went somewhere warmer from our Susitna River and wide white-capped Goose Creek. Dad, Mom, and we kids spent many days this summer pulling in our fill of the abundant fish. Mom even used red tape on her hook one time when she ran out of bait and Dad was out of town. She yelled down the bank at us kids, "This one's mine!" A big beautiful silver jumped out of the water as Mom gracefully pulled it in with the fly rod.

Steve and Lori got to go to camp with Dad in June to the mouth of Sheep Creek on horseback. They came home with several king salmon the next day that were longer than me and the biggest fish I had ever seen.

We worked on our new house all the time, making the reality of it more believable. My siblings and I were so excited about having real bedrooms and a basement. Running water was unimaginable in my eleven-year-old mind as, like my other siblings, I was used to having to haul it up from the spring in five-gallon buckets. We all had rock-hard muscles on our arms and legs, leaving no room for extra weight. Devan was the only husky one of us kids, and her nickname was moose. She was my twin, and boy, was I glad she was.

Dad told all of us kids to carry up the biggest river rocks we could find on the banks of the slough so he could build a real fireplace in our new house. Then he and Steve made cement and put it in between the different-shaped rocks that were stacked in a perfect circle deep and wide for the start of it in the daylight basement. The skinned logs were piled high and ready for a good stretch of weather to get us into the cabin by next summer.

It was fun to play on the concrete wall Dad built to the walk in the dark root cellar that was adjacent to the new house, which was close to the bank of the slough. Devan, Kristi, and I walked far into the cool wood-sided root cellar where we would be able to store more vegetables and meat all year round. We could never have electricity out here, but I heard Dad talk about a big generator someday.

With seven kids, it was getting more crowded in our small shack-like house. Devan and I barely fit in the short bed that was next to Lori's room in the trailer. Timmy and Mikey outgrew the built-in bunks, so Mom and Dad got a set of real bunkbeds to replace Kristi's twin bed by the wall in the living room. Our little brothers got the bunk beds, and Kristi had to sleep in a sleeping bag on the living room floor next to Steve, who was too tall now for the couch.

One wonderful, warm week in July made this last summer my favorite of all time to always stay in my memories.

Steve, Lori, Devan, Kristi, and I got to go to Victory Bible Camp up past Palmer toward Glennallen. All our friends from Talkeetna Bible Church were there, even Chad Valentine, whom I had a big crush on and liked to sit next to on the school bus. Devan and I both liked John Calhoun, who was short and had brown hair and sincere brown eyes. He was my best friend Patsy's older brother and Pastor Gary's son. He was shy and didn't seem too interested in either one of us.

Dad agreed to take Jude and CJ to the Bible camp and leave them so Steve could give horseback rides to all the kids. Because of that, we got to go for the first time this year as it would normally cost too much for all of us to attend.

So Mom and Dad took us up to the campsite with the horses in the trailer and all of us kids in the bed of the pickup.

Victory Bible Camp was situated on a gorgeous reflective lake, with mountains surrounding it and where enormous tall spruce trees towered above us and were much too fat to climb with no lower limbs. There were cute little log cabins close together that were built around the thick trees. Back behind the cabins was a beautiful blue lake where canoes were tied off at the docks.

After we pulled into the camp, Dad found the stables and parked the pickup in front of them, which were right next to the counselor's cabins.

We kids got out of the pickup as strange faces walked by us in a group as a counselor was giving them a tour. Mom and Dad told us older five kids to join the tour and then come back for our belongings, which were three outfits each and a toothbrush in a paper bag.

We did what we were told and followed a young guy who had caught my eye when I first looked at him. Then Devan and I gave each other the look.

He said his name was Mike, and he was tall and handsome with long blond hair and blue eyes. He took us all around the camp where we saw the cabin we were going to sleep. They were assigned to us by age and gender. The cabins had a small porch and a screen door. Each one had four bunk beds for eight kids. The cute counselor called out names as we passed each cabin to tell us which one we were staying in. I thought I saw him wink at me as he called out mine and Devan's names together for a cabin with other girls our age, including Patsy.

Steve and Lori got to stay in the high schoolers' cabins, and Kristi stayed with the younger girls. After that we walked around the lake and hiking trails.

By the time we got back, Dad had the horses unloaded, and they were leaving with Timmy and Mikey in the red Ford pickup. We older kids unloaded our belongings and said goodbye to them for a whole week.

Dad leaned out the window of the driver's side and told us, "You kids have fun and mind your manners." None of us had been away from home for this long but were looking forward to no chores.

The whole camp came together for canoeing, swimming, and BBQs, as well as crafts and hiking. Devan and I had a blast! Lori hung out with her friends as Steve had to give rides every day on Jude and CJ, which he wasn't very happy about but still had a good time.

We all got to join in the war games (Capture the Flag) played at night in the woods by the solstice light. Mike was in charge of the running game where grabbing the flag from the other team was the object. I got to play on his team, and he told me I was the fastest runner there, and I think I really was.

One night while sitting by myself on the dock that floated out into the lake after the war games were over, Mike came walking over to me and asked me to take a walk. My young heart began to beat fast as I followed him into the woods on my shaking legs. All I could think about as I looked at his long curly blond hair and perfect profile was, "Is this really happening to me?" I quickly looked ahead as we walked farther away from the cabin where my twin was probably worried about me.

Mike stopped and took my hands as he faced me just like in the Harlequin Romances I had read. I licked my dry lips and looked into his mesmerizing baby-blue eyes. Mike leaned in with both of his hands cupping my face, and then as if rehearsed, he pressed his soft lips onto mine. It was my first kiss and I wanted to get it right, so I slipped my hands around his neck and gave him a long closed-mouthed kiss with my eyes closed.

Afraid we might get caught, we both let go and just stood there, wondering what to say to each other. Mike asked me quietly, "How old are you?"

I knew better than to lie, especially at Bible camp, and so I looked up at my Prince Charming and said, "I'm almost twelve."

Mike didn't seem to like my answer and told me as we walked back to the cabins, "Well, I'm eighteen, and you are too young for me to be kissing."

At that moment, I wished I was older, but at the same time it just felt good to have someone like Mike think I am pretty enough for him to kiss.

That night in the cabin with Devan and the other girls, I told them about my first kiss, and we stayed up most of the night giggling and exchanging stories. The next day one of the girls told the head counselor about me kissing Mike, and he was given a lecture. Thank goodness Dad never found out, or Mike would have had to answer to him also.

The fun-filled week at Victory Bible Camp ended where we also enjoyed a ton of delicious food that was prepared by the counselors. Hamburgers, baked beans, watermelon, cookies, and much more were served to us, and then we were all assigned cleanup duties.

The day before we left, every single kid and counselor got together in the grass under the tall spruce trees for one last church gathering. A cool breeze blew past me through my short fine blond hair as they invited us to give our testimonials. Being the most passive and shy of all my siblings, I was the last one they would have thought would stand up.

Something compelled me to express the joy that filled my heart when I received the best gift of all, which was eternal life.

I stood up in front of all the many kids' faces looking straight at me and told them my testimonial with a shaking voice.

I told them Devan and I got down on our knees at four years old to receive the gift of salvation and how it made us feel grateful. From that day forward, my fear was gone and my voice was finally heard.

44

HOT WINTER'S NIGHT

STEVE

M om always said, "There are really only two seasons in Alaska, winter and the Fourth of July!" After surviving nine hard winters here on our homestead, we all knew it was true.

It was November, and Dad had just left again for the North Slope and this time would be gone for several weeks. Every winter he had to go to work away from home with no way of contacting us and seemingly for longer periods of time. I could tell Mom was tired of being alone.

Often we would run short of dry wood to burn in the woodstoves and the old shack could barely hold off the severe cold that was seeping into every crack.

When none of the vehicles would start, there was no way to get to town for much-needed groceries and supplies for a big family and feed for the horses.

One night after Dad had left, I heard Mom praying in their bedroom to God. "You have to get us out of here!"

The big barn was the only shelter for our four horses who huddled together during the many blizzards. Our family and our four dogs did the same in the living room around the barrel stove.

Our Polaris was one of the only means of transportation in the winter, and right before Dad left for the slope, it wasn't starting up.

He had me help him drag our only snow machine into the house to warm the engine. We pulled it on its skis right into the living room, barely squeezing it through the front door. Then when Dad tried to start it, to our surprise, a spark caught onto the gas-drenched snow machine and ignited the whole engine on fire.

Dad and I quickly grabbed the skis with our bare hands and dragged the burning Polaris outside as the rest of the family ran into the kitchen.

By the time we got it out the front door by the garage, it was sitting there in four feet of snow, engulfed in flames. We both had blisters for days from the burns on our hands.

The next day Dad and I dragged the Polaris that had been faithful for nine years out to the woods toward the spring with all our other vehicles that had died, which included the Rambler and the Galaxy.

The Millers gave us a station wagon that was a late sixties model that we used in the summer. It was frozen to the ground outside the front door by the garage with the deep snow up to the windows.

We also had a new little white Volkswagen that Uncle Doug left for us to use that had burned up also.

On Halloween day after Dad had left for the slope, the snow on our road was packed down and Mom wanted to try to get out to the highway with the little Volkswagen since Dad had the pickup. It wouldn't start in the below-zero weather and I knew it was a bad idea, but we were desperate.

With Lori's help, Mom and I tried warming up the engine on the little car with heat pots and a propane torch in a twelve-inch stove pipe. We didn't know the Volkswagen had a gas leak until the whole car burst into flames with just enough time to push it away from the house and for us to get out of the way.

Mom, Lori, Devan, Dawn, Kristi, Timmy, Mikey, and I stood outside in the cold, watching yet another vehicle go up in flames.

Even though it was a tragic situation, Mom ran into the house to grab the camera out of her purse to take a Polaroid picture. All of us kids stood outside, feeling the warmth of the big fire and watching a whole car burn up for the first time. The orange flames poured out of every window of the little white car that stood in the snow, releasing big puffs of black smoke.

Without the snow machine, Timmy and Mikey had to stay home, but Mom let us older five kids hike out to the Halloween party at the community center. Besides hiking out in the deep snow, I had to pack the twelve-gauge shotgun over my shoulder with my sisters behind me.

At thirteen and a half now, I could shoot any of Dad's guns, including his new .41 magnum pistol with the long barrel. I'd say my aim was sure and steady with a fast draw, which was required in these parts of the woods. Besides shooting a moose or a caribou while hunting with Dad, I was fortunate to only have shot the guns to scare various wild animals away.

My sisters and I hustled through the snowed-over trail as we had lost time and were running late for the party. The girls were excited and chattering loudly, forgetting the cold for a moment.

Doug Lindstrand had been in his cabin and saw us hurrying by in the dark moonlit evening.

He opened his door and stood in the lit-up doorway as his breath stood still in the air like ours as he waved us over for candy. We all liked him a lot and eagerly ran over to his cabin.

Mom and Dad went over to his cabin one time and sat with him to look at his art. Doug asked them questions about us and the homestead. He told Dad we were good kids and he enjoyed our company. They were glad to have a nearby trustworthy neighbor, which is valuable in the bush.

We siblings dressed up in homemade costumes since money was scarce with seven kids. I went as a cowboy since I got boots for one of my last birthdays. I could fit them inside of my snow boots without the liners. Dad gave me his extra cowboy hat to wear in which my ski mask fit snugly under. I was tired of being cold all the time in the winter. No matter how many layers of clothes I put on, I couldn't ever keep warm. I looked forward to the warm summers as we all did.

When it was snowing and the temperatures reached under thirty below, we all had to wear our ski masks to protect our faces from the beads of ice that blew in the high winds. They grew like crystals clinging onto the wool material of our masks, hardening into solid ice with cracks where our faces were formed. Hiking out a mile and a half to the bus seemed like five miles with the wind hitting your face, especially when we had the snow machine and had to duck our faces down against the wind just to breathe.

I appreciated the days when Mom and Dad let us miss school and stay in our warm house by the woodstoves. Dad called it buckling down. We kids called it board game day.

Lori thought she was too old at fourteen and a half to dress up for Halloween, so instead she helped make costumes for our younger sisters.

It's amazing what you can do with coat hangers, tin foil, paper bags, and paint. Of course we had to wear our winter coats over the costumes, hoping to get there in one piece. The twins went as angels, and Kristi was a cat with pointy black ears and a tail made of black yarn.

We were all practically running through the snow on our trail to keep warm. After another delay of moose running across the trail only yards in front of us being chased by two large timber wolves, we finally made it to the party.

None of us kids will ever forget the fun we had bobbing for apples, the costume contest, the haunted house, hanging out with friends, and of course, the huge table filled with food! To us kids it was worth the long hike home late in the night through the dark woods.

Thanksgiving came and went as December rode in with freezing temperatures and life-changing events.

It was a Sunday afternoon on December 7, 1975. Mom and we kids were all buckled down in the cold house barely warmed by the struggling barrel stove. It hadn't snowed for a week, bringing in fifty-below-zero strong wind. Being outside was only bearable for a short time.

Not even the tar paper on the outside of the old shack could fight off the strong wind, taking the warmth that our two woodstoves were trying to provide. Our noses were red, and we had our coats on even inside the old house.

The living room was lower and less insulated than the kitchen. Mom said to me and Lori while eating an early supper by the propane lanterns, "Why don't we put the barrel stove in the kitchen and see if it keeps the house warmer?"

Lori looked up from her goulash and said to me, "Can we do that without Dad here?"

I looked across the big table at both of them and said with confidence, being the man of the house, "All we have to do is remove the stove pipes and then switch the stoves."

After supper, Devan and Kristi did the dishes with some of the few gallons of water we had left that wasn't frozen.

Dawn got the boys ready for bed into their two-piece pajamas, leaving their socks on to keep their feet warm.

For the next hour, Mom and Lori helped me put the fires down, and then we carefully unhooked the stoves from the big round pipes that went up through the ceiling. It took all of us to move the heavy barrel stove from the living room to the kitchen. The small, black iron woodstove in the kitchen wasn't much lighter as we carried it into the living room.

By the time I got both of the woodstoves hooked firmly back up to the stove pipes, Gary Calhoun pulled up into our plowed driveway. He was there to get Mom for a special evening service at the Talkeetna Bible Church. The icy wind came in the door with Gary and an armload of our birch wood to add to the stack in the living room.

Mom and Gary left in his pickup, sliding around on the hard-packed road with the big headlights shining on the four-foot snowbanks.

I used a lot of kindling to get the two fires roaring again while the girls got ready for bed. Then we all sat around the red-hot barrel stove in the kitchen and had hot cocoa and popcorn that Lori made us in a cast iron skillet.

It was nearly ten o'clock, and Timmy and Mikey were asleep on the bottom bunk together. Lori looked up from her book and told the twins to get in their sleeping bags that were on the floor by the black iron stove in the living room. Kristi picked up her big doll and followed her sisters.

As I took off my coat and boots, Lori had put her book away and climbed up into the top bunk, covering up with her wool blanket. Her own bedroom was too cold this time of year.

It was just another freezing night where I did my usual routine of checking the doors to make sure they were shut tight and turning down the two propane lights.

Meardha was asleep in her big easy chair, and Goldy, Lucky, and LuLu were on the floor asleep in the kitchen by the barrel stove.

The hard floor was cold as I walked back over to the couch to get in bed. As I lay there looking around ready to fall asleep, I decided to get up and stoke the fires one more time.

When I climbed off the couch and opened the iron stove door in the living room, I could hear my sisters and brothers snoring already. After shutting the small door to the little woodstove, I turned to go into the kitchen.

Instantly my nose filled with the smell of smoke that was pouring out of the top of the stove pipe up by the low white ceiling above the barrel stove.

My snow boots were by the couch, and I hurriedly shoved my socked feet into them and ran outside the kitchen door and off the little porch to see the roof.

Running backward into the snow, I could see red flames coming out of our roof right around the chimney stack. Panic started to set in as I knew the lives of my siblings were in my hands, and so I ran frantically back up the wooden steps to the kitchen. *Where was Mom?* I thought quickly in my mind. I ran over to the barrel stove under the black smoke billowing out into my face. Moving my head around, I was terrified when I looked up the three-foot stove pipe and saw that the ceiling was red hot with a ring of sparks around the chimney jack.

There were only seconds to grab the last two gallons of water in a five-gallon bucket sitting on the floor by the stove and run back outside to try to put the fire out.

When I got out the kitchen door, I climbed up onto the wooden porch railing, and while holding the large bucket, I scurried quickly onto the pitched tin roof. By now there were two-foot flames coming out of the roof around the little red-hot tin chimney stack. A huge cloud of black smoke poured out into the freezing wind.

The small bucket of water didn't even slow the flames, and then I knew we were in trouble.

In a panic, I was off the roof and back into the kitchen, ripping the burning ceiling mat down, trying to somehow put out this horrible fire. Right when I did that, the scorching flames made their way into the house and started spreading across the low ceiling toward the trailer.

Then complete terror set into my mind as this was something I wasn't prepared to handle in the bush with six siblings and our parents gone.

My whole body started to shake out of control, and I was barely able to scream out to my sisters and brothers that were still asleep in the living room. "The house is on fire!"

That was the moment our lives changed forever as Lori, Devan, and Dawn sprung out of their warm safe beds, screaming like I'd never heard when they saw the huge red flames engulfing the kitchen.

"Wake the boys up!" Lori yelled over to the twins who were standing there in shock. I threw my coat on and swung two of Dad's rifles over my right shoulder as the fire continued to grow rapidly. The twins jolted into reality and ran over to the bunks to get Timmy and Mikey safely out of the house. They swiftly put their coats on and searched the living room floor through the thick black smoke that was filling the house for their snow boots. Then Dawn yelled through her tears, "Where's Kristi?"

My heart skipped a beat as I scanned the floor for her sleeping bag, having to duck down onto the by now hot floor.

Lori was nowhere in sight either as I saw Kristi's red hair sticking out of her sleeping bag shoved almost all the way under the bunks.

Springing up out of the smoke, I yelled to the twins across the room, "Get in the station wagon!"

Then I busted through the black smoke and reached down and grabbed Kristi's sleeping bag, pulling her out from under the bunk beds, waking her up. "The house is on fire!" I yelled to her face-to-face with sweat pouring down my terrified face.

I never saw my little sister move so quickly as she leaped out of the sleeping bag and ran for her coat.

Devan and Dawn came running back into the house without the boys to grab their raggedy Anne dolls and some of Dad's paintings off the walls in the living room where the flames were starting to enter.

I still couldn't find our sister Lori, whom I thought I saw run into the trailer. The kitchen was almost completely on fire, and I knew the back door to the trailer in her room was nailed shut for the winter.

"Oh, God!" I cried out loud as the crackling of our house burning and the thought of losing one of my brothers or sisters made me want to die right there.

Handing the guns to Devan as the twins ran out the front door again with a few paintings and no dolls, I ran through the overpowering smoke that was taking over the house.

The whole kitchen was on fire, including the floor, in only minutes since the nightmare began and was spreading across the living room ceiling. "Lori! Lori!" My lungs filled with smoke, and I started to cough uncontrollably as I dove through a pocket of hot orange flames to the open trailer door.

Lori was crawling around on her hands and knees on the floor next to Mom and Dad's big bed. I thought maybe she had lost her mind when I yelled at her to get out of the house. She looked up at me with a certain terror in her big green eyes and said quietly through tears streaming down her pale face, "I have to get Mom's clothes."

Tears welled up in my eyes as I felt the burning heat behind me from our only house on fire, and my sister was not acting right.

Boom! Boom! One of our propane tanks blew up and flew off into the air like a bomb! My adrenaline rose even higher as I reached down and wrapped my arms around Lori's stomach and pulled her up against me, dragging her through the trailer door.

I felt like my hair and my coat were on fire as I pulled my sister through the flames surrounding the entry to the living room. She yelled at me as we made it into the smoke-filled room, "Meardha's on the chair!"

I let go of Lori and grabbed Meardha by her collar and pulled her off the easy chair that was starting to burn and headed for the door, grabbing Dad's .41 pistol and his old twenty-gauge rifle. The only one I couldn't grab was my .22 rifle Dad had given me.

Lori found her boots by the door and threw them on while Kristi was still looking through the pile for hers with our broken wind-up clock in her hands. The entire ceiling quickly became covered with lapping flames in the living room as Lori pushed Kristi out the door into the snow with only her nightgown and her boot liners on.

Just as the last of us piled into the long station wagon that was parked close to the garage, another loud explosion went off. We could see through the now defrosted window our last propane tank landing somewhere in the back of the burning house.

I just sat there in the station wagon as my siblings held on to each other, sobbing and shivering, watching the only home we knew on our beautiful homestead burn to the ground right before our eyes. I wasn't sure what to do next.

The propane explosion had fed the burning flames as they ate away at the birch siding and moved onto the roof of the garage.

The windshield of the station wagon was melting from the extreme heat as I was trying to think of where we could find shelter from the bitter cold.

Lori was back to herself and looked over at me as our four dogs were barking, feeling the heat inside the car, and said, "We should go to the big barn." I knew we had to get out of the station wagon as I watched most of our house crash to the ground in a heap of tall flames. The trailer was burning now, and the whole garage too.

Lori and I got out of the hot brown station wagon into the freezing wind to get our siblings somewhere safe and warm. Missy and one of her kittens jumped out of the car at the same time as our dogs.

Mikey, who was only two years old, was crying as he wasn't sure what was happening as Timmy rocked him in the back seat.

We hurried the twins and Kristi out of the car and sent them toward the barn with the dogs. They took the only wool blanket we had that Lori grabbed from her bunk on her way out of the burning house.

Then I pulled my four-year-old brother Timmy out of the back seat as he didn't want to let go of Mikey. Lori reached in from the other side and picked little Mikey up into her arms.

We both left the towering flames that were destroying our house as we watched it burn, sending billows of black smoke up into the tall trees.

On our way to the big barn, I saw our big John Deere tractor get so hot it was burning the rubber off its huge tires.

With the freezing wind, there was no time to think about why Mom wasn't home or how Dad would feel about his dream being shattered in a minute.

Lori and I helped the girls into the big pile of loose hay that was close to Dungo, Jude, CJ, and Star, who were running around the barn floor like they knew something terrible was happening.

After the girls sat deep into the hay, we handed them the boys to keep them all together warm.

I was still shaking like a leaf and could see the tall flames and hear the cracking of the wood and the bending of metal as the trailer started to collapse. Lori was shaking uncontrollably in her coat and, like me, had no gloves on. Our younger brothers and sisters had mittens sewn into their coats, thanks to Mom, and most of them had their snow boots on.

Dawn found both liners but only one of her boots. Kristi only had her liners and no boots. None of us had a hat on.

I could tell by the way my body temperature was dropping rapidly that it was at least fifty below zero.

Lori was huddling down into the hay with our younger siblings when I said to her with stagnant breath, "I'm going for help." My older sister looked down at me, standing by the horses who were now somewhat calm, and said, "Be careful, Steve. Take one of the guns."

I knew the half-mile trail to Doug Lindstrand's cabin like the back of my hand but still didn't want to leave my brothers and sisters here to freeze while I ran for help. The loose hay and somewhat enclosed barn would only keep them warm for a short time.

So I sprinted across our driveway with the twelve-gauge tucked under my left arm as fast as my numb legs and feet would take me.

I passed the burning house and garage and ran into the dark woods, keeping my cold face forward. Still in shock from the tragedy at hand, I still couldn't wrap my mind around it.

By the time I reached Doug's cabin and saw the dull yellow light from his small lantern in the window, I was out of all my breath and felt like I could collapse.

That didn't stop me as I knew time was of the essence as I rushed up to his faded brown door. Somehow my heavy right arm made its way to his window that was framed into the door we always saw him come out of.

Doug didn't answer right away as he was not expecting anyone this hour of the night. Frantically, I yelled through the door at him, "Our house is on fire!" Those words made me want to cry even at thirteen as Doug jerked open his door, looking surprised to see me standing there.

He ran outside past me as I stood there holding the rifle, shivering in the freezing wind. Doug looked toward our house, which he could see the high flames and billowing smoke. "Oh my god!" Doug turned around to me like the speed of sound and said with his eyes like saucers, "Where is your mom and dad?"

I felt my stomach drop to the ground as I said back to him, shaking like a leaf, "Dad's on the North Slope, and Mom went to a church service in Talkeetna."

I already knew he wanted to know about my siblings, so I said to him urgently, "My brothers and sisters are in the barn where I left them, and Mom will be home soon and she'll be worried."

Doug wasted no time and threw on his big heavy coat and his hat, pulling one off the rack for me as he grabbed a couple of wool blankets. He wrapped one around my shoulders and carried my rifle for me until we made it back to our house that was now a red glow of fire filling the dark sky.

My sisters and brothers were still in the big pile of hay in the barn and were getting numb from the inevitable frostbite setting in. I already felt the sting on my ears and fingers from just hiking to Doug's cabin.

Lori, Devan, Dawn, Kristi, Timmy, and Mikey got up out of the hay stack as soon as they saw us come into the barn with Doug's flashlight.

As we all stood there shaking and looking distraught, Doug spoke up. He picked Timmy up into his arms and wrapped his unzipped coat around him. "Let's get to my cabin!"

I picked Mikey up into my coat as well, and the girls followed us out of the barn, and then we hiked by the burning sawdust-insulated old shack we called home.

When we got past the still burning garage, I thought I heard something coming from my sisters. I turned around to see them all crying, even Lori, as they bravely hiked through the cold dark woods. Lori and the twins had laid Kristi with no boots up across their extended arms while they walked close together with a wool blanket over all of their shoulders.

Dawn gimped along in the deep snow with one foot covered with only a boot liner with great courage.

Timmy and Mikey were both sobbing quietly as we carried them away from their short-lived memory of life on the homestead.

Doug Lindstrand's cabin never felt so warm and inviting as we all rushed in and shut the door. We all immediately ran over to his woodstove and warmed our hands seriously but ironically by the blazing fire. Doug heated water on the stove and wrapped us all in warm blankets as we ripped our boots off. We kids knew there was frostbite under our socks and waited to warm our feet first before taking them off.

Doug put his heavy coat back on and his gloves, heading for the front door of his cabin. He looked at our clan all alive, sitting around his stove, and said with compassion in his eyes, "Sure glad you kids all made it out of that fire. I'm going back, hopefully before your mom gets there, to let her know you are all safe."

That's what our great neighbor did that horrible night as Mom rode up in Denny Miller's pickup at 11:00 p.m., an hour after the fire had started.

EVELYN

After a special service at Talkeetna Bible Church, everyone attending went to the Calhoun's house for refreshments. Afterward Denny Miller offered to drive me home as it was getting late. We could see a huge red glow in the sky as we were traveling down the highway. I said to Denny, "Someone's house is on fire!" He gave me a concerning look and kept driving.

When we approached the turnoff to our dirt road, a horrible frantic feeling came over me, gripping me in a state of hysteria. I knew it was our house!

All I wanted to do was get out of the car and run to our seven kids, as I beat on the car door, unable to catch my breath.

Denny tried to calm me as he drove as fast as he could down the longest two miles of my life. "Have faith, Evelyn. Have faith."

I knew that was the right thing to do and remembered to send up a quick, frantic request.

Then I realized again how late it was and just knew the kids were in bed for the night. That sent me into another round of crying and hysteria, "My kids, my kids are gone!"

We finally rounded the last corner of the two-mile road. All I could see was the huge red glow of our burning house on this cold winter's night.

As we roared up, feeling the searing heat, we could see a man standing by our big barn, waving his arms. I barely took notice of him as it was dark and my gaze was fixed on the large lashing flames, looking for any sign of my children's lives. Denny came to a screeching halt next to the man standing in the smoke. It was Doug Lindstrand! He quickly leaned down into my open window before I could even open the door and said through labored breath, "The kids are okay!" Those were the best words I've ever heard in my life.

Collapsing back in the seat with relief, I shouted with thankfulness for the safekeeping of our kids. As Denny, Doug, and I stood close to the burning garage, trailer, and house, none of us spoke as the devastation surrounded us. Doug had tried to push our John Deere Tractor away from the house without success. It was engulfed with flames as well as our station wagon that Doug said the kids had initially taken shelter in. All of our things including pictures from years gone by and just about everything we owned was crackling and exploding inside our burning house. Nothing was as important as our kids though, and I was just grateful all seven had made it out alive.

STEVE

That same night we went to Denny Miller's house eight miles up the main highway and stayed there for a short time. Dad came home from the North Slope as soon as word got to him the next day.

I think a piece of all of us kids was devoured by the angry flames that dark, cold, devastating night on the homestead—like unfinished business that gets swept away with the ashes.

The only life that we kids knew was gone. With a large family, Dad knew this was the end of our journey on Goose Creek, where we had planned to live forever.

We were torn away from the endless emerald-green fields and years of forts being built by hand, the endless trails to all the still waters, the deep dark woods, windrows, ice castles, wildflowers, memories; and most of all, we said goodbye to the ghosts of Goose Creek.

> Hast thou not known? Hast thou not heard, that the everlasting God, the Lord, the creator of the ends of the earth, Fainteth not, neither is weary?
>
> There is no searching of his understanding.

He giveth power to the faint; And to them that have no might he increaseth strength.

Even the youths shall faint and be weary. And the young men shall utterly fall:

But they that wait upon the Lord shall renew their strength;

They shall mount up with wings as eagles; They shall run, and not be weary; And they shall walk, and not faint. (Isaiah 40:28–31)

Car Fire
DEC

Lori Clark

Kristi, Joy, and Dougie

Pastor Lloyd and Ruth in front
of Talkeetna Bible Church

Lori, Devan, Kristi, Dawn, Steve 1969

Dennis and Mikey

Steve, Dawn, Kristi, Devan,
Lori in Oregon 1967

Lori, Dawn, Kristi, Devan, Steve

Lori, Joy, Dawn, Devan, Kristi, and Steve October 1969

Devan and Dawn (the twins)

Timmy and Mikey

Dennis and Evelyn with Lori and baby Steve 1962

Dennis and Evelyn 1960

Dennis Clark and Vern Stanton

Lori, Wendy, Steve, Devan (middle),
Dougie, Kristi, Joy, Dawn, and Lad (dog).

Kristi, Dennis, Evelyn, Steve, Lori, Devan, Dawn 1967

ABOUT THE AUTHOR

Kristi Clark is a single fifty-three-year-old mother of three adult children and has two grandsons. She is a registered nurse who spent part of her childhood in the bush of Alaska with six brothers and sisters in an old shack where survival was learned at a young age. Stories of life in the bush were shared among the siblings for years, and finally Kristi was encouraged by them to write the unforgettable story. After many journeys back into the bush with the family and on her own, Kristi made the old homestead her home again. As she relived the memories through herself and her family, a new author found her love for writing. Feeling the joy and struggle as the memories unfolded, the story came back to life, allowing herself and all the bush kids to always remember how strong they really were.

CPSIA information can be obtained
at www.ICGtesting.com
Printed in the USA
BVHW031441270220
573544BV00001B/1